The Financial Crisis and
Federal Reserve Policy

The Financial Crisis and Federal Reserve Policy

Lloyd B. Thomas

THE FINANCIAL CRISIS AND FEDERAL RESERVE POLICY
Copyright © Lloyd B. Thomas, 2011.

First published in 2011 by
PALGRAVE MACMILLAN®
in the United States—a division of St. Martin's Press LLC,
175 Fifth Avenue, New York, NY 10010.

Where this book is distributed in the UK, Europe and the rest of the world,
this is by Palgrave Macmillan, a division of Macmillan Publishers Limited,
registered in England, company number 785998, of Houndmills,
Basingstoke, Hampshire RG21 6XS.

Palgrave Macmillan is the global academic imprint of the above companies
and has companies and representatives throughout the world.

Palgrave® and Macmillan® are registered trademarks in the United States,
the United Kingdom, Europe and other countries.

ISBN: 978–0–230–10846–2

Library of Congress Cataloging-in-Publication Data

Thomas, Lloyd Brewster, 1941–
        The Financial Crisis and Federal Reserve Policy / by Lloyd B. Thomas.
            p. cm.
        Includes bibliographical references and index.
        ISBN 978–0–230–10846–2
        1. Global Financial Crisis, 2008–2009. 2. Financial crises—United
    States. 3. Monetary policy—United States. 4. Board of Governors of the
    Federal Reserve System (U.S.) I. Title.

HB37172008.T46 2011
330.9′0511—dc22   2010029624

A catalogue record of the book is available from the British Library.

Design by Newgen Imaging Systems (P) Ltd., Chennai, India.

First edition: March 2011

10 9 8 7 6 5 4 3 2 1

Printed in the United States of America.

To Sally, Liz, and Sophie

Contents

Illustrations

Figures

Tables

Preface

Financial crises often ensue on the heels of extended periods of economic calm. It has been said that "stability breeds instability," a view borne out by the extraordinarily stable quarter century immediately preceding the Great Crisis of 2007–2009. In fact, economists refer to this benign period as "The Great Moderation." Of the dozen post–World War II recessions, the two experienced in this period were the mildest and briefest, and the longest continuous economic expansion in history extended from 1991 to 2001. In the two decades prior to the Great Crisis, the nation's unemployment rate was appreciably lower than in the previous twenty years, on average. Also, the inflation rate remained unusually low, averaging only 2.5 percent per year. By the year 2000, Federal Reserve chairman Alan Greenspan had been dubbed "The Maestro" for his ostensibly flawless orchestration of this new era of prosperity and unprecedented stability.

Unfortunately, as has often been the case in the past, this period of good times and heightened economic stability led to hubris. Lenders, borrowers, investors, regulatory authorities, the Federal Reserve, and others mistakenly assumed that esoteric instruments developed by a new breed of financial engineers had effectively reduced risk in financial markets and reallocated remaining risk to those most willing and able to incur it. This development, together with improved conduct of monetary policy, had rendered episodes of severe unemployment and high inflation obsolete—or so it was thought. Overconfidence lulled some economic actors into complacency and induced others to sharply increase risk-taking in pursuit of quick profits—both setting the stage for the catastrophe to come.

The decision to write this book was motivated by the simple fact that I am an economist and the financial crisis that began in 2007, together with its aftermath, constitutes the most important economic event of my lifetime—indeed of the past 75 years. This book, which aims to provide clear and straightforward answers to crucial questions surrounding the

Great Crisis, is written for a broad audience of motivated readers, including those without formal training in economics. It should also be of considerable interest to students in the field, and to professional economists who are not specialists in the areas of finance and monetary economics.

Key questions addressed here are the following:

- Why did the Great Crisis happen and why are financial crises recurring features of capitalism?
- Why did the crisis, which began in the United States, spread throughout the world?
- What were the channels through which the crisis spilled over to cause the recession that was the most severe of the numerous economic contractions since the Great Depression of the 1930s?
- Why are economic contractions associated with financial crises more severe than other recessions?
- What actions did the Federal Reserve take to cut short the cascading events that in September 2008 were poised to result in Great Depression II?
- How did the Fed's performance during the Great Crisis compare with that in the Great Depression?
- What problems are likely to confront the Federal Reserve as it conducts its "exit strategy" in coming years—that is, as it sells off the mortgage-related bonds and other assets it accumulated as it dramatically expanded its balance sheet to stem the contractionary forces of the Great Crisis?
- In what ways have the events of the first decade of the twenty-first century increased the prospects for substantially higher inflation in the years ahead?
- What financial reforms would increase the likelihood that future crises will be less frequent and less severe than the Great Crisis, and how well did the reform legislation enacted in 2010 address the problems?

This book seeks to provide insight into these important questions. Intensive study of the Great Crisis is warranted by its enormous costs. Loss of national output and income during 2008, 2009, and 2010 has been estimated to have been of the order of magnitude of 6 percent of potential levels. In an economy with an annual potential gross domestic product (GDP) of $15 trillion, this loss has likely been in the vicinity of $900 billion per year. Over the three-year period, this amounts to a per capita loss of income in the United States of more than $8,000. Such losses are diminishing only slowly, as even the more optimistic analysts believe it will take almost to mid-decade for economic activity to again approach full-employment levels.

Of course, these costs have not been shared equally across the population. They have been concentrated disproportionately among the more than eight million people thrown out of work. Especially damaging is the fact that the percentage of the labor force in long-term unemployment—those continuously out of work for 27 or more weeks—was five times higher by October 2010 than its average in the 20-year period ending in 2007. Such long-term unemployment is particularly debilitating and costly inasmuch as skills and motivation of the affected workers tends inevitably to atrophy over time. Many individuals of middle age and older, thrown out of work through no fault of their own, may never recover from the debacle.

Yet the costs of the Great Crisis were hardly limited to those denied jobs. Few Americans were not significantly impacted in one way or another. For example, many families whose breadwinners retained their jobs nonetheless lost their homes. The median U.S. family's principal source of wealth has traditionally been its equity in the family home. The unprecedented drop in house prices wiped out $7 trillion of this wealth. The decline in stock prices, in conjunction with the contraction in housing equity, meant that millions of Americans approaching retirement were forced to postpone their decision. And many of those recently retired either re-entered the work force or faced sharply reduced economic circumstances.

The cost to cities and states has been without precedent in modern times. Nearly all 50 states suffered a significant contraction in tax revenues, necessitating imposition of austerity programs. Tens of thousands of school teachers have been let go, with adverse implications for the long-term well-being of their young students. Prisons have released thousands of inmates owing to lack of funds to continue their incarceration. Roads and water systems have deteriorated. Essential services to some of the nation's most vulnerable citizens have been terminated.

Unlike states, the federal government is normally unconstrained in its expenditures by the revenues at hand. Nevertheless, the severe drop in federal tax receipts, combined with stimulus programs aimed at reducing the severity of the economic contraction, sharply boosted the federal deficit in the United States and many other countries. By 2009, the U.S. deficit exceeded 10 percent of GDP, a level unprecedented except in times of all-out war. The magnitude of the deficit placed the fiscal plight of the United States in proximity to that of Greece, Ireland, Spain, Portugal, and other nations experiencing the simmering European sovereign debt crisis—itself a consequence of the worldwide Great Crisis—that surfaced in spring 2010. An increasing number of respected economists expressed the view that the United States was by no means immune to sovereign debt crises. The fear that foreign investors might lose confidence in the U.S. commitment to fiscal responsibility was sufficiently palpable to prevent the implementation of urgently needed fiscal stimulus as the fragile economic recovery showed clear signs of faltering in the second half of 2010.

Early chapters of this work discuss the types of financial crises that have occurred in various nations over the centuries and provide a framework that explains the forces that periodically combine to produce bubbles in credit and asset prices whose inevitable collapse initiates financial crisis. To place in context and shed light on the recent Great Crisis, previous U.S. crises are analyzed, including the Savings and Loan crisis of the late 1980s, the Great Depression, and the Panic of 1907—which directly led to the creation of the Federal Reserve System.

Chapter 4 analyzes the developments that led to the twin bubbles in house prices and the volume of credit extended to homebuyers and other borrowers. This chapter discusses the role played by the forces of "animal spirits" and the myopic belief that, unlike the price of stocks, oil, or gold, house prices are inflexible on the downside—they just cannot fall. Important contributing forces in the inflation of the twin bubbles include imprudent and reckless behavior on the part of both lenders and borrowers, absence of reasonable oversight by regulatory authorities, incompetent and perhaps fraudulent analysis of mortgage-backed securities by ratings agencies, and an almost unbounded supply of credit available to the housing sector. This explosion of credit resulted from a combination of forces. Among these were the securitization of mortgages into marketable bonds and related esoteric instruments, the rapidly emerging and largely unregulated shadow banking system, the search for investment outlets in the United States for funds accumulated by China and other countries that had amassed vast holdings of dollars through persistent trade surpluses vis-à-vis the United States, and extraordinarily easy monetary policy maintained by the Federal Reserve.

Chapter 5 outlines the chain of events that transpired after housing prices began declining in mid-2006 and the volume of credit began contracting. It demonstrates how the vicious cycle of falling house prices, mortgage foreclosures, and forced home sales begat a cascading series of destructive events. This process culminated in the demise of such icons of the financial world as Lehman Brothers and Merrill Lynch, a run on the nation's money market funds and various shadow-banking institutions, and the insolvency and government takeover of Fannie Mae and Freddie Mac, the nation's government-sponsored but privately owned housing agencies. Chapter 6 details the numerous avenues through which the crisis led to severe contractions in consumption, investment, and other forms of expenditures, thereby accounting for the deepest and longest recession since the Great Depression.

Relative to other books about the Great Crisis, a distinguishing feature of this work is its extensive analysis of Federal Reserve policy. This is warranted in part because of the central responsibility accorded the Federal Reserve historically in dealing with financial crises. In part, it is warranted because the extraordinary and heroic actions taken by the Federal Reserve that very likely prevented a massive economic collapse were crowded out in the contemporary media reports and subsequent analyses by attacks focused principally on banks, the "government," and other alleged villains. An in-depth analysis of the Federal Reserve's response to the Great Crisis is presented and contrasted with Fed behavior in the Great Depression. To facilitate this objective, Chapter 7 provides a broad sketch of the framework of Federal Reserve monetary control, explains how the Fed is able to determine short-term interest rates and the trend growth rate of the nation's money supply, and outlines the tools the Fed uses to exert this control.

Chapter 8 discusses the events of the Great Depression of the early 1930s and analyzes the forces that account for the 30 percent contraction in the money supply from 1929 to 1933. Economists believe this development was instrumental in the onset of severe price level deflation that was the signature characteristic and predominant force accounting for the severity and duration of the Great Depression. The chapter discusses several crucial policy mistakes made by the Fed and looks into the mindset of Federal Reserve officials that might account for these costly mistakes. This chapter is of special interest given that Ben Bernanke, who became Federal Reserve chairman in 2006 and presided over the Fed during and after the Great Crisis, earned his reputation as an economist of the first rank in large part through his research into the Great Depression and the role of the Federal Reserve therein.

Chapter 9 explains the actions taken by the Fed to prevent the Great Crisis from degenerating into Great Depression II. As banks and other economic agents became engulfed in fear with the demise of Lehman Brothers in the fall of 2008, the money multiplier that links the monetary base to the nation's money stock declined even more precipitously than in the Great Depression. The Fed compensated by dramatically expanding its balance sheet, first through innovative lending programs to entities being shut off from normal sources of credit, and shortly thereafter through massive acquisition of mortgage-backed bonds and other securities. These actions by the Fed produced sufficiently rapid increases in bank reserves and base money to prevent the money supply from declining and ushering in a potentially devastating episode of price-level deflation.

Chapter 10 analyzes the tools the Federal Reserve is poised to deploy as the economic recovery eventually becomes sufficiently robust for the Fed to initiate its "exit strategy," intended to prevent the enormous quantity of funds it injected into the banking system during the crisis from unleashing an inflationary increase in bank lending. In this endeavor, the Fed is entering uncharted waters. The chapter examines the political and economic forces that will challenge Fed policymakers as they attempt to navigate the recovery from the Great Recession without experiencing a damaging episode of appreciably higher inflation. Chapter 11 discusses the case for replacing discretionary monetary policy with a monetary policy rule. It analyzes the Taylor rule in depth, and employs it as a standard for purposes of evaluating Fed policy in the years leading up to the Great Crisis as well as in the Great Depression and other episodes in which the Fed has been charged with committing important policy mistakes.

Finally, Chapter 12 examines the way in which a series of socially perverse incentives joined forces to contribute to a pattern of behavior that brought on the Great Crisis. It explains why, pending correction of these misaligned incentives through legislation and other means, economists believe that recurring severe financial crises are inevitable.

In sum, this work aims to provide a comprehensive perspective on the Great Crisis. It is hoped that the dedicated reader will emerge with a substantially firmer grasp of the causes and consequences of the Great Crisis, the role of monetary policy in minimizing its consequences, and the financial reforms that would reduce our vulnerability to future damaging crises. If so, the effort expended in writing this book will have been worthwhile.

Acknowledgments

This work could not have been accomplished without the assistance and encouragement of numerous individuals. Yunyun Lv's almost daily efforts on behalf of this project went far beyond the call of duty of a research assistant. Yunyun is responsible for processing a vast amount of data, constructing almost all of the figures in this book and dozens more that were not used, conducting numerous empirical experiments, and performing other tasks too numerous to mention. Her dedication, perseverance, and loyalty are greatly appreciated. Lisa Taylor also provided timely and able assistance, including construction of the figures in Chapter 11.

I am indebted to Bruce Jaffee for arranging for me to spend my sabbatical leave in the Department of Business Economics and Public Policy at Indiana University. His friendship and support is highly valued. Christina Robertson of IU cheerfully typed the tables in the book. I was fortunate to share an office at Indiana with Jurgen von Hagen, whose remarkable knowledge of the recent literature, both immediately and tangentially related to this work, benefitted the author. Thanks go to Michael Baye, Michele Fratianni, Eric Rasmusen and Catalin Stefanescu of Indiana University and Patrick Gormely, Ed Olson, and Dennis Weisman of Kansas State University for helpful conversations, encouragement, and references to pertinent literature. Dennis Weisman also provided a rigorous and constructive critique of the chapter on financial reform. Mike Greenwood, my former colleague and long-time good friend, has always been an important source of inspiration and support. Dave Mandy, economics department head at the University of Missouri, kindly made an office available to me during the critical month of June, 2010 and Jack Morris, Dean of the College of Business and Economics at the University of Idaho, provided an office in July. Laurie Harting, my editor at Palgrave Macmillan, provided guidance and encouragement, and Tiffany Hufford, assistant editor, helped lift my spirit numerous times with her upbeat e-mail messages in response to myriad inquiries.

My greatest debt is due my wife, Sally, whose generosity, loyalty, and support accounts for anything I have been able to accomplish. She endured many days in which my engrossment in this project meant that I was not there, even at times we were in the same room. Sally also created the art which forms the cover of this book. My daughter, Liz Thomas-Horn, always provides needed encouragement. In addition, she meticulously reviewed each chapter and her considerable talents have appreciably improved the organization and clarity of exposition of this work. My siblings—Martha, Ellen, Mimi, Charlie, and Jeannie—are always an important source of support and encouragement. Finally, Sophie Horn, age 19 months, has been a source of inspiration. Her smile makes hard work seem worthwhile.

Abbreviated Terms

AIG	American Insurance Group
AMLF	Asset-Backed Commercial Paper and Money Market Mutual Fund Facility
ARM	Adjustable-Rate Mortgage
ATM	Automatic Teller Machine
CBO	Congressional Budget Office
CDO	Collateralized Debt Obligation
CDS	Credit Default Swap
CEO	Chief Executive Officer
CMBS	Commercial Mortgage-Backed Security
CPFF	Commercial Paper Funding Facility
CPI	Consumer Price Index
CRA	Community Reinvestment Act
DDO	Demand Deposits and Other Checkable Deposits
FDIC	Federal Deposit Insurance Corporation
FDR	Franklin Delano Roosevelt
FFR	Federal Funds Rate
FOMC	Federal Open Market Committee
FRED	Federal Reserve Economic Database
FRN	Federal Reserve Notes
GDP	Gross Domestic Product
GSE	Government-Sponsored Enterprise
HUD	Housing and Urban Development
IMF	International Monetary Fund
IT	Inflation Targeting
LIBOR	London Interbank Borrowing Rate
MBS	Mortgage-Backed Security
MMMF	Money Market Mutual Fund
NAFTA	North American Free Trade Agreement
NAIRU	Non-Accelerating Inflation Rate of Unemployment

NASDAQ	National Association of Securities Dealers Automated Quotations
NBER	National Bureau of Economic Research
NRSRO	Nationally Recognized Statistical Rating Organization
PCE	Personal Consumption Expenditures
PDCF	Primary Dealer Credit Facility
PPI	Producer Price Index
RGDP	Real Gross Domestic Product
S&L	Savings and Loan Association
SEC	Securities and Exchange Commission
SIV	Structured Investment Vehicle
SWPs	Liquidy Swap Lines
TAF	Term Auction Facility
TALF	Term Asset-Backed Loan Facility

Chapter 1

Financial Crises: An Overview

I. Introduction

In 2007, problems that originated in the U.S. subprime mortgage market set off a world-wide financial crisis of a magnitude not witnessed in 75 years. In the United States, this calamity ended up throwing millions of people out of work, wiping out trillions of dollars of household wealth, causing countless families to lose their homes, and bankrupting thousands of business firms, including more than 250 banks. The financial crisis led directly to fiscal crises in nearly every state in the union and drove the federal budget deficit into territory previously experienced only in the exigent circumstances of all-out war. Financial crises can be devastating, and this one ranks among the most damaging in its ramifications because, unlike the Latin American and Russian crises of the 1980s and 1990s, it originated in the world's most important financial center.

The crisis was not unique to the United States; it touched almost every nation in the world. In part, this pervasiveness was due to the fact that the same fundamental forces that caused the U.S. crisis were experienced in numerous other nations as well. For another part, crises of this severity and source tend strongly to be contagious. Like the influenza pandemic that began at Fort Riley, Kansas, in 1918 and spread in two years to kill more than 600,000 Americans and an estimated 30 million people around the world, a major financial crisis spirals outward from its source to ultimately impact countless people in far-flung portions of the globe. The effects of the crisis in the United States spilled over to infect countries from Iceland to Spain to the Philippines.

A financial crisis occurs when a speculation-driven economic boom is followed by an inevitable bust. A financial crisis may be defined as a major disruption in financial markets, institutions, and economic activity, typically preceded by a rapid expansion of private and public sector debt or money growth, and characterized by sharp declines in prices of real estate, shares of stock and, in many cases, the value of domestic currencies relative to foreign currencies. Ironically, the same aspects of capitalism that provide the vitality that makes it superior to other economic systems in fostering high and rising living standards— the propensity to innovate and willingness to take risk—also make it vulnerable to bubbles that eventually burst with devastating results.

The 2007–2009 worldwide financial crisis, hereafter dubbed the "Great Crisis," was just one of hundreds of financial crises that have occurred around the world over the past few hundred years. Financial crises date back many centuries to the earliest formation of financial markets. In fact, these crises can be traced back thousands of years to the introduction of money in the form of metallic coins in ancient civilizations. In those times, monarchs often clipped the metallic coins of the realm to forge additional money with which to finance military adventures and other expenditures. Such a debasement of currency often led to severe inflation.

Financial crises come in several varieties; the characteristics, causes, and consequences of each type are sketched in this chapter. Chapter 2 focuses on the particular type—the banking crisis—that characterizes the recent Great Crisis and provides a theoretical framework that enables us to understand the forces triggering banking crises and why such crises occur with considerable regularity.

II. Types of Financial Crises

There are four main types of financial crises: sovereign debt defaults, that is, government defaults on debt—foreign, domestic, or both; hyperinflation; exchange rate or currency crises; and banking crises. In recent decades, sovereign defaults and hyperinflation have been experienced predominantly by impoverished and emerging market economies. While most highly developed industrial nations have avoided sovereign defaults and hyperinflation in the past century, exchange rate crises and banking crises have proven much more intractable. In fact, given the nature of human behavior, these types of crises appear unlikely to someday become extinct. Few economists below the age of 60 believe they have witnessed the last major financial crisis of their lifetime. The recent worldwide financial crisis that was initiated by the U.S. subprime mortgage meltdown—the Great Crisis—is classified as a banking crisis, albeit one in which "banking" is broadly defined to include the "shadow banking system," comprising hedge funds, investment banks, and other nonbank institutions that engage in financial intermediation.

Sovereign Defaults

In a sovereign default, a national government simply reneges on its debt. It fails to make interest and/or principal payments when payments are due. While banking crises have occurred in all countries, sovereign debt defaults in modern times have been rare in highly developed nations. Nevertheless, only a handful of nations—the United States, Canada, Australia, New Zealand, and very few others—can claim to have avoided this type of crisis throughout their entire history. Most highly developed nations today (Germany, Japan, U.K.) have resorted to sovereign debt default at some point. Over the centuries the experience of France, Spain, Russia, Turkey, Greece, and numerous other nations has been one of serial sovereign defaults. Governments of Spain, for example, have defaulted more than a dozen times over the course of the nation's history.

A nation's gross domestic product (GDP) is the total value of all final goods and services produced in the nation in a given year. The worldwide economic contraction of 2007–2009 was the first instance since the Great Depression of the early 1930s in which world GDP—the aggregate GDP of all nations—declined. The fiscal ramifications of this episode, henceforth referred to as the Great Recession, exposed the debt problems of numerous euro-currency nations in 2010. Particularly vulnerable were Greece, Portugal, Ireland, Spain, and Italy. The Great Recession sharply reduced tax revenues and induced the implementation of fiscal stimulus programs in these and other nations in 2008 and 2009. This boosted the deficit/GDP ratios of several euro-currency nations (as well as of the U.K. and the United States) into double-digit territory, putting the debt/GDP ratios of several of these nations on a rising and dangerous trajectory. Table 1-1 indicates the budget deficit/GDP and government debt/GDP ratios for several euro-currency nations, along with the U.K. and the United States, as of the end of 2009.[1]

In the spring and summer of 2010, the fiscal problems of Greece occupied the headlines. The reputation of the profligate Greek government was damaged when it was revealed that it had used esoteric derivative transactions devised by a Wall Street investment bank to disguise the true state of its budgetary problems. While Germany and other members of the euro community debated the terms on which financial support might be extended to Greece to stave off a prospective sovereign default, the credit-rating agencies downgraded the status of Portugal's debt. At

Table 1-1   Measures of Fiscal Condition in 2009 (Selected Countries)

Country	Budget Deficit/GDP (%)	Government Debt/GDP (%)
Greece	13.6	115
Ireland	14.3	64
UK	11.5	68
United States	11.5	81
Spain	11.2	53
Portugal	9.4	77
Germany	3.3	73

Source: Eurostat and FRED database.

the same time, severe fiscal problems experienced by other euro currency countries—notably Spain and Ireland—threatened the harmony and stability of the European community. The contrast between the fiscal circumstances of Germany and those of such euro-currency nations as Greece, Ireland, and Portugal, as illustrated in Table 1.1, is palpable.

As viewed from the vantage point of summer 2010, Greece appeared to be caught in a death spiral resulting from a debt/GDP ratio that exceeded 100 percent, coupled with enormous budget deficits and surging bond yields driven by increasing fears of sovereign debt default. Extremely high bond yields meant that servicing the debt was driving the budget deficit sharply higher and rapidly boosting the nation's debt/GDP ratio. As Greek bond yields approached 20 percent and the tipping point appeared imminent in May 2010, the euro-currency nations and the International Monetary Fund (IMF) put together an enormous rescue package approaching $1 trillion. In return, the Greek government agreed to implement a package of unprecedented austerity, including wage cuts for Greek workers, severe budget cuts eliminating thousands of jobs and numerous perks for government bureaucrats, and major tax increases, coupled with the assurance of a crackdown on widespread tax evasion.

While the announcement of this agreement soothed immediate fears of sovereign default, the financial markets sensed a significant likelihood of the Greek crisis becoming contagious, spreading to Spain, Portugal, Ireland, and other euro-currency nations struggling with large and rapidly increasing debt burdens. The austerity measures implemented by these countries (as well as by the U.K.) to bring down budget deficits threatened to plunge Europe back into recession and impinge adversely on the U.S. economic recovery from the Great Recession. Germany, traditionally the most fiscally conservative of the euro-currency nations, appeared intransigent in its unwillingness to employ stimulus measures that might ease the burden on its neighbors. The European crisis is likely to simmer for years, and it is not clear at the time of this writing (October 2010) whether the 16-nation euro-currency bloc will survive in its 2010 makeup. The possibility of sovereign debt default, even among industrial nations, is alive and well today.[2]

Hyperinflation

A second type of financial crisis, hyperinflation, is essentially a de facto default on debt—a more subtle form of default than sovereign default. With hyperinflation, governments and other debtors pay interest and repay the principal on their debts with units of currency that are worth dramatically less than their values at the times the debts were incurred.[3] Less developed countries and emerging nations are much more prone to hyperinflation than are modern industrial nations.

Nevertheless, if we (arbitrarily) define hyperinflation as inflation at rates in excess of 100 percent per year, few nations can claim they have never experienced hyperinflation. Germany experienced such extreme inflation in the early 1920s that billions of marks were needed in 1923 to purchase a good or service that a single mark had purchased ten years earlier. Poland and Russia also experienced episodes of inflation at rates in excess of 10,000 percent per year in the early 1920s, as did Hungary, Greece, and China in the mid-1940s. In the 1980s and 1990s, such Latin American nations as Argentina, Bolivia, Brazil, and Peru were plagued by bouts of inflation at rates in excess of 1,000 percent per year. And even the United States had one experience with hyperinflation—a brief period of inflation with annual rates in excess of 150 percent in 1779, during the Revolutionary War.[4]

Hyperinflation typically occurs in a nation with an unstable and often corrupt government, a poorly developed financial system, and a rudimentary or virtually nonexistent tax system. Without a satisfactory tax system, a government must borrow to finance itself—it is forced to deficit spend. But given the absence of developed bond markets, along with a dearth of savings among the populace in poor countries and a widespread distrust of government in such nations, governments typically finance deficits through the exploitation of subservient central banks. The government borrows directly from the central bank or simply prints large quantities of the currency to finance expenditures. Therefore, the money placed in the private sector as the government spends is not recouped, either through tax receipts or through sales of bonds to private sector entities. The quantity of money increases as the government makes payments for goods, services, and salaries of government employees.

Rapid expansion of the money supply typically leads to rapid increases in expenditures, driving up prices of goods and services. After a period of high and rising inflation, hyperinflation sets in. To see how this happens, consider that inflation essentially imposes a tax on money (checking accounts and currency), the tax rate being the rate of inflation. Money depreciates in real value each year at a rate equal to the rate of inflation. As inflation rises, the tax rate increases and people respond by reducing demand for money—that is, they are less willing to hold wealth in the form of money. After reaching a critical threshold, rising inflation expectations begin to cause people to spend money more quickly to beat the anticipated price hikes. They rid themselves of it more rapidly to purchase goods and services and real assets. The velocity of money increases, and prices begin increasing even more rapidly than the nation's money supply. Once this mechanism sets in, it is extremely difficult to eradicate inflation. In many instances, hyperinflation is followed by a collapse of the monetary economy, as the unwillingness of people to accept money as payment means that the process of exchange reverts to a system of barter. The extreme inefficiency inherent in a barter economy means that depression is almost inevitable.

Exchange Rate Crises

A third type of financial crisis is an exchange rate crisis or currency crisis. Emerging economies—those not as rich as the United States and other highly industrialized nations but not as poor as most African countries—seem especially susceptible to exchange rate crises. In the past 20 years, currency crises have occurred in such countries as Mexico in 1994; Thailand, Malaysia, Hong Kong, Indonesia, the Philippines and South Korea in 1997 and 1998; Russia in 1998; and Argentina and Turkey in 2001. In addition to encompassing asset price declines and severe problems in the banking sector, exchange rate crises are characterized by large-scale capital flight as funds are withdrawn and placed in countries that exhibit more favorable economic prospects. The outflow of financial capital triggers exchange rate depreciation, higher inflation, rising interest rates, falling asset prices, and increasing bank failures.

Exchange rate crises are typically preceded by a period of large and sustained inflows of financial capital from other nations. These capital inflows often arise in response to the liberalization of markets, in which competition is promoted through dismantling of government controls, privatization of government-owned industries, and removal of impediments to international trade in goods and services. Such reforms often lead to perceptions that the economic outlook and rates of return on assets in the nation are likely to be superior in the foreseeable future. Agents in foreign nations invest in countries in which expected returns are highest, and economic liberalization of a previously repressed economy tends to create such opportunities. Following a series of annual capital inflows, a nation has accumulated large debts to foreign nations, typically amounting to a significant percentage of its GDP. The nation that is the recipient of these capital inflows thus becomes vulnerable to unexpected shocks. A shock eventually occurs that reverses the inflow of capital, leading to a depreciation of the nation's currency.

Mexico's currency crisis of the early 1990s provides a clear example. Following a major debt crisis in 1982, a consensus was reached in Mexico in the mid-1980s that prosperity and growth could be best achieved through a policy of market liberalization. State enterprises were privatized, tariffs were reduced, and import restrictions were lifted.

A regime headed by Carlos Salinas and staffed by Ph.D. economists trained at American Ivy League universities ascended to power in 1988. Shortly thereafter, the Brady Plan of 1989 called for forgiveness of much of the foreign debt accumulated by Mexico in the previous decade. The North American Free Trade Agreement (NAFTA), originally negotiated between the United States and Canada, was extended to include Mexico. Prospects for future Mexican exports to the United States and Canada brightened. It appeared that Salinas's free trade initiatives and market liberalization would bring permanent benefits to Mexico. Taken in tandem, the extension to Mexico of the NAFTA treaty, the Brady Plan for debt forgiveness, and the market liberalization program of the Salinas regime produced a major change in the outlook for prosperity in Mexico. Foreign capital began flowing into the country, including more than $30 billion in 1993 alone.

In the case of Mexico, early hints of an impending crisis began to appear as the emergence of large budget deficits and rapidly increasing government debt began to make foreign holders of government bonds wary of possible sovereign default on this debt. Anticipation of economic repercussions associated with an impending government default rendered privately issued debt also unacceptably risky to foreign investors. For Mexico, the tipping point came with the March 1994 assassination of the charismatic presidential candidate Donaldo Colosio, heir apparent to Salinas, together with a rebellion in the poverty-stricken state of Chiapas. These events dashed hopes of sustained political stability and contributed to the capital flight.

In such situations, the government typically does not have sufficient reserves of foreign currencies to prevent currency depreciation. In many instances, emerging nations fix their exchange rate to the U.S. dollar to hold down inflation and contribute to stability. Especially in a fixed exchange rate regime, strong signals of impending problems in an emerging nation lead to a one-sided speculative attack on the currency because it is clear to speculators that the domestic currency will either be devalued or the exchange rate will remain unchanged. (Devaluation means that a unit of domestic currency buys fewer units of foreign currency.) There is virtually no prospect that the currency will be revalued—that is, changed in value so that a unit of domestic currency buys *more* units of foreign currency. This circumstance presents speculators with a "heads I win, tails I break even" proposition. These one-sided speculative attacks often force the country to devalue its currency.

While devaluation or depreciation of a nation's currency makes its products more competitive in world markets, it also creates problems. In emerging economies such as Mexico, Argentina, and Russia, debts of firms are often denominated in foreign currencies such as dollars rather than in domestic currencies such as pesos or rubles. Because a devaluation of the peso means that the peso buys fewer dollars, it takes more pesos to fetch the dollars needed to pay the debt. The devaluation increases the indebtedness (liabilities) of domestic firms, as measured in units of domestic currency. The net worth of domestic firms is thus reduced. This means that more firms that are indebted to banks are likely to become insolvent. A major depreciation of the domestic currency results in increased bankruptcies of domestic firms and other borrowers, along with widespread loan defaults. These developments often lead to increasing bank failures.

In addition, the collapse of the currency typically results in higher inflation as the prices of imported goods, measured in units of domestic currency, immediately increase. The credibility of a central bank in emerging countries is often low to begin with because of past experience. The currency depreciation and associated initial increase in inflation is likely to quickly boost inflation expectations, which may trigger additional downward pressure on the exchange rate. A vicious cycle of inflation and currency depreciation can easily develop in such instances. Unless the devaluation of the currency is accompanied by implementation of reforms that convince market participants that things are well under control, this process is likely to feed upon itself. The country is thus susceptible to a devastating pattern of capital outflows, currency depreciation, inflation, and additional capital outflows and associated currency depreciation.

This is exactly what happened to Mexico, as massive capital outflows led to a 50 percent depreciation of the peso. This sharply increased the peso value of debts that were indexed to the U.S. dollar, thereby raising the specter of default on debt. Interest rates increased sharply as lenders required a premium to compensate for risk, thus exacerbating the government's fiscal problems. The sovereign debt crisis spilled over to the real economy. A severe recession ensued, with Mexican output falling nearly 8 percent and thousands of business firms going bankrupt.

The 2001 currency or exchange rate crisis of Argentina strongly conforms to this general outline of the cycle of events. For many decades, Argentina had a history of chronic government budget deficits, financed by money creation. Inflation was endemic. In the 1980s, for example, inflation was extremely high. It increased from annual rates of around 100 percent at the beginning of the decade to more than 2,000 percent by 1989. But in that year, a new president, Carlos Menem, ascended to power. His administration implemented a set of policies that met with sufficient early success to dramatically improve the economic outlook.

The Menem government attacked the formidable inflation problem through several initiatives. First, it reduced the budget deficit through a combination of spending cuts and higher taxes. It established a currency board in which the peso was tied rigidly to the U.S. dollar, fixing the peso–dollar exchange rate at $1 per peso. In the currency board, Argentineans were permitted to exchange their pesos for dollars on a one-for-one basis, and the central bank was required to maintain a sufficient stock of dollars to make this feasible. By requiring that each peso in circulation be backed by one dollar of reserves, the new currency board ensured that the Argentine government would be unable to finance new expenditures through money creation. Given the currency board, Argentina's monetary fate would be tied to that of the United States. The radical decision to adopt the currency board provided essential credibility that helped bring down inflation expectations in Argentina, thus reducing the cost of policies aimed at eradicating the severely entrenched inflation. The Menem administration also implemented a major economic liberalization program, dismantling trade barriers and privatizing formerly state-owned enterprises.

For a time, the policy worked amazingly well. Inflation fell precipitously, reaching an annual rate of less than 5 percent by 1994. Confidence in the government's program and the economy soared as output increased by more than 20 percent in three years and the unemployment rate fell sharply. Foreign capital flowed into the country as foreign banks began buying Argentinean government bonds and foreign private investors purchased bonds issued by the newly privatized corporations. This capital inflow, coupled with the decline in inflation expectations, resulted in lower interest rates. This, in turn, facilitated the government's deficit reduction efforts by reducing interest expenses incurred in servicing the debt. The makings of a virtuous cycle began to form.

Unfortunately, however, the good times were short lived. Problems soon began to reappear. Government spending in Argentine provinces, outside the central administration's control, expanded rapidly, causing the nation's aggregate government budget deficit to increase. Perhaps most importantly, while inflation had come down sharply in the early 1990s, it remained higher than inflation in the United States. Given that the peso–dollar exchange rate was rigidly fixed, this meant that the *real* Argentine exchange rate, expressed as dollars per peso, was appreciating. The peso increased by more than 50 percent in real terms, placing Argentina at a severe disadvantage in international trade. Net exports declined sharply. A lesson learned through this episode is that a country like Argentina that is forced to devalue its currency should ensure that the devaluation is of sufficient magnitude that the country's export products are strongly competitive in international markets.

Following Mexico's experience of a few years earlier, capital began flowing out of Argentina and other Latin American nations. This reduced the supply of loans and boosted interest rates in Argentina, thus adversely impacting consumption and investment spending and increasing the cost of servicing the debt. Coupled with the decline in net exports, this resulted in a severe recession in the mid-1990s. The unemployment rate moved above 15 percent and the severe decline in economic activity boosted the nation's budget deficit as tax receipts plunged.

Soon, visions of possible sovereign default and currency devaluation became established. Capital flight increased. This intensified the nation's problems. In late 2001, the government stopped making payments on its debt. This triggered a severe banking crisis in Argentina as the value of government bonds held by domestic banks plunged, adding to the loss of bank capital arising from increasing loan defaults attributable to the ongoing decline in output and increase in unemployment. Then things took a dramatic turn for the worse. Given the absence of deposit insurance and visions of escalating bank failures, depositors panicked and attempted to withdraw their funds from banks. A full-scale banking crisis was now underway. The government reacted by placing severe restrictions on withdrawal of funds from banks, leading to a major political crisis. Civil unrest escalated, and riots and looting became widespread in December 2001.

The president resigned, the currency board was terminated, and the peso plunged in the foreign exchange markets as speculators attacked the currency en masse. This triggered a sharp increase in the cost of imports and a decline in living standards. A major increase in the peso value of dollar-denominated debts caused by the currency depreciation resulted in an increase in corporate bankruptcies in Argentina. By the end of the severe 2000–2002 recession, the unemployment rate exceeded 20 percent. Ultimately, the depreciation of the peso began to reverse the downward momentum of economic activity, and recovery set in as exports expanded strongly after 2002. But the financial crisis exacted a huge price in terms of hardship as measured by massive unemployment and associated loss of output and income in Argentina.

Banking Crises

The final category of financial crisis, and the most prevalent and seemingly intractable type for highly developed nations like the United States, Great Britain, and major European nations, is the banking crisis. The United States suffered major banking crises in 1819, 1837, 1857, 1873, 1893, 1907, and 1929–1933, as well as the Great Crisis of 2007–2009.

In a banking crisis, large-scale defaults on bank loans induced by unexpected changes in underlying economic conditions systematically reduce the capital or net worth of numerous banks. A bank's capital is the amount by which the value of its assets exceeds the value of its liabilities. The predominant assets of the typical bank are its loans, while its main liabilities are its debts in the form of customers' deposits and other borrowed funds. Banks borrow from those entities with surplus funds on hand, such as depositors, and lend them to those needing access to such funds to expand a business, buy a house, and so forth. As more of a bank's loans go bad during hard times, the value of its total assets drops, thus reducing its capital by a like amount. In the event a bank's total assets fall below its total liabilities, the bank's capital is negative and it is insolvent.

All nations suffer the vicissitudes of business cycles—the age-old rhythmic pattern of economic life in which periods of high prosperity are followed by periods of hard times that ultimately give way to recovery and rising prosperity in a never-ending cycle. Once an economic downturn sets in, or in times when other serious economic shocks occur, many banks suffer a decline in capital as a result of escalating loan defaults, banking panics, or both. As economic circumstances deteriorate and increasing numbers of borrowers find themselves unable to make payments on bank loans, defaults increase. Borrowers' assets posted as collateral—houses, commercial property, shares of stock, and so forth—are seized by the bank. These assets are dumped on the market, sometimes at fire sale prices. This process may trigger a vicious cycle of falling property prices, additional collateral calls and loan defaults, and escalating bank failures. The contraction of bank capital, coupled with the inevitable deterioration in the economic outlook as perceived by bank management, results in a tightening of lending standards. To make matters worse, households and firms become increasingly averse to incurring debt as output, employment, and both business and consumer confidence deteriorate. These forces feed into a downward spiral of economic activity. In a negative feedback loop, rising unemployment and declining economic activity lead to additional loan defaults, more bank failures, and additional credit tightening by lending institutions.

The banking crisis of 1929–1933 was the result of a contagious banking panic in which the public, fearing for the safety of their banks, rushed to withdraw uninsured deposits. Because banks hold only a small fraction of their deposit liabilities in cash and highly liquid assets, they were forced to call in loans and sell bonds in an effort to satisfy their depositors' demands for cash. As banks called in these loans and refused to renew others, many legitimate borrowers were shut off from essential credit, thereby disrupting business activity, triggering an economic downturn, and increasing the incidence of bad loans. And as thousands of banks sold bonds in the scramble to obtain cash for their panicked depositors, bond prices fell sharply. This reduced the value of assets of all banks holding such bonds, worsening the financial condition of many banks, including those that had few bad loans on their books. This process was contagious because failure of a particular bank led depositors at other banks to fear for their safety as well, thereby increasing the likelihood of a run on those banks. In addition, because the failure of numerous banks results in a contraction in economic activity, previously sound loans in thousands of banks to go bad, weakening those banks. All told, more than 9,000 banks failed and bank loans declined sharply in the Great Depression of the early 1930s.

The Great Crisis of 2007–2009 was initiated by falling house prices. Prior to the Great Crisis, house prices in the United States and numerous other countries were bid up in a speculative frenzy to untenably high levels. As these prices began falling, households that had purchased homes with little or no down payment received calls from lending institutions for more collateral. Many of these households, unable to comply, lost their homes. Banks repossessed the houses and put them on the market for sale. Such actions became widespread, leading to a self-reinforcing downward spiral in housing prices that was of unimaginable proportion. Bonds made up of pools of individual mortgages and owned by banks and other financial intermediaries declined sharply in value, imperiling the financial condition of hundreds of institutions, including several of the nation's largest banks. As aggregate bank capital declined, thousands of banks began reducing loans, a process known as deleveraging.[5] Loans that had been extremely easy to obtain during the preceding boom now were almost impossible to obtain in many instances, in spite of extraordinary efforts by the Federal Reserve to provide banks with ample funds. Through this and other channels, the Great Crisis led to the Great Recession.

III. Conclusion

This book tells the story of how numerous factors conspired to create enormous bubbles in credit and house prices in the United States and several other nations in the decade extending from 1996 to 2006. It describes the chain reaction that was ignited as the twin bubbles began deflating, giving rise to the most devastating contraction in economic activity since the Great Depression. The story recounts the almost inexplicable failure of the Federal Reserve to contain the wave of bank failures that was instrumental in causing the Great Depression, and contrasts this failure with the remarkable feats of the Federal Reserve and other major central banks in preventing the Great Crisis of 2007–2009 from degenerating into an economic cataclysm rivaling the earlier debacle. The story goes on to tell how these forceful and creative efforts were however unable to prevent the Great Recession—the deepest economic downturn in 75 years. Our tale ends on a cautious but hopeful note: cautious because financial crises are recurring events, endemic to capitalism and not to be eradicated; hopeful because financial reforms being put in place by the United States and other major nations stand a fair chance of rendering the next crisis less devastating.

Chapter 2

The Nature of Banking Crises

I. Introduction

The United States has experienced more than ten banking crises since the beginning of the twentieth century. This chapter begins by outlining a theory that helps us understand why such crises occur over and over again in nations throughout the world. These crises are also seldom confined to a single country—they strongly tend to occur in clusters, with numerous nations almost simultaneously experiencing the same problems. The Great Crisis of 2007–2009 proved to be contagious, quickly spreading from the United States to many parts of the globe. The underlying forces behind this phenomenon and the various channels through which crises are transmitted from country to country are explored in this chapter. Because the Great Crisis caught U.S. officials by surprise, this chapter discusses the contentious issue of whether careful monitoring of emerging patterns may make it possible to foresee or predict crises, and thus take measures to lessen their impact. Finally, the chapter analyzes the macroeconomic fallout from banking crises and explains why the associated economic contractions tend to be more damaging than recessions that occur in the absence of financial crises.

II. The Minsky Theory of Financial Crises

In a series of works published in the 1980s and early 1990s, Hyman Minsky developed an important theory of financial crises.[1] This theory helps us understand the forces that create financial crises and explains why these crises occur with such regularity. Minsky spent most of his career at academic institutions such as Brown, Berkeley, and Washington University in St. Louis. He died in 1997. Perhaps because the United States and other highly developed nations experienced an unusual period of sustained economic stability in the quarter century extending from the severe 1981–1982 worldwide recession through the mid-2000s, Minsky's work received relatively little attention during his lifetime. However, because his theory of financial crises turned out to be remarkably prescient in accounting for the unfolding of the chain of events of 2007–2009 throughout the world, Minsky's work is now widely admired and increasingly cited by economists.

Minsky argued that capitalism contains a critical flaw: recurring financial crises and economic instability are inherent characteristics of the system. He believed that the nature of banking and financial institutions, in becoming increasingly interdependent over time, would inevitably lead to major crises that wreak havoc on the nation's overall economy. In Minsky's framework, the supply of credit plays the central role in accounting for financial crises.

Credit Expansion in the Upswing

In the early portion of the expansion phase of the business cycle, firms become aware of potential payoffs from prospective new investment projects. This change in outlook typically stems from what Minsky terms a "displacement"—an event such as emergence of an important new technology, the financial liberalization of a country, the end of a war, or other salient development.

This "displacement" boosts the expected returns on a number of prospective investment projects. These initial investments, financed primarily through borrowing, soon result in an increase in the nation's rate of economic growth. This contributes to an improving economic outlook, leading more business firms and prospective entrepreneurs to revise upward their expected rates of return on a broader array of investment projects, thus driving many of these expected returns appreciably above the rate of interest on loans. Existing firms and emerging entrepreneurs increase their demand for loans to take advantage of the promising investment opportunities.

In step with borrowers, lenders also become increasingly optimistic, revising downward their assessment of risk associated with prospective loans. They ease lending standards, thus accommodating the growing demand. And with prices of stocks and real estate typically appreciating during this phase, the value of collateral posted by current and prospective borrowers increases, further supporting expansion of bank credit. Risk aversion on the part of both borrowers and lenders declines, and bankers soon begin granting loans they had previously deemed too risky.

As optimism about the economic outlook increases and demand for credit escalates, new banks are formed and other lenders emerge.[2] This new competition may induce established banks to expand loans in an effort to maintain market share. Economic activity becomes increasingly robust as the economy enters the boom phase of the business cycle. Loan losses at banks and other lending institutions decline, encouraging these institutions to reduce minimum down-payments for purchase of real estate and ease margin requirements for purchase of stocks. Assets appreciate strongly, financed by increased indebtedness. In the beginning stages of the process, the increased borrowing may not significantly increase the leverage (debt/net worth or debt/income) of borrowers because asset appreciation tends to boost net worth and income. Soon, however, rising indebtedness means an appreciable increase in leverage takes place. Debt increases relative to borrowers' income and net worth, making borrowers vulnerable to any future deterioration in economic conditions.

In the manic phase of inflation of the bubble in credit and asset prices, borrowers are lured into seeking quick capital gains. Making money now appears to be easy. People observe friends and others becoming wealthy through real estate, stock market, and other ventures and seek to join in. They purchase these assets not for the stream of income expected to be returned over the years from them but rather out of expectations that the assets can quickly be resold at higher prices. Attempts to turn quick profits on stocks, houses, and other assets become increasingly prevalent. Day trading in stocks by neophyte speculators operating online through discount brokerage firms becomes increasingly widespread.[3] In the euphoria of the moment, past episodes of financial disappointment are forgotten. People are now purchasing condominiums before the construction has commenced—with the intent of reselling them upon completion of construction. Total credit outstanding increases strongly in this phase. The apex of the cycle is at hand.

Credit Contraction in the Downswing

The ensuing downturn may begin spontaneously, or it may be triggered by a negative shock such as announcement of an important corporation's bankruptcy, an unexpected increase in interest rates initiated by the central bank, or myriad other developments. Even in the absence of a specific shock, the economy inevitably begins to slow at some point. Like a bicycle that is slowing in speed, things become unstable before the speed reaches zero. The trajectory of asset prices often swings from positive to negative with little or no transition period of stability. Perhaps because the nation's output growth inevitably slows as the level of production approaches capacity, actual rates of return on assets begin to decline, and expected returns quickly follow. These actual and expected rates of return soon fall below the interest rates being paid by borrowers, which were elevated by market forces during the boom phase. Because loans are no longer profitable for the borrowers, following a short period of this "negative carry," they begin liquidating assets to repay loans.

Prices of stocks, real estate, and other assets therefore begin declining as well. This initially creates problems for heavily leveraged borrowers, including those who took out zero or low down-payment mortgages on homes as well as speculators who borrowed heavily to purchase stocks and other assets. The contraction in real estate and stock values reduces the value of the collateral supporting the loans. Lenders issue collateral calls to borrowers, inducing forced sales of assets and further driving down their prices. Homeowners who are "underwater" with negative equity in their homes begin defaulting on their mortgages. This process feeds on itself as bank foreclosures and liquidation of houses adds to the downward pressure on prices.

Soon, the economy is in recession and unemployment is rising. The drumbeat of negative economic news becomes incessant and confidence wanes. Stock prices plummet, thus reducing wealth and feeding into the pattern of dwindling expenditures, falling output, and declining employment. As unemployment increases, more and more bank loans go bad, reducing bank capital and forcing banks to liquidate assets in weak markets in order to meet capital standards. Bank failures increase, and a vicious cycle of falling asset prices, increasing debt defaults, rising unemployment, and additional bank failures becomes established. Optimism has given way to profound pessimism. Demand for loans declines as consumption and investment expenditures decline. In addition, banks tighten lending standards, and loans that were once plentiful become extremely difficult to obtain. Demand for goods and services, output, and employment all take a nosedive, exacerbating the contraction of asset values, economic activity, and credit outstanding. The cycle reaches its nadir.

Hedge, Speculative, and Ponzi Financial Arrangements

Minsky spoke of three types of financial arrangements engaged in by individuals and firms that borrow. He termed these arrangements "hedge finance," "speculative finance," and "Ponzi finance." In hedge finance, the borrower is able to make all of the payment obligations of interest and principal out of cash flows from the investment. Thus, a corporation that issues bonds to finance expansion of the firm pays the annual interest as it comes due, and also pays off the principal at maturity from the cash flows derived from the project. In speculative finance, the borrower is able to meet the interest payments on the loan as they come due but makes no progress on reducing the principal on the loan. The principal is never repaid out of the proceeds from the project and the loan must be refinanced at maturity. In Ponzi finance, the corporation is unable to generate sufficient cash flows from the investment to pay even the interest on the loan. Unpaid interest must be added to the principal, which must be rolled over periodically in ever-larger magnitudes. The Ponzi borrower is gambling on solid and persistent appreciation in the value of assets acquired with borrowed funds. If there is no appreciable increase in the value of these assets as expected, the individual or firm is headed for serious trouble.

In terms of mortgage debt, a borrower engaging in hedge finance makes regular payments on a fully amortized mortgage, so that a part of each monthly payment reduces the remaining principal on the debt. When the mortgage reaches maturity, the homeowner owns the house free and clear, having paid off the entire debt. In a speculative finance venture, the homeowner takes out an "interest-only" mortgage and at maturity must take out a new mortgage of the same magnitude as the original mortgage. In this type of finance, the homeowner runs the risk that interest rates and monthly payments at the time the mortgage is to be refinanced may be higher than on the initial debt, as well as the risk that the value of the home may have declined sufficiently to put the homeowner underwater. If this happens, prospects for renewing the mortgage are endangered. In Ponzi finance, payments on the mortgage are insufficient to meet the monthly interest due on the loan. In this negative amortization loan, the mortgage balance rises over time, without limit. If the value of the house fails to increase in line with the size of the mortgage, the borrower finds himself underwater. The lender may then demand additional collateral, likely forcing the borrower to default.

Minsky's key hypothesis is that over periods of sustained prosperity, the financial system gradually transitions from financial relationships that are consistent with a stable system to those that lead to financial instability. Over a lengthy period of good times, a financial structure dominated by conservative hedge finance inevitably gives way to the one in which speculative and Ponzi finance play ever-larger roles. This makes the system increasingly unstable and fragile. A crisis becomes an accident waiting to happen. For example, if the central bank raises interest rates during an economic boom in an attempt to reduce inflation in the presence of significant elements of speculative and Ponzi finance, assets must be liquidated in order to meet the higher interest obligations. Many of those initially practicing speculative finance will be forced into Ponzi status, and those already in Ponzi status will almost surely be forced to liquidate assets financed by the loans. This is likely to result in a chain reaction of falling prices of stocks, bonds, and real estate, with associated rising debt defaults and bank failures.

In essence, Minsky argues that long periods of economic stability inevitably lead to episodes of serious instability. This results from the human psychological propensity to exhibit herding behavior, in which people buy a particular asset not because of its fundamental value, but simply because others are purchasing it. Because such behavior is inconsistent with the tenets of rational expectations, the predominant assumption of macroeconomic analysis since the "rational expectations revolution" of the 1970s, Minsky's theory did not accord with contemporary economic analysis during his lifetime. Once again, however, because of its prescience in accounting for the recent worldwide crisis that commenced in 2007, the theory has gained increasing attention and respect.

As indicated, Minsky's framework accounts for the events of 2002–2006 quite well. The remarkable economic stability experienced in the two decades prior to the development of the twin bubbles in credit and house prices led to overconfidence and complacency on the part of borrowers, lenders, the Federal Reserve and the various regulatory authorities. Economic agents increasingly became convinced that advances in the art and science of monetary policy, together with the new financial technologies that ostensibly had both reduced risk and reallocated remaining risk to those most capable of assessing and incurring it, had brought forth a "new economy" that would be devoid of the severe cycles of the past.

Just as Minsky's model predicts, however, reckless behavior increased as financial arrangements evolved from a preponderance of hedge finance to increasingly prevalent elements of speculative finance, and ultimately to a considerable element of Ponzi finance. To cite just one aspect of this transition, traditional, thoroughly documented 20 percent down-payment fixed-rate mortgages increasingly gave way to nondocumented low and zero down-payment, variable-rate mortgages, and negative amortization loans. In the latter stages of this transition, overly optimistic households overreached, purchasing second homes or trading up to much larger, more expensive homes that turned out to be unaffordable. Increasingly aggressive mortgage lenders of questionable integrity lured unsophisticated borrowers into nondocumented, zero down-payment, and negative amortization loans, many of which featured higher mortgage rates than the buyers were qualified for.

III. Clustering, International Transmission, and Predictability of Banking Crises

There is a strong tendency for banking crises to emerge in clusters. This clustering—half a dozen or more countries almost simultaneously experiencing crises—occurs for two reasons. First, numerous countries often experience the same forces that are ultimately responsible for the crises. Secondly, financial crises are highly contagious, tending to spread from the country of origin—the epicenter—to numerous other nations. The fact that banking crises share many common characteristics and are so costly has led economists to begin exploring whether financial crises can be predicted. If they can be, perhaps policies could be put in place to reduce their severity and ameliorate their consequences. These ideas will be discussed in this section.

Clustering of Banking Crises

Many historical episodes of important financial crises that were experienced nearly simultaneously in numerous countries can be cited. In many cases, a shock common to numerous countries explains the clustering. For example, commodity prices are determined in world markets. If the price of oil, copper, cotton, coffee, or rubber were to decline sharply, numerous countries would experience elevated exposure to crisis as firms producing these commodities experience severe problems and default on loans. The banking crises of 1907, the early 1930s, and the early 1980s were triggered by major drops in commodity prices. For example, in 1907 a sharp decline in copper prices that initiated a panic in the United States (detailed in chapter 3) simultaneously impacted other copper-producing countries like Chile and Mexico. In the Great Depression of the early 1930s, real (inflation-adjusted) commodity prices fell in half, heavily influencing emerging market nations dependent on commodity exports, such as Argentina, Brazil, Mexico, and China. In a similar fashion, the severe worldwide recession of 1981–1983 resulted in a dramatic fall in commodity prices, causing both banking and sovereign debt crises in Argentina, Brazil, and Mexico, as well as in Colombia, Ecuador, Uruguay, and the Philippines.

In the years immediately preceding the recent Great Crisis, housing bubbles—the proximate source of the U.S. crisis—formed not only in the United States, but in numerous other nations as well. In fact, the real price of houses increased even more rapidly during 2002–2006 in France, Spain, Denmark, Poland, Iceland, and New Zealand than in the United States. In the age of the Internet and instant worldwide communication, waves of sentiment that drive bubbles are unlikely to be confined to a single country. It is therefore not surprising that the bursting of housing bubbles directly led to banking crises in all of these nations.

A factor that often fuels multicountry credit and asset-price booms that are the prelude to banking crises are large and sustained inflows of foreign capital. The United States exhibited large current account deficits and associated capital inflows during the decade leading up to the Great Crisis.[4] In the same period, Ireland, Spain, the United Kingdom, Iceland, and New Zealand also experienced large capital inflows that helped fuel dual credit and housing bubbles in these nations. In addition, as detailed in chapter 1, sudden reversals of capital inflows, caused by a change in the economic outlook, led to currency and banking crises in Latin American nations in the mid-1990s (Mexico, Argentina, and Brazil) and in the emerging Asian countries in the late 1990s (Hong Kong, Malaysia, Taiwan, Thailand, and Vietnam).

International Transmission of Banking Crises

Contagion contributes powerfully to the clustering of financial crises. A crisis-induced recession in a major nation like the United States or Japan spills over through several channels to appreciably reduce economic activity and weaken banking systems in countries whose livelihood depends on exporting to these large-economy countries. For example, the Great Recessions in the United States and Europe directly lowered demand for Asian exports, thus weakening Asian economies and increasing their exposure to banking crises. In addition, as the U.S. economy slowed in 2007 and moved into recession at the end of the year, U.S. interest rates fell sharply, leading initially to depreciation of the U.S. dollar in foreign exchange markets. The corresponding appreciation of currencies of U.S. trading partners raised the prices of their export products in U.S. markets, thus exacerbating the contraction in these nations' exports and boosting their vulnerability to crises.[5]

In such countries as Mexico, Guatemala, Colombia, and Nicaragua, remittances sent home by migrant workers in the United States constitute an important source of purchasing power. When employment opportunities dried up for migrant workers in construction and other U.S. sectors hammered by the Great Recession, Latin American nations were adversely affected as well.

Money markets around the world are highly interconnected. When a major country experiences financial problems, this tends to quickly ripple through world money markets to disrupt events elsewhere. For example, when Lehman Brothers, one of the large U.S. investment banks, filed for bankruptcy in September 2008, the commercial paper—short-term debt issued by reputedly safe corporations to fund daily operations—that Lehman had issued became worthless. Because money market funds around the world are major holders of this paper, news of Lehman's failure triggered an international panic in that market. Interbank markets in which large banks around the world lend to each other became impaired as banks with funds available to lend became fearful that their prospective counterparties might be holding large quantities of commercial paper issued by Lehman and thus be unable to repay the loans. Interbank lending rates quickly jumped by four percentage points and this market became nearly dysfunctional. This, in turn, made it impossible for many banks to obtain funds to loan viable business firms seeking bank credit.

Of critical importance, major financial institutions around the globe own large blocks of securities issued in other nations. In the nineteenth century, Great Britain was the world's foremost economic power. In the 1840s, British railroad bonds were in vogue, held by financial institutions around the world. When many of these bonds went bad, major losses were suffered by these institutions, contributing to banking crises in several nations. In connection with the recent Great Crisis, large quantities of AAA-rated mortgage-backed bonds and related securities issued in the United States were held by banks, pension funds, and other institutions throughout Europe, Asia, and elsewhere. As these bonds became toxic with the decline in U.S. house prices, the financial conditions of these foreign institutions deteriorated. The infection of lending institutions in Europe was particularly damaging because European corporations rely more on banks for access to credit than their U.S. counterparts, who can normally also obtain funds directly in capital markets by issuing corporate bonds, commercial paper, and equities. As major European banks experienced large losses, their subsidiaries in such far-flung nations as Hungary, Ukraine, and the Baltic nations tightened lending standards appreciably. The U.S. crisis was thus transmitted from the United States to Western Europe and ultimately to numerous eastern European nations.

Can Financial Crises Be Predicted?

There are several leading indicators that tend to be precursors of financial crises. As indicated, such crises are typically preceded by the formation of a bubble during a manic period of euphoria in which expectations become fanciful. Bubbles always deflate, often triggering crises because a bubble is by definition an unsustainable increase in the price of one or more classes of assets. Most financial crises of the past century have been preceded by the following four developments: abnormal price appreciation of such assets as real estate and/or stocks, rising leverage of households and firms as indicated by such metrics as debt/income or debt/net worth, large international capital inflows and associated current account deficits, and a slowdown in output growth. Some of these indicators become increasingly pronounced during the manic phase of the cycle as expectations become unhinged from reality.

A financial crisis typically follows on the heels of the development of a certain hubris or overconfidence that has become fairly prevalent among the population. Characteristically, the belief that "this time is different" becomes widespread.[6] That is, the view that fundamental developments unique to the contemporary era fully warrant the high valuation of assets becomes the conventional wisdom. This overconfidence often seems to spring almost inevitably from rising expectations of future prosperity triggered by a major technological innovation, financial liberalization in a country, or other seminal event.

The U.S. stock market bubble of the late 1920s represented the culmination of a period of rising confidence in the U.S. economy throughout that decade. The United States had reigned victorious in World War I. Assembly-line automobile production, initiated by Henry Ford, had resulted in a sharp reduction in car prices and a nationwide road construction program. While the dream of automobile ownership and the freedom to travel were becoming a reality for the masses of middle-class Americans, widespread electrification and introduction of telephones and radios in homes added to the newfound feeling of euphoria that contributed to the stock bubble formation.

The phenomenal U.S. stock market bubble of the late 1990s—the biggest in U.S. history—was largely the result of two important developments. First, the advances in telecommunications and information technology that gave us the Internet and e-mail made instant worldwide communication accessible to billions of individuals around the globe. The information technology revolution transformed the way business is conducted, leading to an acceleration of productivity in a broad array of applications. This development appears to have been comparable in economic significance to the building of railroads and development of the internal combustion engine. Secondly, the erroneous perception that we had entered a "new economy" in which major recessions and episodes of severe inflation had been rendered obsolete by new financial technologies and advances in the conduct of monetary policy also played an important role in the development of the 1990s bubble. Given perceptions of a permanent increase in economic stability, assessment of risk in a multitude of prospective endeavors was imprudently revised downward.

Unlike many earlier bubbles, however, the credit and housing bubbles that preceded the Great Crisis were not grounded in fundamental technological improvements. Houses built in 2005 offered negligible improvements in quality relative to those built in 1990. This boom was a fairly rare, purely speculative bubble, leaving in its wake vast tracts of unoccupied and rapidly deteriorating houses rather than significant and lasting improvement in economic fundamentals.

By 2005, the indicators of impending financial crisis were flashing red in the United States and several other nations. House prices, as indicated by conventional measures, had reached bubble levels. As will be discussed in detail in chapter 4, credit—the other side of debt—expanded at unsustainable rates after 2002, both in the private and public sectors of the U.S. economy. In the buildup to the crisis, the United States had experienced a series of large capital inflows and current account deficits that soared as high as 6 percent of GDP as indebtedness to foreign countries—especially China—expanded rapidly. And economic growth slowed appreciably during 2000–2007 relative to the robust growth of 1994–1999, making it more difficult to service the rapidly expanding debt. Thus, numerous indicators reveal that a financial crisis was being signaled, albeit one whose timing was totally unpredictable.

The most prominent precursor of the Great Crisis was the dramatic increase in real estate prices in the United States and numerous other countries in the period extending from 2000 to 2006. Figure 2-1 illustrates the history of real U.S. house prices—house prices adjusted for inflation—over the period from 1890 through 2009. As indicated in the figure, the real price of U.S. homes, which had increased at an average rate of less than one percent per year in the prior century, nearly doubled in the decade ending in 2006.

Given the heavy costs of financial crises, it would clearly be of great value if economists and government policy officials were able to reliably detect incipient bubbles early enough to implement measures that might at least partially attenuate their severity and thereby minimize the ultimate damage to the nation. Stimulated by the Great Crisis, a literature on predicting financial crises is emerging. Using such indicators as the extent of appreciation of asset prices, the magnitude of public and private debt expansion, the magnitude and duration of international current account deficits, and measures indicating recent changes in economic activity, models have had some success in accounting for the incidence of past crises around the world after they had happened. However, such models have been unsuccessful in predicting the *timing* of such crises.

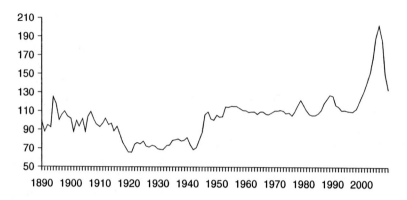

Figure 2-1   Real U.S. home price index, 1890–2009
Source: Robert Shiller and Standard and Poor's.

Often, circumstances accumulate to the point where a crisis becomes inevitable, pending some form of shock that sets if off. Given that such shocks are inherently unpredictable, it is unlikely that forecasting the timing of future crises will be successful.

Moreover, it is very difficult to ascertain with confidence, especially in the early and intermediate stages, whether an abnormal increase in asset prices is warranted by changing economic fundamentals. And the time lags inherent in the use of monetary and fiscal policies for purposes of attempting to nip bubbles in mid-development are problematic. It is therefore not clear that active use of these tools represents the optimal approach to dealing with formation of costly bubbles.[7] Regulations and other measures aimed at constraining the outsized growth of credit and associated leverage in the intermediate and advanced phases of the Minsky cycle, as financing arrangements evolve from hedge to speculative and Ponzi status, seem more likely to meet with success. Regulatory proposals that might make advanced countries less susceptible to financial crises are discussed in detail in chapter 12.

IV. The Macroeconomic Fallout from Financial Crises

As is intuitively plausible, economic downturns associated with economic crises are almost always more severe than the more typical recessions that are caused by such forces as an exogenous decline in consumer confidence or higher interest rates implemented by the central bank. The 1990–1991 U.S. recession was caused by a sharp decline in consumer confidence.

This occurred as Saddam Hussein took control of the oil fields in Kuwait in 1990, and appeared set to also invade Saudi Arabia. Real output in that recession declined by a modest 1.4 percent, as measured from peak to trough of the unusually mild and brief 8-month recession.

The United States next suffered a recession in 2001 as investment expenditures on information technology equipment plunged. Buoyed by tax cuts, strong consumption spending, and timely monetary stimulus implemented by the Federal Reserve, real GDP declined by a miniscule 0.3 percent in the 8-month downturn. In contrast to the mild and brief 1990–1991 and 2001 recessions, real GDP in the United States declined by 3.8 percent in the 2007–2009 crisis-related recession that lasted some 18 months. This marked the largest percentage decline in real output, as well as the lengthiest recession, in the United States since the Great Depression.

Economic crises add several dimensions to the normal forces that typically exert downward pressure on consumption and investment expenditures in recessions. In large part, these additional forces are related to the surge in debt and leverage, and the associated inflation of bubbles in prices of real estate and other assets that precede financial crises. Real estate finance is almost always a highly leveraged undertaking. When real estate prices decline appreciably, many of those with mortgages come under pressure and defaults increase. If severe, this phenomenon impairs the capital of the financial institutions that granted the mortgages. As these institutions suffer a loss of capital, they typically must either raise additional capital or reduce assets in order to meet capital standards. Because financial institutions often face difficulty in raising capital in times of crisis, and because loans make up two-thirds of bank assets, banks are typically forced to tighten lending standards and reduce loans during periods of crisis. A vicious cycle of falling house prices, increasing mortgage defaults, rising unemployment, additional loan defaults and bank failures, and tightening lending standards tends to be set in motion.

During this process, stock prices almost inevitably decline as sales and business profits drop, unemployment increases, and consumer and business confidence wane. With the exception of bonds issued by extremely secure firms, corporate bond prices typically fall as risk premiums in the form of higher yields increase due to deteriorating economic conditions and the associated elevation of credit risk. Thus, three important components of household wealth decline in times of financial crisis: stocks, bonds, and equity in homes.

Declining wealth, along with falling consumer confidence and rising unemployment, depresses consumption spending. Lower stock prices also mean that firms are less willing to issue new shares to finance investment expenditures. Declining business confidence, tighter lending standards at banks, and higher yields on corporate bonds owing to elevated credit risk typically result in a marked contraction in business investment spending. As the recession sets in, revenues flowing to state and local governments decline, inevitably forcinag cutbacks in their expenditures. In these ways, financial crises typically lead to severe recessions or exacerbate existing downturns.

In an empirical study of past financial crises, Reinhart and Rogoff examine 21 major financial crises in order to establish benchmarks for comparison.[8] The set of countries included in the study was determined by accessibility of reliable data covering such essential variables as house and stock prices, output, unemployment rates, and government budget deficits and debt. The sample of crises studied includes those experienced by such advanced industrial nations as Spain (1977), Norway (1987), Finland (1991), Sweden (1991), and Japan (1992), along with the countries that experienced the severe Asian crises of 1997–1998: Thailand, Hong Kong, Indonesia, South Korea, Malaysia, and the Philippines. The set of countries also included Colombia (1998) and Argentina (2001), as well as several countries that experienced the Great Crisis of 2007–2009: the United States, U.K., Ireland, Austria, Iceland, Spain, and Hungary. Data pertaining to the average experience of these nations forms a baseline that facilitates comparison of the severity of various financial crises, including the recent blockbuster.

Reinhart and Rogoff report that both the antecedents and consequences of crises have been similar for advanced nations and emerging economies. In fact, many of the consequences are strikingly consistent across countries. First, declines in asset prices are typically deep and prolonged. On average, the inflation-adjusted prices of homes fell 35 percent over a lengthy period that lasted six years. Even if Japan, where housing prices declined for 17 consecutive years, is omitted from the sample, house prices continued to fall for more than five years before stabilizing, on average. Real equity prices fell by 55 percent as stock prices continued to decline for about 3.5 years.

Real GDP declined on average by 9 percent over a period that lasted about two years, while the unemployment rate increased by 7 percentage points in the sample of experiences. The rising unemployment typically continued for four years, substantially outpacing in longevity the contraction of output. This discrepancy is likely due to growth of the labor force over time, together with reluctance by firms to hire additional workers until a recovery is solidly in place. Reinhart and Rogoff found that the contraction in real output in advanced countries tends to be less severe than in emerging economies. This is likely the result of the fact that emerging economies rely more heavily on credit supplied by foreign sources. The characteristic sudden reversal of inflows of foreign capital in emerging nations presents problems not typically experienced by advanced industrial nations.

Perhaps most striking is the propensity for government budget deficits to explode during major financial crises, with the ratio of government debt to GDP rising sharply. On average, the real value of government debt expanded by a stunning 86 percent in the first three years of economic contractions associated with these major financial crises. This is largely the result of plunging tax revenues that occur during recessions, although discretionary fiscal stimulus programs implemented in response to crises often contribute to the expansion of deficits and debt. The automatic fiscal stabilizers operate more strongly in nations with high and steeply graduated marginal income tax rates than in nations like the United States and Japan, which have lower income tax rates and less progressivity in the tax structure.[9]

One might be skeptical of the general applicability of these benchmark findings to the Great Crisis of 2007–2009 on a couple of grounds. First, it should be noted that most of the crises included in Reinhart and Rogoff's sample of nations were either confined to a single nation or a relatively small region of the world. In contrast, the Great Crisis was clearly a systemic, worldwide episode in which major financial problems in one country spread quickly to numerous other nations. In a crisis restricted to a single country or region, a nation might be able to extricate itself through expansion of exports (through exchange rate depreciation and other measures) and foreign borrowing. Such options are foreclosed in major worldwide crises. This consideration suggests that one might expect the recent crisis to have had larger consequences than Reinhart and Rogoff's baseline findings, other things being equal. On the other hand, those in charge of monetary policy in many nations have had more flexibility in recent years than in earlier crises in which exchange rates were pegged across a larger spectrum of nations.

Due largely to the implementation of monetary and fiscal stimulus of unprecedented magnitude, the macroeconomic consequences of the Great Crisis for the United States appear to be less severe than the baseline case. Unemployment in the United States increased by about 5 percentage points, as contrasted to 7 points in the baseline. Real output fell by about 4 percent over a period of about six quarters, in contrast to the 9 percent norm over a two-year period in the baseline case. On the other hand, the decline in U.S real house prices roughly matched the 35 percent baseline contraction. The trajectory of the U.S. debt/GDP ratio, while very severe, falls a bit short of the baseline explosion. And demographic forces unrelated to the financial crisis account for a portion of this alarming fiscal development.

V. Conclusion

Banking crises have occurred with regularity over the past 200 years in the United States and even longer in the older European nations. Prior to the recent Great Crisis, conventional wisdom seemed to be that exposure to severe banking crises had been permanently reduced by advances in monetary policy and such financial innovations as credit default swaps and other instruments developed by financial engineers in the past quarter century. Former Fed chairman Alan Greenspan and others heralded the alleged beneficial role of this new financial technology in facilitating the distribution of risk to those entities most capable of evaluating and bearing it. The view that our susceptibility to severe crises has been reduced, however, is belied by the devastating experience of the Great Crisis. The consensus today is that the "financial weapons of mass destruction," in Warren Buffet's apt words, were instrumental in creating the crisis, accelerating its spread, and amplifying its severity. Minsky's analysis indicates why such crises are likely to remain endemic to capitalism, transcending any conceivable new financial technologies as well as efforts to prevent crises through regulation. Upcoming chapters probe more deeply into these issues by analyzing several examples of important U.S. financial crises.

Chapter 3

The Panic of 1907 and the Savings and Loan Crisis

I. Introduction

Banking crises go back hundreds of years to the origin of fractional reserve banking. In such a system, banks and other depository institutions maintain only a small fraction of their deposit liabilities in the form of reserves, defined loosely as cash on hand and deposits in other banks. As the story is told in textbooks, fractional reserve banking began with English goldsmiths. Turning the clock back nearly 400 years, the East India Company and other recently chartered British organizations involved in long-distance trade began amassing large amounts of gold around 1650 AD. These companies, along with merchants and other wealthy individuals in seventeenth-century London, needed a place to store their precious metals—mostly gold and silver coins. Goldsmiths were private firms that originated as jewelers. Because they owned impregnable safes in which to store their jewelry, goldsmiths provided the logical place in which to store the increasing stocks of gold and silver.

Goldsmiths built prosperous businesses warehousing the precious metals. They held the gold and silver until requested by the owner, and issued paper notes to depositors. These notes were receipts acknowledging rights to a specific amount of gold or silver coins, payable by the goldsmith on demand to the bearer of the notes. Because these notes were fully redeemable, they quickly became as acceptable a medium of exchange for the purchase of goods and services as the gold and silver coins that backed the paper notes.

The goldsmiths soon discovered that only a very small portion of the gold or silver would typically be withdrawn in any given week or month. It became clear that it was unnecessary for the paper notes to be backed

100 percent by gold and silver. Goldsmiths became bankers as they began to grant loans by issuing paper notes in amounts greater than the amount of gold and silver held in safekeeping. They began to loan these notes to businesses and other worthy borrowers, earning a handsome income in the form of interest payments in the process. Moreover, some of the benefits of this new practice could be returned to the owners of the precious metals in the form of reduced service charges for safekeeping the metals. Everyone came out ahead—depositors, borrowers, and goldsmiths.

In view of the fact that failure to honor note holders' requests to exchange notes for gold would cause the business to fail, how much should a prudent goldsmith loan out in the form of newly issued notes? Twenty percent of the value of gold in storage? Five hundred percent? The former figure seems quite conservative inasmuch as the goldsmith would be easily able to honor all requests as long as an overwhelming majority of note holders did not ask to redeem the notes in gold and silver. A more aggressive goldsmith, tempted by the prospect of earning robust profits during heady economic times and periods of high interest rates, might grant loans amounting to several times its holdings of the metals. This consideration illustrates the tension between bankers' conflicting goals of scrupulously maintaining safety on the one hand and achieving greater profitability on the other. This tension has challenged bankers throughout the course of history.

Extrapolating Minsky's theory of the credit cycle backward to the seventeenth century, a long period of good times would inevitably lead goldsmiths to revise downward their perception of risk and therefore to leverage themselves more highly by increasing the volume of notes issued relative to gold held in their safes. This periodic easing of credit contributed to the formation of costly bubbles in financial and real asset prices.

This chapter analyzes the nature of fractional reserve banking and discusses the nineteenth-century U.S. banking crises that culminated in the Panic of 1907. The latter episode led directly to the creation of the Federal Reserve System. In addition, the chapter analyzes the U.S. savings and loan crisis of the 1980s. Later chapters examine the Great Depression and the recent Great Crisis in detail.

II. Fractional Reserve Banking and Recurring Panics in U.S. History

These English goldsmiths were forerunners of modern fractional reserve banking systems that exist in all developed nations today. In such systems, reserves of each bank constitute only a small fraction of the bank's deposit liabilities. In the case of the goldsmith system described above, as well as in modern fractional reserve banking, the quantity of money in the nation is not tied rigidly to the stock of precious metals. Such a system provides certain clear advantages.

First, abandonment of a commodity-based system like a gold standard means that fewer resources need to be allocated to the production of a nation's money. This frees up resources for more worthwhile uses, such as producing food, clothing, and an array of services. As a nation grows over time, the quantity of money needs to grow in line with the growth of economic activity in order to maintain a stable price level and overall economic stability. Consider the inefficiency and wasted resources in a society in which a significant portion of the nation's workforce is employed in simply extracting exhaustible and increasingly inaccessible resources of gold or silver from the earth to provide the requisite quantity of money.

In addition, the ability of a nation to manage the quantity of money for purposes of contributing to economic stability brings potential benefits to an advanced society. Leaving the quantity of money and the nation's economic fate to the vagaries of gold discoveries seems archaic and outmoded in an age of high technology and general affluence.

However, a fractional reserve banking system also has certain drawbacks. For one thing, political forces can induce policymakers to provide excessive growth of a nation's money supply, unleashing all the problems associated with inflation. As indicated in the discussion of hyperinflation in the previous chapter, history is replete with examples of central bank misconduct associated with political expediency.

But there is another important implication of fractional reserve banking. It has proven to be prone to recurring episodes of banking crises. In the absence of certain institutions such as a credible deposit insurance system and a competent central bank, a fractional reserve banking system seems to inevitably experience periodic episodes of panic that spill over to adversely affect economic activity. Indeed, even in the presence of such institutions, modern industrial nations have been unable to avoid the scourge of banking crises, albeit typically in different forms than in earlier times.

Because only a small portion of deposit liabilities in a fractional reserve system banking system are available to be withdrawn at any point in time, the system is inherently unstable. The banks simply do not have the funds on hand. They are tied up, mainly in the form of loans. If a significant portion of depositors simultaneously attempt to withdraw funds from their deposit accounts, unless some mechanism is in place to inject additional reserves into the system, the entire banking system is likely to collapse and bring the economy down with it. Throughout history, periodic contagious banking panics have occurred, causing severe consequences for nations' economies.

A modern depository institution may maintain perhaps 3 percent of its total deposit liabilities in reserves—cash and deposits at the central bank—with most of the remaining 97 percent having been loaned or used to purchase government bonds and other securities. As was the case with the early goldsmiths, this is not necessarily imprudent because only a small percentage of depositors typically withdraw funds in any given period, and any such withdrawals are normally roughly balanced by incoming reserves associated with new deposits.

However, if a significant portion of depositors simultaneously withdraw funds from a bank, in order to obtain the funds with which to pay depositors, the bank will be forced to sell securities from its portfolio and call in existing loans or refuse to refinance loans that are due for renewal. A major, rapid withdrawal of funds—a "run" on the bank—typically occurs when depositors are not fully covered by a credible deposit insurance program, and are given reason to suspect that the bank may be in impaired financial condition.

Runs on banks tend to be contagious. A run on a particular bank, resulting from a rumor about its condition that may or may not be true, tends to cause depositors of other banks to also withdraw their accounts. A multitude of banks are naturally subject to the same set of fundamental economic forces. A national economic downturn that causes loans to go bad in one bank, for example, is almost inevitably having a similar effect on other banks. Also, banks are interlinked, with many banks holding deposits in other banks in correspondent banking relationships. Failure of a bank in which other banks are holding deposits may imperil these other banks. Individuals who observe a bank in the region being closed down, or even hear rumors that a neighboring bank may be in trouble, naturally tend to be increasingly apprehensive about the condition of their own bank. This is perfectly rational because many banks in a region are normally influenced by the same regional economic forces, and because even those banks that are very prudently managed can become impaired by the spillover effects from problems experienced by other banks. For these reasons, banking runs tend to become contagious, self-fulfilling prophecies. The fear that some banks are in trouble can trigger the demise of other banks that would have remained healthy save for the fear factor.

In the absence of a central bank or other organization capable of supplying cash to the banks, a banking panic is likely to have disastrous economic consequences. This has been demonstrated time and again throughout U.S. history. When banks are selling securities en masse to obtain cash for depositors in response to a banking run, the price of the securities is likely to fall appreciably. This reduces the value of assets and capital of all banks that own such securities, including those banks initially in excellent condition and not subject to the run. As banks call in loans to obtain cash for panicked depositors, businesses and other borrowers are often seriously disrupted. For example, businesses that depend on bank loans may be unable to purchase new equipment, maintain an adequate stock of inventories, or make payroll.

By reducing credit availability in this way, a banking panic inevitably feeds back to impair economic activity. Aggregate spending and output decline and unemployment increases, causing borrowers to default on loans made by banks that were initially in robust condition. The resulting erosion of bank capital leads to additional bank runs, bank failures, and tightening of bank credit. A vicious cycle may set in, leading to a cascading downward spiral of economic activity in the nation.

In terms of money mechanics, this process of a panic-induced credit contraction causes the nation's money supply to contract as well. As banks unload securities and call in loans to obtain cash for panicked depositors, checks are written to the banks by the buyers of the securities and those repaying loans. This means that demand deposits in the nation's banks are being extinguished. The money supply, defined to include aggregate demand deposits and currency in the hands of the public, falls. Aggregate spending declines, leading to a period of depressed economic activity.

A fundamental consideration in understanding the fractional reserve banking system is that any one bank, *acting alone*, can obtain additional reserves by liquidating assets. But this does not apply to banks collectively. To assert otherwise is to commit the fallacy of composition. A bank that sells some of its Treasury bonds or receives repayment of a loan will receive cash or witness its deposit account at a correspondent bank (or the central bank in modern times) credited as the check written to the bank is cleared in the bank's favor. This bank gains reserves, but these reserves are obtained at the expense of the reserves held by the banks of those who buy the securities or repay loans.

When thousands of banks around the nation are selling securities or liquidating loans in times of panic as reserves decline in response to the public withdrawal of cash from deposits, the banking system gains no additional reserves. In the absence of a central bank or other entity capable of providing reserves to the banking system, the system cannot obtain the needed additional reserves to satisfy their customers. The futile effort to do so leads to a destructive contraction of credit, money, and the banking system, as demonstrated repeatedly in the nineteenth and early twentieth centuries. The most fundamental role of a central bank is to serve as the lender of last resort to the banking system. In the absence of a reliable central bank, this function may not be served.

III. Early Banking Panics, the Panic of 1907, and the Creation of the Federal Reserve System

The nineteenth century was a time of periodic systemic banking panics in the United States. Major panics occurred in 1819, 1837, 1857, 1873, 1884, and 1893—an average of about one serious crisis every 17 years.[1] The panic of 1907 bears a strong resemblance to the earlier panics. It is of great historical significance because it led directly to the creation of the Federal Reserve System, the central bank of the United States.

Nineteenth Century Banking in the United States

Episodic booms and busts characterized nineteenth century U.S. economic history. Typically, real estate prices would increase rapidly during periods when the building of canals, expansion of railroads, or growth of cities created surging demand for land. Credit would expand rapidly in such periods of prosperity as economic fundamentals and irrational exuberance joined forces to occasionally inflate real estate and stock prices to astounding levels. Real estate and stocks typically served as collateral for bank loans, and rising prices of these assets facilitated expansion of credit during the booms.

After a period of extraordinary increases in asset prices, an event would occur that would pierce the bubble. In a typical case, this might involve a rumor of an impending insolvency of a famous speculator, bank, or brokerage house. Land and stock prices would then begin to fall as speculators unloaded assets in an attempt to preserve their profits. As the existing value of collateral declined below the amount of a bank loan, the bank would ask the borrower for additional collateral. Inability to supply the necessary collateral typically led to default on the loan. Increasing loan defaults led to bank failures and panics in the form of runs on suspect banks. The most severe nineteenth century crises occurred in 1873 and 1893. These crises were followed by a period of depression characterized by increasing bankruptcies, rising unemployment, bank failures, and credit stringency as debt deflation was set in motion.

The early years of the twentieth century were times of rising prosperity. Having recovered from the severe panic and accompanying depression of 1893, the U.S. economy was again booming by the early 1900s.

But signs of trouble began to emerge in 1905 and 1906, and by the summer of 1907 the economy was again in a precarious condition. The National Bureau of Economic Research later determined that a recession had begun in May. The stock market began falling in March and the shares of Union Pacific Railroad, widely used as collateral for loans, declined sharply. New York City teetered on the brink of bankruptcy and an offering of new bonds by the city in June failed to attract buyers.[2] The copper market collapsed in July, and in August it was announced that Standard Oil had been fined the enormous sum of $29 million for violation of antitrust regulations. U.S. stocks were down sharply and banking runs had recently occurred in Germany, Japan, and Egypt.

In those days, credit conditions exhibited a distinct seasonal pattern, due in large part to the predominant role of agriculture in the nation's economy. Credit demands typically increased in the autumn as grain dealers in Midwestern states sought credit to purchase grain from farmers. This normally led to a seasonal outflow of funds from New York to agricultural regions and an increase in interest rates and tightening of credit on the Wall Street, but in most years, a flow of funds from Europe to New York would largely attenuate the seasonal credit strains. However, special problems prevented that development in 1907. Many San Francisco buildings had been insured by companies located in London, and the devastating earthquake of 1906 had led to a sustained outflow of funds from London to America. This resulted in a shortfall of credit in England and Europe. The Bank of England had been boosting interest rates since the end of 1906, and the normal seasonal flow of credit from London to the United States dried up.

Trust Companies and Banks

Prior to the Civil War, all of the nation's banks received their operating charters from the individual states. The National Banking Act of 1863 authorized the chartering of banks by the federal government, thus establishing the dual banking system. The banks chartered by the federal government were known as national banks and were subject to regulations specified in the Banking Act. Banks chartered by individual states were governed by state banking regulations. In the absence of a central bank, organizations known as clearinghouses were formed in large cities like New York. These organizations were established by groups of individual banks that joined forces to pool resources to guarantee bank deposits and lend cash when needed to sound banks that were members of the clearinghouse. The clearinghouses served to modestly reduce the propensity of local banking panics to become systemic.

In New York, organizations known as trusts grew rapidly during the decade preceding the panic of 1907. Trusts were initially established to manage the estates of very wealthy clients in the gilded age. Originally conservatively managed, they were thought to be safe and were therefore subject to fewer restraints on permissible activities than regular banks. They were less constrained in the types of assets they could purchase and were not subject to significant reserve requirements. This meant trusts could invest a larger portion of their deposits in earning assets than banks. Being subject to less stringent regulation, they could also purchase riskier assets.

Trusts were more profitable and paid a higher rate of return to depositors than banks. As economic activity again became robust and memories of the banking panic and depression of 1893 dimmed, these trusts began to make riskier investments. They earned handsome returns in the early years of the twentieth century. Taking note of the superior returns, depositors began flocking to these trusts, spurring their growth. In the period from 1895 to 1907, total assets of trusts in New York expanded more than twice as rapidly as those of New York banks and reached approximate parity with these banks by 1907. As suggested by Minsky's hypothesis, periods of rising prosperity tend to lead to overconfidence on the part of both borrowers and lenders. This was manifest in increasingly risky behavior by the New York trust institutions. As economic activity boomed in the early 1900s, these trusts began speculating in the stock market and real estate ventures. At first, returns were phenomenal. Then conditions changed for the worse. The Panic of 1907, which originated in the New York trusts, soon threatened to spread throughout the nation's banking system.

The Panic of 1907

In the spring of 1906, Fritz A. Heinze arrived in New York City from the West. Heinze was a high-rolling speculator who had amassed a fortune in the copper mining business in Butte, Montana. Upon arriving in New York, Heinze joined forces with Charles Morse, a banker whose reputation—like Heinze's—was less than impeccable. Together, they became affiliated with numerous banks, trusts, and insurance companies, gaining control of several and serving on the board of directors of many others.

Heinze owned a great number of shares in the struggling United Copper Company back in Montana. Discovering that speculators had heavily shorted stock in United Copper—that is, had borrowed shares and sold them with the intention of repurchasing them later at a lower price, Heinze and his brother devised a scheme to enhance their personal fortunes by executing a short squeeze on the speculators. In this plan, the brothers would drive up the price of United Copper through massive purchases of the shares, using funds borrowed from banks with which they had connections. They hoped to force the short sellers to cover by repurchasing shares, most of them from the Heinzes, at much higher prices. If the scheme worked, the Heinze brothers would bankrupt the short sellers and enrich themselves.

Heinze had previously established a banking relationship with Charles Barney, president of the Knickerbocker Trust Company, one of New York's largest and most respected trust organizations. Although Barney had financed previously successful speculations by F.A. Heinze, he turned down the brothers' request for a large loan. The undaunted Heinze brothers went ahead with the short squeeze, using personal funds and funds borrowed from other banks with whom they had close connections. In mid-October of 1907, they began purchasing shares of United Copper, pushing the price up sharply. But the brothers had misjudged the market. Those who had shorted the stock had already obtained shares to cover their short sales at prices sharply below the elevated prices resulting from the Heinze brothers' purchases. Within two days, the price of United Copper declined by more than 80 percent and the Heinze brothers suffered huge losses.

At the time, the State Savings Bank of Butte, owned by Heinze, was holding a large amount of collateral in the form of shares of United Copper posted by those to whom the bank had granted loans. When the shares crashed, the bank demanded additional collateral, which the borrowers were unable to provide. As a result, the loans went bad and the bank was declared insolvent. News about its demise triggered a massive run on Mercantile National Bank in New York, recently acquired by Heinze, which had a correspondent relationship with the Butte bank. In addition to attacking Heinze's banks, depositors withdrew a large amount of funds from trusts and banks owned by Morse, Heinze's partner.

The State Savings Bank of Butte was just one of many smaller banks throughout the nation that had established correspondent relationships with larger city banks, many of them located in New York. In these relationships, the small banks held deposits in large banks in New York and other cities in return for services provided by the city banks. When news of the panic in New York spread, many of these smaller banks withdrew their funds from New York banks. In the scramble for liquidity, several banks and trust companies, including many of those affiliated with Morse and Heinze, were subject to runs and forced to close. In an effort to prevent a systemic panic in the larger banking system, the New York Clearinghouse forced the resignations of Heinze and Morse from banking boards in New York. This served to forestall panic for a short time.

However, people became increasingly concerned about known and rumored links between notorious speculators, brokerage houses, and trusts and banks. Banking is based on confidence, which was starting to break down. On Friday, October 18, rumors spread that Charles Barney had been involved in the Heinze brothers' disastrous attempt to corner the short sellers in United Copper. This triggered a sustained run on Barney's Knickerbocker Trust Corporation, which was forced to close on October 22. The following day, the run spread to the Trust Company of America, the nation's second largest trust. It is likely no coincidence that Barney was a prominent member of its board of directors.[3]

John Pierpont Morgan was the principal owner of the U.S. Steel Corporation and the most respected, knowledgeable, and wealthy banker in New York. He had no direct financial interest in the trust companies. But he realized that this growing panic had the potential to bring about a disastrous systemic crash and massive depression if it were allowed to spread to the larger banking system. The key link involved call loans that trusts had made to stockbrokers. Such loans can be called in at the discretion of the lender. Morgan anticipated that continued runs on the trusts would force a large-scale recall of such loans, which would trigger forced sales of shares of stock. As the decline in stock prices began to push the value of collateral below the amount of the loan, banks would systematically call in the loans, forcing brokers to dump stock, even at fire sale prices, to repay the loans. This, in turn, would create a self-perpetuating cycle of falling bank capital, bank failures, additional runs on banks, and more loan liquidation, credit tightening, and falling asset prices. The final outcome would likely be a major depression.

Reckoning that failure of the Trust Company could ignite a disastrous nationwide banking panic, Morgan convened several of the city's top bankers in a series of late-night meetings in his home. Essentially, the healthy banks were asked to ante up millions of dollars to shore up the Trust Company of America and other trusts and banks that appeared vulnerable to imminent runs. Morgan agreed to put in $25 million of his personal funds, and John D. Rockefeller volunteered to put in up to $40 million if needed. The U.S. Treasury came up with $25 million, and other large banks also contributed to the effort.

On October 24, Wall Street observers noted workers carrying bags of gold and paper currency from the U.S. Treasury's New York facility to the trusts and banks designated for help. The word spread and public psychology quickly changed. It turned out that the effort spearheaded by Morgan was sufficient to carry the day. While there remained a few bumps and challenges, the Panic of 1907 ended in early November. It had lasted only 6 weeks, and while two dozen trusts had failed, only a handful of banks had closed down.

The panic contributed appreciably to the recession that extended from May 1907 to June 1908. In this period, national output declined by about 10 percent and the nation's unemployment rate increased from 3 to 8 percent. But things would have been far worse had it not been for J.P. Morgan's wisdom and forceful leadership. Morgan, together with a few banking colleagues and Treasury officials, had essentially performed the most fundamental role of a central bank—serving as a lender of last resort to the financial system in times of panic. However, it was apparent to thoughtful observers that it would be foolish for the young nation to continue to rely on the wisdom and benevolence of a single individual for its economic health, especially when that individual may not be entirely free of conflicts of interest. Clearly, the time was at hand to establish a central bank.

The Creation of the Federal Reserve System

In the spring of 1908, Congress enacted the Aldrich-Vreeland Act. This legislation created the National Monetary Commission, which was mandated to investigate the causes for the periodic banking panics and to develop a set of proposals and regulations aimed at reducing the frequency and severity of banking crises. Both England and France had established central banks more than a century earlier. Senator Nelson Aldrich, chairman of the National Monetary Commission, soon departed for Europe to engage in an in-depth study of the operation of central banking systems there. Upon his return to the United States, Aldrich arranged a secret conference of top banking authorities on an almost-deserted island off the coast of Georgia in November 1910. In attendance were such financiers as Charles Norton, Paul Warburg, and Benjamin Strong, who was representing J.P. Morgan. Strong was later to become president of the Federal Reserve Bank of New York and de facto leader of the Federal Reserve System.

The final report of the National Monetary Commission was submitted in early 1911, but for two years Congress wrangled over the details of the proposed new central bank. The major points of contention centered on the appropriate division of power over decision-making in the proposed central bank between the government and the private sector, between urban and rural interests, and among bankers, nonbank businesses, and the rest of society. The final outcome represented a delicate balance among these competing interests. On December 22, 1913, Congress passed the Federal Reserve Act. President Woodrow Wilson signed the legislation the same day. After more than 135 years in existence, the United States now had a permanent central bank. However, as the nation learned fewer than 20 years later, creation of the new central bank by no means put an end to severe banking crises. Indeed, the most severe financial crisis in U.S. history was to occur during 1929–1933. This episode is analyzed in chapter 8. Here, we examine a more recent and less catastrophic crisis.

IV. The Savings and Loan Crisis of the 1980s

In the United States, the goal of widespread homeownership has long been considered a worthy one. It is believed that homeownership promotes personal responsibility, a sense of pride, a strong work ethic, commitment to education, and social solidarity. The rate of homeownership has traditionally been significantly higher in the United States than in European and other nations, in part because the United States has extended numerous subsidies to homeowners that are not available to renters. To encourage homeownership among middle-class Americans, Congress fostered savings and loan associations (S&Ls) in the 1930s. It created the Federal Home Loan Bank Board to regulate and supervise the S&Ls and the Federal Savings and Loan Association to insure their deposits.

S&Ls have traditionally borrowed funds from masses of individual households by issuing savings and time deposits, using the overwhelming portion of these funds to finance long-term mortgages at fixed interest rates. To retain depositors, rates paid to the households must remain roughly competitive with short-term market yields—for example those available on Treasury bills and money market mutual fund shares. To cover the salaries of employees and other operating expenses and remain profitable, an S&L must earn a rate of return on its portfolio of mortgages a percentage point or two above the average rate paid to depositors.

S&Ls, like commercial banks, "borrow short and lend long." Their cost of funds depends on short-term interest rates while the rate of return they earn on assets has traditionally depended on long-term rates. Assume the average cost of funds to an S&L is 3 percent. Assume also that the average return on the portfolio of mortgages on its books is 6 percent. As long as the cost of funds remains stable, the S&L works with a comfortable margin or "spread"—3 percentage points in this example. As long as the yield curve is upward sloping, with long-term interest rates significantly higher than short-term rates, and as long as short-term rates do not rise rapidly, S&Ls are likely to exhibit healthy profits. From the 1930s to the 1970s, inflation and interest rates were relatively low and stable. The yield curve was almost always upward sloping. Thus, S&L managers could exhibit a fine lifestyle without being especially bright or creative.

But the original S&L concept was flawed from the beginning. S&Ls were heavily regulated. Unlike commercial banks, they were prevented from diversifying their asset structure. In particular, they were required to put 85 percent of their assets in mortgages, and variable-rate mortgages were generally not authorized until the 1980s. If the yield curve were to become inverted—with short-term rates higher than long-term rates—for a significant period, or if short-term rates (and their cost of funds) were to rise sharply, the S&Ls would incur severe operating losses. If these losses persisted for a significant period, many S&Ls would see their capital wiped out and become insolvent. In retrospect, it is a bit surprising that the S&L crisis did not occur before the early 1980s.

For about four decades extending from the late 1930s through the mid 1970s, S&Ls were stable and prosperous. Interest rates trended upward from the mid-1960s through the mid-1970s, but the increase was mild and gradual enough that S&Ls remained in healthy condition. Unfortunately, economic conditions changed dramatically in the late 1970s. Economic stability gave way to severe instability. As a result of enormous increases in crude oil prices in 1973 and 1979 and an accommodative policy stance on the part of the Federal Reserve, U.S. inflation rose into double-digit territory by the late 1970s, causing a dramatic spike in interest rates. Long-term rates rose as a natural response of bond market participants to rising inflation expectations. And short-term rates increased sharply as the Federal Reserve, under the leadership of Paul Volcker, implemented a highly restrictive policy from the late 1970s through the early 1980s in an ultimately successful effort to bring down the unacceptably high rates of inflation. The 90-day Treasury bill yield jumped from around 6 percent in March 1978 to more than 15 percent two years later. By December 1980, the Fed had pushed the federal funds rate above 19 percent. The yield curve became inverted in 1981 and 1982.[4]

This meant that the S&Ls, through no fault of their own, were in a very tight bind. They had to sharply raise interest rates paid to depositors to prevent their defection to the newly established money market mutual funds that were now paying very handsome yields to shareholders.[5] Yet the S&Ls could not raise interest rates on those fixed-rate mortgages already on their books. They could of course raise rates on new mortgages, but issuance of new mortgages in an average year amounted only to about 15 percent of a typical S&L's total stock of mortgages owned. S&Ls could try to shift the increased cost of funds, payable to *all* depositors, only on to *new* homebuyers. Moreover, prospective new homeowners are sensitive to mortgage rates. When rates on fixed-rate mortgages rise sharply, many prospective buyers are forced to postpone purchase of a home. By the end of the 1970s, conditions were in place for the nation's S&Ls to experience unprecedented operating losses.

One can think of the Treasury bill yield as a crude proxy for the rate of interest that an S&L must pay depositors to remain competitive with money market funds and retain depositors. The rate of return on an S&L's portfolio of mortgages may be approximated by the average rate on mortgages issued in recent years. When the margin by which the average rate earned by an S&L on its mortgage portfolio exceeds the Treasury bill yield is very low or zero, the S&Ls will experience losses. When the spread turns negative, they will experience large losses that vary in amount with the magnitude of the negative spread. When the spread is positive and greater than one or two percentage points, the S&L will typically earn profits.

Figure 3-1 illustrates the relationship, for the period extending from 1976 to 2010, between the contemporaneous Treasury bill yield and the average rate on 30-year fixed-rate mortgages over the previous five years. This period encompasses the crucial 1979–1982 interval in which S&Ls experienced tremendous stress and the crisis developed.

The figure illustrates the dramatic upsurge in short-term Treasury security yields during the late 1970s and early 1980s as the Federal Reserve responded aggressively to booming economic activity and the onset of double-digit inflation. The Treasury bill yield rose from less than 5 percent in March, 1977 to more than 15 percent three years later. While this rate returned to single digits for a few weeks in mid-1980, it again spiked in August and averaged more than 12 percent during the next two years. The Treasury bill yield moved above the lagged 5-year moving average 30-year mortgage rate in January 1979 and the negative spread remained for most of the following three-and-a-half years. This spread, which averaged positive 3.9 percentage points from 1985 to 2010, was *negative* 1.5 percentage points, on average, for the period extending from January 1979 through June 1982.

This negative spread, together with elevated loan defaults resulting from high unemployment during the back-to-back 1980 and 1981–1982 recessions, resulted in huge operating losses for S&Ls. Aggregate net losses for the S&L industry amounted to $6 billion in 1981 and $5 billion in 1982, with 85 percent of S&Ls experiencing losses in 1981 and

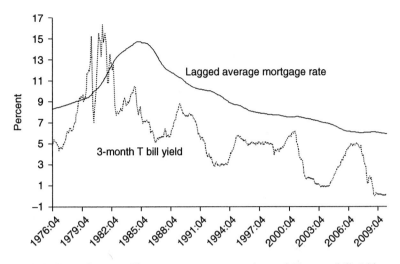

Figure 3-1   Lagged average 30-year mortgage rates vs. 3-month Treasury bill yield.
Source: Data from FRED database, at http://research.stlouisfed.org/fred2/

more than two-thirds losing money in 1982. Given the huge operating losses incurred in 1981 and 1982, erosion of S&L capital was sufficiently strong that some 60 percent of all S&Ls were technically insolvent by the end of 1982. By then, approximately one quarter of the 3,500 S&Ls that were in operation in the 1970s had either been closed down or merged with stronger institutions. Estimates indicate that the collective net worth of the S&L industry declined from more than $30 billion in 1979 to less than $5 billion in 1982.[6]

But the majority of the insolvent institutions were not shut down. Instead, these "zombie" institutions were allowed to continue in business, and with only minimal supervision. The extent of the problem was not made public. The U.S. government instead essentially engaged in a cover-up, hoping that the S&Ls would be able to pull themselves out of insolvency as the nation recovered from the severe 1981–1982 recession and as short-term interest rates declined toward normal levels.

In perhaps the most ill-timed financial legislation in U.S. history, Congress enacted the Garn-St. Germain Act in 1982. This legislation, which implicitly acknowledged the role of government regulations in creating the S&L fiasco, heavily deregulated the industry. Given the horrendous financial condition of most of the nation's S&Ls, this gave rise to the ultimate example of moral hazard. The S&Ls were no longer required to maintain the bulk of their assets in mortgages. The door was open. With nothing to lose and with supervisory agents nowhere to be seen, many of the zombie institutions gambled recklessly with depositors' money in a desperate effort to pull themselves out of insolvency before the authorities caught up with them and shut them down. As would be expected, these gambles overwhelmingly failed, and S&Ls dug themselves deeper into the red. Finally, shortly after the 1988 presidential election, the government publicly acknowledged the problem and began closing down the insolvent institutions. The eventual cost to U.S. taxpayers was approximately $150 billion.[7]

Given that the federal government had established S&Ls in the 1930s and provided them a mandate to put 85 percent of their assets in fixed-rate mortgages, and considering that government policy was the principal cause of the severe inflation of the 1970s, which triggered the massive increase in interest rates, it is reasonable to argue that government bears primary responsibility for the S&L debacle. Such was not the case in the recent Great Crisis. Albeit with some assistance from government, Wall Street firms, mortgage lenders, and other actors in the private sector are mainly responsible for this disaster.

V. Conclusion

Banking crises have plagued the U.S. economy throughout history. Fractional reserve banking systems are inherently susceptible to panics in which depositors attempt to withdraw funds from banks perceived to be in financial difficulty. In the absence of credible deposit insurance and a lender of last resort, such loss of confidence becomes a self-fulfilling prophecy as it results in a wave of contagious bank failures, declining money supply and credit availability, and contracting economic activity. Prior to the 1913 establishment of the Federal Reserve System, major banking crises occurred every 15–20 years. Following the Panic of 1907, Congress implemented legislation that established the Federal Reserve. Although the new central bank failed to prevent the banking panics and the Great Depression of the early 1930s, the ensuing 40 years rolled by without major banking problems.

The savings and loan crisis of the 1980s was a fundamentally different animal than earlier banking panics. It originated in flawed regulations that prevented S&Ls from diversifying their assets, together with government policies that resulted in the severe escalation of inflation and interest rates during the late 1970s and early 1980s. The risk of rapidly rising interest rates, which today has been partially shifted by S&Ls and other mortgage lenders onto borrowers through issuance of variable-rate mortgages, was previously borne almost entirely by S&Ls and other thrift institutions that were required to put the predominant portion of their assets in fixed-rate mortgages.

The shortness of memory of those CEOs and managers at the top of American financial institutions and other officers responsible for critical investment decisions is remarkable. For just as the S&L debacle of the 1980s resulted from borrowing short and lending long, so resides the cause for much of the damage wrought in the recent financial crisis. In the latter instance, the initiating force was primarily liquidity risk arising from the inability of institutions to refinance maturing short-term debt instruments. This inability arose from the spreading recognition in 2007 and 2008 that many financial institutions had become subject to risk of insolvency because of declining value of mortgages and mortgage-related securities on their books. Financial institutions had not given adequate consideration to the risk they would be unable to roll over their debt. This underestimation of risk stemmed ultimately from the irrationally low probability assigned to the possibility that real estate prices might decline significantly. The Great Crisis of 2007–2009 is examined in the following two chapters.

Chapter 4

Development of the Housing and Credit Bubbles

I. Introduction

The economic downturn that began in December 2007 was the lengthiest and most severe recession since the Great Depression of the early 1930s. It cost the country more than 8 million jobs and some $2,000 billion of income ($6,500 per person, on average) over the course of 2008 and 2009 alone. Plummeting tax revenues forced states and localities throughout the nation to fire teachers, allow roads and bridges to deteriorate, and eliminate essential services for its most vulnerable citizens. The Great Recession of 2007–2009 and the fiscal measures implemented to combat it pushed the already tenuous federal budget deficit well into the danger zone. A consensus among economists suggests that these costs are likely to diminish only slowly in the coming years. If we hope to prevent a crisis of such magnitude from recurring, it is important to think about the development of the forces that caused this economic disaster.

The proximate cause of the Great Recession was the bursting of the housing and credit bubbles that began to develop during the last years of the twentieth century and inflated rapidly during 2002–2006. The initial decline in home prices after the spring of 2006 acted as an accelerant that set off a conflagration. This fire took down homeowners, financial institutions, and thousands of business firms, including such icons as Merrill Lynch and General Motors. By initiating a vicious cycle of falling home prices, foreclosures of homes on which owners had ceased making mortgage payments, and subsequent liquidation of houses, the crisis spread to the financial system. Commercial banks as well as more highly leveraged investment banks, hedge funds, and other institutions came under severe financial strain. This led to a severe tightening of lending standards, exacerbating the economic downturn.

This chapter discusses the numerous elements that contributed to the formation and growth of dual bubbles in credit and house prices, the inevitable bursting of which led to the broader economic calamity. The most fundamental forces behind the twin bubbles were an irrational and widespread belief that house prices can only increase, along with an increased willingness on the part of lenders to extend credit and borrowers to take on debt. These forces, combined with increasing access to credit and extremely low interest rates, ultimately led to herd behavior that produced the housing bubble by driving the demand for housing—and the associated extraordinary demand for (and supply of) credit.

It is important to note that the causal nexus between rising home prices and increasing credit is bi-directional. Increasing availability of credit on easy terms boosted home buying, driving up house prices. The housing and associated mortgage boom stimulated the introduction by Wall Street and the mortgage industry of financial instruments that boosted the supply of funding for houses and eventually led to a search for borrowers of marginal financial viability. A multitude of financial innovations such as mortgage-backed securities (MBS) and arcane instruments derived from them contributed strongly to the inflation of the credit bubble. Also contributing were the rapid growth of the shadow banking system, a massive inflow of funds from China and other countries exhibiting large trade surpluses vis-à-vis the United States, and extremely low interest rates maintained by the Federal Reserve during 2002–2005.

In addition to these new instruments that artificially inflated home prices, securitization of commercial mortgages, credit card loans, auto loans, student loans, and other items helped fuel a massive expansion of credit used for nonhousing purposes. This helps account for the increase in the share of the nation's output devoted to consumption goods and services from 67 percent in 1998 to more than 70 percent by 2004.

Of paramount significance was a major increase in risk-taking on the part of financial institutions in the form of acquisition of nontraditional and little-understood financial instruments and in sharply increased leverage. A growing hubris on the part of Wall Street firms developed out of the belief that new financial technologies had made it possible to accurately quantify risk and take measures to alleviate it. These developments coincided with and were abetted by the ascent of increasingly zealous free-market, antiregulatory philosophy in Washington. In the quarter century preceding the crisis, American public policy took an increasingly laissez-faire approach to government regulation and supervision. This trend started with the election of President Ronald Reagan, and continued through both Democratic and Republican administrations, culminating with that of George W. Bush (2001–2009).

An increase in imprudent and irresponsible behavior on the part of lenders, borrowers, and regulators was epitomized by the emergence and increasing issuance of "ninja" (no income, no job or assets) mortgage loans. Antiregulatory zeal was evidenced by acquiescence of regulators in the deterioration of lending standards in the mortgage industry and the proliferation of "2-28" adjustable-rate mortgages. These mortgages, which featured rates fixed for the first two years, led to predatory exploitation by lenders of unsophisticated borrowers, whose likelihood of default soared with the sharp increase in monthly payments almost certain to occur after the initial two years of the loan. Another sign of "malign neglect" on the part of those responsible for overseeing the financial system was acquiescence in the process allowing private firms that rate mortgage-backed securities (MBS) and the securities created from them to be paid for this service by the very investment banks that created and marketed the instruments.[1]

In short, in accounting for the housing and credit bubbles, there is plenty of blame to go around. In this chapter, we examine the confluence of events that contributed to the credit and housing bubbles that inevitably popped, ushering in an era of hard times for tens of millions of Americans as well as inhabitants of Europe and other countries.

II. The Growth of Credit and Debt

The amount of private-sector debt has grown over the years, not only in nominal and real terms, but also relative to the nation's gross domestic product (GDP). In part, this is due to changes in financial technology. The introduction and proliferation of credit cards has enabled households to spend more than they earn. Issuance of commercial paper allows major corporations to more cheaply finance inventories and payrolls than by going to financial intermediaries such as banks, and money market mutual funds emerged in the 1970s to purchase much of this paper. Critically important has been the phenomenon of securitization—the packaging of individual mortgages, auto loans, credit card balances, and other forms of debt into multimillion dollar securities. These securities, collateralized by the debt instruments contained in them, were perceived by prospective investors to be very safe. Because their yields appreciably exceeded those of Treasury securities and other debt instruments, they were in great demand by investment banks, hedge funds, and pension funds with multibillion dollar blocks of funds to invest. This new technology enhanced the availability of various loans and the terms on which they were available to the public. Figure 4-1 illustrates the growth of

U.S. household and financial sector debt relative to GDP over the past 35 years.

Note that household and financial-sector debt have grown more rapidly over the years than GDP. Beginning in the late 1990s, these trends accelerated. Household-sector debt increased from an average annual rate of 6.3 percent during the first seven years of the 1990s to a rate of 9.6 percent per year in the following decade. The corresponding annual growth rates of financial-sector debt are 10.7 percent and 11.5 percent, respectively. Expressed as ratios to GDP, the upward trend of household debt increased modestly until the late 1990s, and more rapidly thereafter. Financial sector debt exhibits a similar trend, although its growth rate has been higher since 2000 than the household-sector ratio. Household-sector debt grew from about 66 percent of GDP in early 2000 to 96 percent of GDP in 2008 and 2009. The financial-sector debt/GDP ratio increased from 76 percent to more than 110 percent over the same interval.

Focusing more narrowly on aggregate household mortgage debt, the data reveal that the amount of this debt fluctuated within a relatively narrow range of 57 to 60 percent of aggregate household disposable income in the 1990–1998 period, and then climbed sharply to a peak of 99 percent in 2007. While a small portion of the upward trend of the mortgage debt/disposable income ratio is attributable to an increase in the homeownership rate after 2000, this sharp upward trend constitutes one of several red flags suggesting that American households were becoming overextended in expenditures on housing.[2]

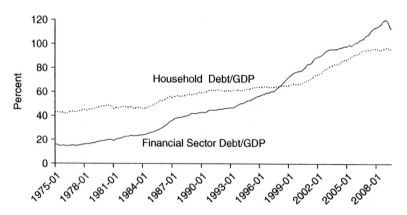

Figure 4-1 U.S. household and financial sector debt as percentage of GDP.
Source: Federal Reserve System, Flow of Funds Accounts.

III. Forces Contributing to the Housing Bubble

Specific factors that contributed to the dramatic rise in home prices in the 2000–2006 period include increasing awareness of the historically strong financial returns from homeownership, along with several forces that worked to expand the availability and reduce the cost of mortgages. These forces included a lowering of lending standards, the advent of securitization of mortgages, development of the subprime mortgage market, activities of government-sponsored enterprises (GSEs), and the rise of the shadow banking system.

Home Buying as an Investment

Over the long run, increases in house prices in the United States have outpaced growth of the nation's price level by about one percent per year. This fact, coupled with favorable tax treatment of homeowners vis-à-vis renters and the psychological benefits of owning a home, helps explain the appeal of ownership. Almost from its very beginning, America has had a higher home ownership rate than European countries and other nations. Home equity constitutes the largest single source of wealth of the median American household. When house prices increase rapidly, as was the case from the late 1990s until 2006, owning a house provides a phenomenal rate of return on investment.[3]

Consider the economics of purchasing a $200,000 home with a 5 percent down payment of $10,000. If the house appreciates 10 percent a year for five years, its value has risen to $322,102, for a gain of $122,102. The $10,000 initial investment in the home has earned a tax-free rate of return of 65 percent per year over the five-year period! If the value of the home rises 14 percent per year, as was the case on average in 20 large U.S. cities during the first five years of the twenty-first century, the investment has returned 79 percent per year.[4] Even if the home appreciates at a modest 5 percent annually, the rate of return exceeds 40 percent per year. Such is the nature of leverage, and the typical new homebuyer is heavily leveraged.

The above considerations, coupled with the widespread belief that house prices could never fall, helps explain the turn of events that created the financial crisis and the Great Recession of 2007–2009. Prior to 2006, average house prices in the country as a whole had not declined in any single year since the Great Depression of the early 1930s. As time passed, house prices consistently increased, albeit at considerably different rates across the country. In the early years of the twenty-first century, house prices began rising more rapidly. Speculation became an important factor boosting demand for homes. After several years of above-normal price increases, the present value of expected future capital gains on houses began to get built into the current prices of houses. At this point, the bubble was on. Figure 4-2 indicates the inflation rate of U.S. house prices as the bubble escalated from 1998 until early 2006.

As indicated in the figure, the national house price inflation rate ratcheted up from about 8 percent in early 2002 to more than 14 percent in 2005. Note that inflation of house prices in larger U.S. cities, as indicated by the 20-city home price index, has been consistently higher than that for houses in the nation overall, on average.[5]

It became an article of faith, especially in large coastal urban areas, that house prices could not fall. In the conventional wisdom, a growing population living on a fixed amount of land, coupled with inexorably rising living standards and a robust income elasticity of demand for housing, meant that the likelihood of a significant decline in home prices was nil and could safely be ignored. This view seemed to be almost universal among borrowers, lenders, and regulators. Coupled with the economics of house price appreciation indicated above, this view was instrumental in the introduction of several innovations on the part of mortgage lenders that facilitated home purchases. It seemed that the benefits of homeownership could be extended to a significantly larger portion of American households.

Figure 4-2   Inflation rate of U.S. houses, 1998–2006. Case-Shiller indexes.
Source: Standard & Poor's.

The Demise of Lending Standards

Traditionally, the predominant constraints limiting homeownership have been making the initial down payment and meeting the monthly mortgage payments. The mortgage industry relaxed lending standards and introduced innovations that eased both of those constraints. Mortgage lenders implemented "creative financing." This took numerous forms, some of which would have been prohibited by alert and conscientious regulators. These include undocumented ("liar") loans, zero down-payment loans, negative amortization loans, and "teaser rate" adjustable-rate mortgages (ARMs). The latter instruments feature mortgage rates that were initially fixed and very low (often less than 3 percent) for the first two years but adjusted upward after that.[6] Other mortgages were designed as "interest-only ARMs" and "option ARMs." By granting the homeowner the option to make monthly payments on the ARM that did not even fully cover the interest portion normally due, option ARMs brought monthly mortgage payments sharply below normal payments. The shortfall in monthly payments was tacked on to the principal balance, so that the balance on this negative amortization (Ponzi) loan increased over time.

As the housing bubble inflated, the conventional 30-year fixed-rate mortgage relinquished its traditional role as the predominant mortgage instrument in many parts of the country. Exceptionally low short-term interest rates maintained by the Federal Reserve gave impetus to the rise of teaser-rate and other ARMs. Consistent with Minsky's theory of credit bubbles, mortgage finance transitioned from hedge finance to speculative finance, and eventually to Ponzi finance. Interest-only and option ARMs increased their share of the nationwide mortgage market from less than 10 percent in 2000 to more than 30 percent in 2005. In that year, more than half of all mortgages made in San Francisco were of these forms, as were more than 40 percent in Phoenix, Seattle, and Denver, and Washington, D.C.

The Role of Securitization

In earlier times, a local bank or savings institution that made loans to local citizens held on to the loan until maturity. Not infrequently, the loan officer had known the borrower for several years and felt a strong sense of moral obligation to be straightforward with the borrower about the details and risks involved in the loan. Incentives were efficiently aligned because default on the part of a borrower would accrue adversely to the bottom line of the lending institution. Starting more than 30 years ago, mortgage lenders began moving to the "originate to distribute" model of mortgage finance. In this model, mortgage lenders originate the mortgages and collect the monthly payments but quickly sell the mortgages to investment banks and other institutions that package the individual mortgages into huge bond-like securities. Over the course of the decade ending in 2006, the aggregate value of securitized mortgages outstanding tripled, from about $2,400 billion to more than $7,200 billion.

These securities were marketed to large banks, insurance companies, pension funds, hedge funds, and foreign buyers. They were appealing to these investors because they featured attractive interest payments not far below those paid on the individual mortgages, and appeared to offer the safety of diversification made possible by the pooling of thousands of individual mortgages. Barring an unthinkable significant drop in house prices, the AAA-rated mortgage-backed securities appeared nearly as safe as Treasury bonds in spite of their superior yield. The Federal National Mortgage Association (Fannie Mae), a GSE, had long securitized prime mortgages—those made to borrowers who had met rigorous standards. Fannie guaranteed the debt service on these securities, thus protecting the buyers of the MBS. At the same time, it imposed standards for creditworthiness on the borrowers whose mortgages were to be packaged. Regulations prevented Fannie from securitizing subprime mortgages.

Given the loss of underwriting activities in stocks that resulted from the bursting of the stock market bubble in 2000–2002, major investment banks like Goldman Sachs and Morgan Stanley were searching for new profitable lines of business. They sharply increased their activities in the lucrative securitization business, concentrating on securitizing subprime mortgages. Subprime mortgages are those extended to individuals with blemished credit histories and higher-than-normal perceived risk of inability to make payments. Such households generally have lower income and are unable to make down payments of the magnitude typically required in the prime mortgage market. Alt-A loans are those made to homebuyers who have good credit histories but lack asset or income verification or are self employed. Investment banks increased their securitization of subprime mortgages dramatically in 2003–2006. The share of new residential mortgages designated as subprime or Alt-A increased from less than 10 percent in 2000 to more than 40 percent in 2006. The annual value of mortgage-backed securities issued during the 2000s by private firms like Goldman Sachs is shown in Figure 4-3.

These mortgage-backed securities provided major benefits to lending institutions. Banks and other institutions, which collected handsome fees as they initiated individual mortgages, could now sell these mortgages soon after they were made. This reduced risk to the lending institution and provided funds to grant additional mortgage loans. In

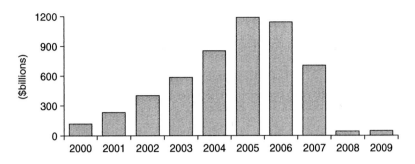

Figure 4-3   Issuance of non-agency mortgage-backed securities.
Source: Federal Reserve System, Flow of Funds Accounts.

earlier times, because the mortgages remained on the balance sheet of the lending institution, a natural limit was placed on the amount of mortgages that could be issued. As the institution reached its quota, issuance of additional mortgages ceased. With the advent of securitization, there was no longer any limit on the granting of mortgages as long as buyers for mortgage-backed bonds existed anywhere in the world. The securitization phenomenon strongly contributed to the costly frenzy of mortgage issuance during the critical period extending from 2003 through 2006.

The securitization development stood to benefit households in that it increased the supply of funds available for mortgages, thus providing more loans at more favorable terms for home buyers. These mortgage-backed securities and the instruments derived from them appeared to spread any slight risk to those lenders willing and able to accept somewhat higher risk in return for a relatively attractive yield. And even those risks could ostensibly be hedged through purchase of credit default swaps and other insurance instruments.

A critical drawback, however, was the fact that mortgage originators had less incentive than formerly to scrutinize the financial circumstances of prospective borrowers. The mortgage originators quickly sold the mortgages, passing any risk down the line. Lenders who suspected that uninformed recipients of the new undocumented loans and teaser-rate ARMs would likely experience difficulty making payments could soothe their consciences via the rationalization that, with continued appreciation, homeowners could use the increasing equity to later refinance the mortgage on better terms or increase the mortgage balance and use the proceeds to continue making payments. This misalignment of incentives resulting from mortgage securitization played a crucial role in creating the credit and housing bubbles.[7]

Subprime and Alt-A Mortgages

One of the goals of the past several presidential administrations has been to spread the benefits of homeownership to additional households. To achieve this goal, more mortgages were extended to subprime and Alt-A borrowers—those whose circumstances made them more risky than the median homebuyer. To compensate for the elevated risk, subprime and Alt-A mortgage loans carry mortgage rates that are typically 3–5 percentage points higher than those on prime mortgages.[8] Some unethical lending institutions gave bonuses to officers who steered unwary borrowers into mortgages featuring higher rates than those for which the borrowers were qualified.

As the housing bubble began to inflate in the early years of the twenty-first century, borrowers sought ways to purchase a home with low down-payments and affordable monthly payments. Lenders looked for ways to expand their businesses. Guidelines underlying mortgage standards in the subprime market deteriorated. Many lenders began to rely heavily on credit scoring to evaluate prospective borrowers and neglected the more traditional benchmarks such as income and employment status. Finance companies such as Household Finance Corporation and CitiFinancial, which were often set up as subsidiaries by major bank holding companies like Bank of America and Citigroup, became heavily involved in subprime lending. A large portion of subprime mortgage originations were made by independent lenders that were not federally regulated.

Automated loan approval methods were implemented. Interest-only ARMs, option ARMs, and those with teaser rates proliferated. Some 80 percent of subprime mortgages were ARMs, many with initial teaser rates. By 2006, there were more than 7 million subprime mortgages outstanding, which constituted more than 10 percent of all mortgages. These subprime mortgages had an aggregate value of approximately $1.3 trillion. In 2005, the median down payment on these mortgages was 2 percent of the value of the home, and more than 40 percent of mortgages involved no down payment at all. This degradation of lending standards ensured that any significant decline in home prices would put millions of households underwater on their mortgages.

Government Sponsored Enterprises: Fannie Mae and Freddy Mac

To facilitate the national goal of widespread homeownership, Congress created the Federal National Mortgage Association (Fannie Mae) in 1938. Fannie has traditionally supported the mortgage market by issuing bonds to the public and using the proceeds to buy up mortgages. Because Fannie was established as a government organization, its debt was considered as safe as U.S. Treasury bonds. This allowed it to borrow at relatively low rates which, in turn, meant that mortgage rates would be lower than would otherwise be the case. Freddie Mac was created in 1970 to serve essentially the same purpose and to provide competition for Fannie. While Fannie Mae was privatized as a stockholder-owned corporation in 1968, it implicitly retained the backing of the U.S. government, thus allowing it to continue borrowing at low rates. The activities of "Fannie" and "Freddie," the so-called government-sponsored enterprises (GSEs), constitute one of several subsidies the U.S. government extends to homeowners and industries that supply them.[9]

The Department of Housing and Urban Development (HUD) oversees Fannie Mae and Freddie Mac. In 1995, these privately owned GSEs were given federal tax incentives for buying MBS that included loans to low-income borrowers. In 1996, HUD set a goal for Fannie and Freddie to issue at least 42 percent of new mortgages to households with incomes below the median U.S. household income. This goal was boosted to 50 percent in 2000 and 52 percent in 2005. The combined purchases of low-income household mortgages of these two institutions quadrupled between 2002 and 2006, amounting to $175 billion in 2006.

Previously, in 1977, Congress had enacted the Community Reinvestment Act (CRA), which mandated increased lending to low and moderate-income borrowers. Over the remainder of the twentieth century, default rates were low and CRA lending became a profitable venture. Some critics place the blame for the 2008 demise of Fannie and Freddie, and even the housing meltdown and Great Recession, on the enactment by Congress of this Act. However, the fact that the Great Crisis arrived 30 years after the enactment of CRA casts doubt on this view, as do the problems experienced in the prime residential mortgage market and commercial mortgage market. The CRA did not endorse nondocumented loans or teaser-rate ARMs. Nor did it mandate financing of upscale condominiums in Miami and Las Vegas or require investment banks to become heavily involved in securitizing subprime mortgages.

While Fannie and Freddie did not package individual subprime mortgages into mortgage-backed securities, they purchased a very large amount of these securities from 2000 to 2007. Fannie and Freddie together own or guarantee more than half of the nation's $12 trillion of residential mortgages. As the prices of homes cratered in 2007 and 2008, the value of these mortgage-backed securities fell sharply and markets in which they are traded shut down. Both Fannie and Freddie became insolvent and were taken over by the U.S. government in September 2008.[10]

Fannie and Freddie engaged in the same type of risk-taking as did such firms as Lehman, Bear Stearns, and many others. They became increasingly leveraged, and by 2006 exhibited debt/equity ratios higher than 20. This exceeded the ratios of commercial banks and even approached those of investment banks. Keep in mind that Fannie and Freddie, while government-sponsored, were private corporations. Their CEOs and other top officers stood to make enormous salaries and bonuses tied to annual profits posted by these firms. These officers faced the same incentives for risk-taking as did CEOs of Merrill Lynch, Lehman, and other major privately owned financial institutions.[11]

The Rise of the Shadow Banking System

What is the definition of a bank? It is essentially an institution that borrows funds by issuing claims or IOU's on itself, traditionally in the form of checking and time deposits, and uses these funds to issue loans. These bank loans are made to individuals, business firms, and various levels of government (conventional banks buy municipal bonds and U.S. Treasury securities). Banks facilitate maturity transformation in the financial system by "borrowing short and lending long." Most of the deposits they issue to obtain funds can be withdrawn on demand, or at least on short notice. The assets they acquire are predominantly of longer maturity, consisting heavily of mortgage loans, business loans, and municipal and government bonds. Traditionally, such depository institutions as commercial banks and savings and loan associations were responsible for a major portion of the transfer of funds from the masses of individual savers to those entities that needed access to funds to build factories, purchase homes, or build local schools or libraries.

However, changes in financial technology over the years have facilitated the rapid growth of the "shadow banking "or "parallel banking" sector. Shadow banks serve the function of transferring funds from surplus units to those needing loans. However, rather than financing deficit-spenders by issuing deposits, the shadow banking system typically obtains funds by issuing short-term securities like commercial paper—short-term debt issued by highly rated corporations—and using the proceeds to purchase longer-term instruments like mortgage-backed securities and related securities.[12]

Advances in information technology have increased information available in financial markets and led to the development of new financial instruments and markets. Over the years, financial innovations have squeezed the profitability of depository institutions, both from the liability side of the balance sheet and from the asset side. From the 1930s through the 1970s, statutory prohibition of interest payable on checking accounts and statutory ceiling rates payable on savings and time deposits ensured banks a solid flow of low-cost funds. The elimination of these bank subsidies in the 1980s, coupled with the advent of money market mutual funds (MMMFs), meant that banks were subject to enhanced competition in obtaining funds to lend out. They were forced to pay higher interest rates than formerly to attract depositors.

Financial innovations provided attractive alternatives to many borrowers who had traditionally relied on banks for loans, thus dealing a significant blow to banks' profitability also via the asset side of the balance sheet. By increasing the processing and dissemination of information in financial markets, information technology has facilitated the rise of the commercial paper market, the junk bond market, and the phenomenon of securitization. The development of the commercial paper market was stimulated greatly by the emergence of MMMFs, major buyers of the paper. This meant that highly rated corporations needing loans were now able to circumvent commercial banks and instead borrow directly from other firms and individuals by issuing commercial paper to them. The rise of the commercial paper market has enabled such institutions in the shadow banking market as hedge funds and investment banks to issue short-term asset-backed commercial paper and use the funds to purchase mortgage-backed securities and other long-term assets bearing attractive yields.

Advances in information technology also allowed lower-rated corporations, traditionally dependent on banks for loans, to borrow through the "junk bond" market, now politely referred to as the "high-yield" market. The rise of this market was facilitated in part by technologies that more accurately evaluated risk in such bonds and partly by the advent of pooling of hundreds of individual lower-rated corporate bonds into large units. Through pooling of risk and diversification across industries, these blocks of individual junk bonds provide an attractive outlet for investors willing to incur higher risk than that on AAA-rated corporate bonds in return for higher rates of return. These pools of high-yield bonds are marketed through mutual funds and exchange-traded funds.

These innovations inevitably meant that commercial banks and thrift institutions would play a declining role in the financial system. The share of total credit granted to nonfinancial sector borrowers by commercial banks and thrift institutions, which stood at 53 percent in 1975, declined to less than 30 percent by 2008. The rise of the shadow banking system—hedge funds, investment banks, and other nonbanks that serve the traditional banking function of issuing debt claims to finance loans—accounts for a major part of the declining share of credit extended by commercial banks and thrift institutions. Banks responded to this squeeze by increasing their activity in the commercial real estate market and by increasing loans for corporate takeovers and leveraged buyouts. They also embraced shadow banking by pursuing new off-balance sheet activities.

Tim Geithner, then president of the Federal Reserve Bank of New York, indicated in a mid-2009 speech that the combined assets of the shadow banking system had grown to exceed those of the "regular" banking system. He estimated that the five largest U.S. investment banks had total assets of $4 trillion, assets in hedge funds totaled $1.8 trillion, and assets in an array of instruments that include auction-rate securities, asset-backed commercial paper conduits, overnight repurchase agreements, and other forms added up to $4.4 trillion. This sums to a total of more than $10.2 trillion in the shadow banking system, as compared to total assets of $10 trillion in the commercial banking system.[13] Some analysts believe that Geithner's figures underestimate the relative importance of the shadow banking system, which is relatively unregulated and has grown extremely rapidly since the beginning of the twenty-first century.

The share of total financial intermediation contributed by asset-backed securities issued by investment banks and hedge funds increased from nil in 1984 to 15 percent in 2006. Taking advantage of huge profits to be made in packaging individual mortgages into MBS, privately owned investment banks became increasingly involved in this activity from 2000 to 2005. As indicated in Figure 4-3, more than $5,000 billion worth of these instruments were manufactured by private firms from 2000 to 2007, with the peak year occurring in 2005. After house prices had fallen significantly and the value of these bonds declined and became uncertain due to the dearth of buyers in this market, new issuance of these bonds was negligible in 2008 and 2009. This market had virtually shut down. Only Fannie and Freddie remained actively involved in the securitization business as of summer 2010.

The Role of Leverage

A financial institution's leverage can be defined as the ratio of its total assets or its total debt to its equity or capital. If a bank can earn a rate of return of 1 percent per year on its total assets, and if its ratio of total assets to net worth or equity capital is 12, its rate of return on equity for the owners is 12 percent per year. If an investment bank earns a 1.5 percent rate of return on assets and is leveraged 20 to one, it has earned a phenomenal rate of return of 30 percent per year for the owners. When things are going well, it is tempting to increase the leverage in order to magnify earnings.

As the U.S. economy was rolling along in the 1990s, it experienced falling unemployment, low inflation, surging productivity growth, and rising profits. The profits share of the nation's income increased and stock prices surged in the late 1990s. Ever since the mid-1980s, the U.S. economy had experienced remarkable stability. The variability of both output and inflation declined significantly. The two recessions that occurred in the quarter century extending from 1982 to 2007 were the mildest of the post–Second World War period. This time period, most of which occurred under the watch of Federal Reserve Chairman Alan Greenspan, became known to economists as "the Great Moderation." People began to speak of a "New Economy." They anticipated a future devoid of both severe inflation and high unemployment. Confidence in the future of the U.S. economy grew.

As hypothesized by Hyman Minsky, the mother of economic instability is a long period of high stability. In the words of Nobel Laureate Joseph Stiglitz, "stability breeds instability." Buoyed by the era of the Great Moderation, robust profits, and somnolent regulators, firms began to take on more risk, just as Minsky predicted. This can be done in two ways, both of which were exhibited in abundance on Wall Street and elsewhere: purchasing more risky assets and taking on more leverage. This hubris, overconfidence, or greed was manifest in a widespread increase in leverage by financial institutions worldwide. Figure 4-4 illustrates the growth in leverage in the U.S. financial sector, as exemplified by the debt to equity ratio of the four largest U.S. investment banks during the years extending from 2004 through 2007—the years immediately preceding the onset of the financial crisis.

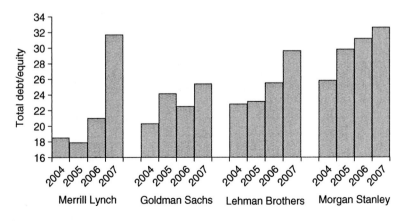

Figure 4-4   Leverage ratios of U.S. investment banks, 2004–2007.
Source: Company annual reports (SEC Form 10K).

Note that Merrill Lynch, which exhibited the most dramatic increase in leverage from 2004 to 2007, experienced severe problems and was subsumed as part of Bank of America in September 2008. Lehman Brothers went bankrupt at about the same time. The company that appears most conservative in regards to leverage, Goldman Sachs, is arguably the strongest of the firms today.[14] The key point is that financial firms engaged in a major increase in risk-taking after 2003, and the nation was still paying the price in 2010 and 2011.

IV. The Role of the Federal Reserve

The housing bubble developed on the heels of the popping of an earlier bubble—the huge run-up of stock prices in the late 1990s. In the longest and strongest bull market in U.S. history, stock values rose dramatically from the early 1980s through the end of the century. U.S. stocks then lost some 45 percent of their value in the first two years of the twenty-first century. Technology stocks, which had experienced an enormous bubble in the late 1990s, dropped more than 75 percent in the "Tech Wreck" of 2000–2002. Some critics charge that the Federal Reserve cleaned up the wreckage wrought by the stock market crash by creating a second bubble, this time in the housing market. The Fed maintained short-term interest rates at extraordinarily low levels during 2003, 2004, and 2005.[15]

Many economists and pundits have noted that the unusually low interest rates were an important source of the bubbles in credit and house prices that eventually burst and touched off the financial crisis of 2007–2009. The conventional interpretation of this episode is that the Greenspan Fed was very concerned at the time that the U.S. economy might be on the cusp of an episode of deflation. Japan had experienced a prolonged episode of price-level deflation in the 1990s and beyond, in which economic activity remained stagnant and unemployment was much higher than the normal level. This episode became known as the "lost decade." Contributing also to fears of deflation was the emergence of China as a huge exporter of goods whose prices often undercut those of U.S. producers. The process of globalization was imposing intense price competition on the U.S. manufacturing sector. Figure 4-5, which shows the actual trend of U.S. inflation in those years, indicates why Greenspan was worried about deflation in 2002 and 2003.

Inflation had been trending downward for several years. The inflation rate of the producer price index (PPI) is a leading indicator of the inflation rate of the consumer price index (CPI). The 12-month core PPI inflation rate trended downward from 1999 to 2003, and became negative by autumn 2002. The core CPI inflation rate also trended downward from

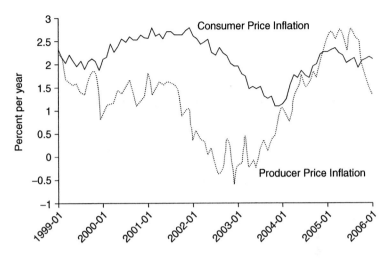

Figure 4-5   Core inflation rates of consumer and producer prices, 1999–2006.
Source: Federal Reserve Bank of St. Louis, FRED database.

about 2.5 percent per year in 2000 to 1.1 percent per year in December 2003, before increasing in the next two years.

Given the shocks provided by the stock market meltdown of 2000–2002, the 2001 recession, and the terrorist attacks in New York and Washington, business and consumer confidence were very low. It is thus not difficult to understand the Fed's decision to maintain short-term interest rates at unusually low levels under those circumstances.

Critics wonder, however, why the Fed kept rates so low for so long. The rate of core producer price inflation began rising in spring 2003, with core consumer price inflation following about six months later. Yet the Greenspan Fed continued to keep the federal funds rate (FFR) at exceptionally low levels. The real FFR was maintained in negative territory from January 2002 until the summer of 2005. This contrasts with the prior 50-year average real FFR of about (positive) 1.8 percent. We will never know if this low interest-rate policy in fact allowed the nation to avert a costly episode of deflation. With the aid of hindsight, it seems unlikely that extraordinarily low rates were needed for such an extended period. Future historians will likely regard the episode as an important policy mistake.

V. Identifying a Bubble

Federal Reserve chairmen Alan Greenspan and Ben Bernanke, in defense of their reluctance to use their policy tools to combat the development of bubbles, emphasized that bubbles are extremely difficult to identify. It is difficult to disentangle the effect on the price of a house or share of stock of fundamental economic forces from that arising from "animal spirits." Nevertheless, certain indicators can shed light on this issue. In the case of shares of stocks, the price–earnings ratio, if far above the historical norm, raises a red flag suggesting evidence of a possible bubble. When the price–earnings ratio of the Standard and Poor's 500 stock index (measuring earnings as a ten-year average) was nearly three times its 50-year historical average, as was the case at the end of 1999, surely the odds were extremely high that a bubble was in force.

In the case of houses, identifying bubbles is more difficult. Nevertheless, there are several indicators that provide useful hints. One plausible indicator is the ratio of home prices to annual rents on homes of similar quality and location. Figure 4-6 shows an index of the price-to-rent ratio from 1997 to 2010, using the ratio of the Case-Shiller National Home Price Index to a measure of owner's equivalent rent.

In the figure, the ratio is expressed as an index number, with 1997 set equal to 100. The ratio depicted increases at a moderate pace from 1997 to early 2003, before accelerating strongly to a peak near the end of 2005. At its peak, this ratio—one indicator of affordability of houses—had increased nearly 80 percent relative to 1997 and 60 percent relative to 2002.

A second kind of indicator focuses on measuring the ability to meet monthly mortgage payments. A good indicator would be the percentage of disposable income the median home-owning family uses to make these

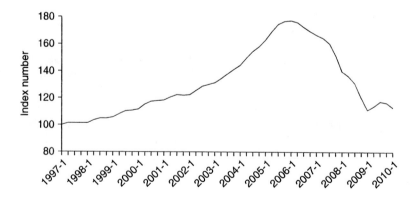

Figure 4-6   Ratio of U.S. national home price index to owners' equivalent rent (1997:1 = 100).

Source: U.S. Bureau of Labor Statistics and Standard & Poor's.

monthly payments, inclusive of taxes and insurance. In several U.S. cities in 2004–2006, the median household was spending over 50 percent of take-home pay, and in some cases, 60 percent, to make the monthly house payments. However, a large percentage of homes sold during the inflating of the housing bubble were made to new owners who took out variable-rate mortgages. This meant that their future monthly payments were highly uncertain and likely to increase. Hence, a better indicator might be the ratio of the price of the house to some measure of disposable income of the household. An index of the ratio of the national home price index to per capita disposable income increased by nearly 60 percent from 1998 to early 2006 before turning down sharply as house prices collapsed.

From 2002 to the middle of 2006, a period in which overall U.S. inflation averaged less than 3 percent annually, house prices in numerous large American cities simply exploded. In the latter stages of the boom, many buyers panicked and stepped in with offers to buy at or above the asking price before it went even higher. House prices more than doubled in this four-and-a-half-year period in such cities as Miami, Los Angeles, Las Vegas, and Phoenix. In eleven of the 20 cities in the Case-Shiller 20-city index, prices jumped more than 70 percent in this brief period. It is hard to escape the conclusion that an alert observer would have concluded that a bubble was in place.

VI. Conclusion

The dual credit and housing bubbles that developed in the first six years of the twenty-first century resulted from the confluence of numerous forces. It is highly unlikely that any one force, acting alone, would have produced the bubbles. The contributing forces include "animal spirits" and the irrational prevailing view that house prices could not fall. Wall Street firms and large banks mistakenly bought into the view that new financial technologies and complex models they had developed had allowed them to accurately measure risk and take measures to nearly eliminate it. Critically influential in the development of the bubbles was a serious degradation of lending standards induced in part by changes in financial technology, the ascent of the shadow banking system, maintenance of exceptionally low interest rates by the Federal Reserve, and a socially inefficient alignment of incentives in numerous areas. Finally, the inevitable lag of the regulatory apparatus behind the rapid change in financial technology played an important role.

Perhaps the most surprising facet of this whole debacle is that it occurred so quickly on the heels of the 2000–2002 meltdown of the enormous stock market bubble of the late 1990s. Memories seem to be getting shorter. If this is the case, the next crisis may not be long in the making. In the next chapter we will look at the Great Crisis—the chain of events that took place in the first couple of years after house prices began falling.

Chapter 5

Bursting of the Twin Bubbles

I. Introduction

The previous chapter examined the interplay of forces that produced the twin bubbles in house prices and the volume of credit. This chapter looks at the events that transpired as these bubbles deflated rapidly in 2007 and 2008 as house prices fell and the process of deleveraging commenced. The following chapter examines the ways in which the popping of the twin bubbles spilled over to create the lengthiest and most severe U.S. economic contraction since the 1930s.

At some point, probably in 2002 or 2003, the persistently robust increases in house prices evolved into what might reasonably be termed a bubble. People began viewing a home as an investment rather than as simply a place to live. Millions of home owners began trading up to bigger homes or purchasing vacation homes. Fueled by low interest rates, easy access to credit, and herd mentality, speculation became rampant. In some parts of the country, homes were being purchased with the intention not of living in them but rather of reselling them, perhaps in only a few months. By the beginning of 2003, house prices in major U.S. cities were rising at double-digit rates, on average, in spite of very low overall consumer price inflation in the country. By 2004, this inflation rate of house prices was escalating toward 15 percent and more.

At the end of the bubble, house prices peaked in most large U.S. cities in 2006, although these prices continued rising in some cities well into 2007. From January 2000 until the peak, house prices more than doubled in such cities as New York, San Francisco, Phoenix, Las Vegas, Washington, Los Angeles, and Miami, nearly tripling in the latter two cities. The Case-Shiller index of house prices in 20 large metropolitan areas increased by 139 percent in this period. This dramatic increase represents the biggest bubble in house prices in U.S. history.

House prices in large coastal cities, along with those in Phoenix and Las Vegas, increased by the largest relative amount during the bubble. Inflation of house prices in the United States exhibits considerable geographic variation resulting from differences in market conditions. The cost of land is a major ingredient in the determination of house prices, and physical limitations on expansion of building space in such cities as San Francisco, New York, and Miami help explain the relatively high and sharply rising cost of houses in those cities. House prices are much lower and have increased more slowly in cities like Dallas and Atlanta, where land is more plentiful and less expensive. In 2010, after the dust had cleared following the housing boom and bust, the real (inflation-adjusted) price of the typical house in New York and Seattle was more than twice its level a decade earlier. In troubled Detroit, it was approximately half of its 2000 value.

Unfortunately, the good times came to an end in summer 2006 as prices began to decline—slowly at first and then more rapidly. They continued to decline in most cities until spring of 2009, falling about one-third in the nation as a whole and much more than that in numerous cities. This wreaked havoc on millions of homeowners and thousands of financial institutions. It spilled over to result in the most severe U.S. recession since the Great Depression of the 1930s, as detailed in the next chapter.

II. Falling Home Prices and Foreclosures: A Vicious Cycle

In the early portion of the first decade of the new millennium, the Federal Reserve slashed interest rates repeatedly in response to the 2001 recession, the terrorist attacks of September 2001, and the stock market crash of 2000–2002. The federal funds target rate reached 1 percent by mid-2003 and was maintained at this level for about a year. In July 2004, nearly three years after the official end of the 2001 recession, the Fed began boosting the rate. In a series of small increments, the target federal funds rate reached 2 percent in November 2004, 3 percent in May 2005, 4 percent in November 2005, and 5 percent in May 2006.

The implications of this increase in rates for many of those unwary or imprudent borrowers who had taken out adjustable-rate mortgages (ARMs) in the rock-bottom interest rate environment of 2003 and 2004 were disastrous. By the spring of 2006, many were seeing their monthly payments bumped up as the ARMs were reset at higher rates, and by the spring of 2007, the number had turned into a flood. A typical subprime homeowner saw monthly payments jump from $1,200 to perhaps $1,500 per month. Hundreds of thousands who were barely able to make the payments at $1,200 could not meet the higher payments. They defaulted on their mortgages and the lenders repossessed their homes. The default rate, running at an annual rate of 775,000 at the beginning of 2006, escalated to 1,000,000 by the end of the year and then jumped sharply to 1,500,000 by mid-2007. From the summer of 2007 to the spring of 2008, it is estimated that the number of vacant homes increased by one million.

House prices began falling, and then tumbling. Home sales declined from an annual rate of 7.5 million at the beginning of 2007 to fewer than 5.5 million by the end of the year. Builders were caught by surprise by the downturn in new home purchases. Rising inventories of newly built homes, together with the increased stock of repossessed homes that lenders were dumping on the market, put severe downward pressure on house prices. The number of homeowners who were underwater—their mortgages exceeding the market value of their home—increased from about 2.5 million in the spring of 2006 to 3.5 million in the spring of 2007, and to 8 million in the spring of 2008. And the job market was now beginning to turn south, thus causing more households to fall behind in making their payments.

In America, home mortgages are nonrecourse obligations in 11 of the 50 states. In case of nonpayment and default, the lender can claim the house it has been holding as collateral, but cannot take possession of the personal assets of the defaulting borrower. Even in the other 39 states, mortgage lenders seldom find it worthwhile to take legal action against defaulting homeowners because of expenses involved and because those who default seldom have significant personal wealth. It is thus clear that there is a strong financial incentive in most instances to walk away from a property that is significantly underwater, even if the homeowner has the ability to keep making the payments. The incentive to just move out and mail in the keys to the bank rises strongly as the value of the house continues to fall and the amount of negative equity in the home increases.

To illustrate a case of the fix that millions of underwater U.S. homeowners found themselves in by mid-2010, take an unlucky (and, in hindsight, unwise) Las Vegas family that purchased a $500,000 home at the May 2006 peak of the bubble. Assume this family made a healthy 20 percent down payment and took out a $400,000 mortgage. Given the extreme (55 percent) contraction of Las Vegas property values, the home was valued at only $225,000 in May 2010. In spite of the hefty $100,000 down payment, this family was underwater to the tune of nearly $175,000. While Las Vegas is an extreme example because of the severity of the decline in house prices there, the initial loan-to-value ratio of 80 percent in the example is lower than the norm of the times. Millions of homebuyers in the twenty-first century made down payments of 10 percent or less. Many others piggybacked a second mortgage on top of the original mortgage to push the loan-to-value ratio close to 100 percent, meaning that even a modest decline in house prices would place them underwater.

Several factors limit the extent of owners' willingness to walk away from underwater homes. These include the psychic cost of moving one's family to a new neighborhood or city, thereby forcing the children to change schools and disrupt friendships; a sense of personal ethical responsibility on the part of most Americans to honor one's debts; and the potential damage to one's reputation, credit score, and future job prospects that defaulting on the home might entail.

The number of households underwater on their homes in mid-2010 was estimated to be about 15 million, or approximately one-fourth of all residential properties with mortgages. Some 5 million of these homeowners were more than 20 percent underwater. Studies suggest that while the great majority of underwater households strive to continue making payments and stay in the home, this commitment tends to break down when the market value of the home falls below 80 percent of the mortgage balance. At some such point, the financial costs of staying in the home overwhelm the previously mentioned costs of defaulting. It is interesting to note that wealthy individuals with mortgages of a million dollars or more have a much greater propensity to walk away from underwater mortgages than those with modest incomes and mortgages.

As indicated, house prices began falling in the summer of 2006. They did so for at least three years as the grinding vicious cycle of falling prices leading to more foreclosures and forced sales, resulting in additional price declines, continued. House prices in many cities bottomed out in the spring of 2009, although prices continued to decline in a few cities throughout the year and beyond. Figure 5-1 illustrates the percentage decline in home prices in a sample of 12 large cities from the peak prices reached in 2006 or 2007 to the price troughs of 2009.

Note that the average house price in Las Vegas and Phoenix declined by more than 50 percent. In six of the 12 cities represented in the figure, prices fell by more than 40 percent. The composite index reveals that the average house declined by approximately one-third in 20 large U.S. cities. Among the cities listed, the range of decline in house prices ranged from 55.5 percent in Las Vegas to 11 percent in Dallas. In general, the cities that had experienced the most appreciation of prices during the bubble

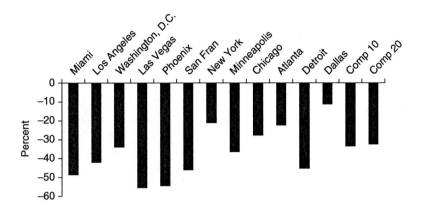

Figure 5-1 Percentage decrease in house prices, 2006–2007 peak to 2009 trough.
Source: Standard & Poor's.

incurred the most loss of value during the crash. A $200,000 home in Miami in 2000 rose to $562,000 in December 2006 before falling to about $290,000 in May 2009. At the other extreme, a $200,000 Dallas home in 2000 appreciated only to about $253,000 at the peak before falling to about $225,000 in February 2009. Given the economic problems experienced by Detroit and the U.S. auto industry, it is not surprising that a $200,000 home there in 2000 appreciated to only $254,000 in December 2005 and then collapsed to $139,000 in June 2008.

The financial crisis that ended up costing the nation more than 8 million jobs and more than $2,000 billion of lost income was triggered by this unprecedented decline in home prices. The decline in house prices led directly to a large decline in the value of mortgage-backed bonds and related derivatives that had been created in the previous 15 years by financial engineers. This, in turn, set off a huge chain reaction that severely impaired the financial condition of many of our financial institutions and triggered a "run" on many bank and nonbank institutions that had borrowed in short-term money markets to purchase the mortgage-backed bonds and other long-term instruments. Almost everyone, including Fed chairman Ben Bernanke and Treasury secretary Henry Paulson, was taken by surprise by the extent to which the financial system was shown to be interconnected. For example, the decision to allow Lehman Brothers to file for bankruptcy almost immediately triggered a run on money market mutual funds, which, in turn, quickly shut down the crucial commercial paper market, denying credit to hundreds of major corporations. We turn now to a discussion of the ways in which the decline in house prices triggered the chain reaction that very nearly led to a catastrophe that may have rivaled that of the 1930s.

III. The Economics of Borrowing Short and Lending Long

Long-term interest rates are typically higher than short-term rates. For example, in the case of U.S. Treasury securities, 10-year and 30-year bond yields have exceeded 90-day Treasury bill yields on about 90 percent of the days in the past 50 years. During this period, the yield margin has averaged about 1.5 percentage points for 10-year Treasury bonds, and about 1.8 percentage points for 30-year Treasury bonds.[1] The same principle applies in markets for private debt securities, as AAA corporate bond yields are typically higher than yields on top-rated short-term commercial paper. Hence, over the years, it has normally been profitable to "borrow short and lend long."

However, this strategy is inherently risky. And sometimes the chickens come home to roost, as was the case in the financial crisis of 2007–2009. Financial institutions that issue short-term debt to finance long-term loans are subject to liquidity risk and interest-rate risk—risks not incurred by firms that finance themselves by issuing long-term debt to make long-term loans. If an institution has funded long-term loan commitments by issuing short-term debt, it is vulnerable in the event it is unable to roll over its debt—that is, if it cannot find buyers when it reissues short-term debt as it comes due. In this situation, the institution will be forced to sell its long-term assets, quite likely under duress and at depressed prices. This is what we mean by liquidity risk. It can cause severe financial problems, as was witnessed repeatedly during the Great Crisis.

Also, to the extent an institution has made long-term loan commitments at fixed interest rates, even if it has no problem finding new lenders as its short-term debt matures, it is vulnerable to a potential increase in interest rates payable on its short-term debt. In this case, its profit margin will be squeezed or eliminated by rising short-term interest rates. If the situation persists, such institutions can become insolvent. The classic example is the U.S. savings and loan (S&L) crisis of the 1980s, as discussed in Chapter 3. A dramatic increase in short-term interest rates in 1979 and 1980 sharply raised S&Ls' costs of obtaining funds, and this increase in costs could not be shifted via higher interest rates onto borrowers who had taken out fixed-rate mortgages in the previous years. Huge operating losses occurred in 1981 and 1982, and more than half of the nation's S&Ls were either closed down or merged with stronger institutions.

As stated previously, the shortness of memory of those CEOs and managers at the top of American financial institutions and other officers responsible for critical investment decisions is remarkable. For just as the S&L debacle resulted from borrowing short and lending long, so resides the cause for much of the damage wrought in the Great Crisis. In this case, however, the initiating cause was primarily liquidity risk arising from the inability of institutions to refinance maturing debt. This inability arose from growing recognition in 2007 and 2008 that many financial institutions were likely on the verge of insolvency because of the declining value of mortgage-related securities on their books. Financial institutions had not given adequate consideration to liquidity risk—the risk they would be unable to roll over their debt. This underestimation of risk stemmed ultimately from the irrationally low probability assigned to the possibility that real estate prices might decline significantly.

IV. Arcane Financial Instruments and the Shadow Banking System

Wall Street churned out a multitude of new financial instruments in the past quarter century. Economists believe that these instruments, by improving the efficiency of the financial system, are in principle socially beneficial. However, many of the complicated and little-understood instruments played an important part in the creation of the credit and housing bubbles. Here, a few of the more important instruments are discussed.

Mortgage-Backed Securities and Collateralized Debt Obligations

A mortgage-backed security (MBS) is a package of either residential or commercial mortgages, collateralized by the mortgages in the bundle and sold like bonds to investors around the world. A collateralized debt obligation (CDO) is a derivative built by financial engineers from packages of residential mortgages, commercial mortgages, auto loans, corporate bonds, student loans, or other types of loans. To build a CDO, loans of a particular type are first securitized. These securities are then divided into *tranches* (a French word meaning "slices") of varying degrees of risk. In descending order of quality, these tranches include the senior tranche, the mezzanine tranches, and the inferior tranche, sometimes known as the "equity" tranche.

The senior tranche has first claim on interest payments from the underlying securities; it therefore bears the least risk and provides the lowest yield. These senior tranches typically constitute more than three-fourths of the face value of the security. They are commonly sold to large banks and pension funds that are regulated in the kinds of risk they are allowed to take and required to invest only in AAA-rated securities. The "mezzanine" tranches, bearing intermediate risk and yield, are typically A-rated securities. They are often sold to insurance companies, which are subject to less stringent regulations than banks. The lowest tranches, typically making up less than 5 percent of the value of all tranches, are the last to be paid interest in the event of problems with the underlying mortgages or other securities. These tranches are unrated and require a higher yield to compensate investors for the greater risk. Hedge funds, because they are expected to earn very high returns for their investors who are willing to incur significant risk in their zeal to reap outsized returns, have typically been the principal buyers of these securities.

CDOs were appealing in that they could in principle be constructed to meet the risk appetite of various investors. For example, a senior AAA tranche of Southwest Airlines bonds might be mixed with a senior AAA tranche of Conoco-Phillips bonds, thus providing a hedge against a major change in oil prices and thereby reducing risk to a potential conservative investor. A CDO might also be formed by combining senior tranches of mortgage-backed securities from different regions of the country to provide safety through geographic diversification. Investors willing to accept somewhat higher risk for higher expected returns might be interested in purchasing CDOs built from mezzanine tranches of diversified mortgage-backed securities or other debt instruments. The conventional wisdom was that the added diversification in such a CDO made it a relatively safe instrument.

Credit Default Swaps

Buyers of these various mortgage-backed bonds, CDOs, and other instruments were able to buy insurance that ostensibly would cover any losses incurred on these investments. Through complex derivatives transactions, insurance instruments known as credit default swaps (CDS) were written by large banks and insurance companies such as American Insurance Group (AIG). The cost of buying such insurance was relatively low—far too low, as it turned out to AIG's (and U.S. taxpayers') dismay. Issuance of CDS grew dramatically after 2000, their notional value (face value of all the properties being insured) reaching more than $60 trillion by 2006.

It appeared that Wall Street had invented new products that had permanently lowered risk in financial markets. Given the perception that the MBS and CDOs were very safe and that any unlikely losses would be covered by the CDS, demand for the securities by investors all around the world surged during 2002–2006. Many of these securities had been given the highest marks of AAA by rating agencies like Standard and Poor's and Moody's, which had apparently bought into the illusion that the securities were very safe. As long as there was demand by large investors for additional MBS and mortgage-related CDOs, the supply of mortgages available to U.S. households was virtually unlimited. The underpricing of risk and the associated surge in worldwide demand for housing-related MBS and CDOs gave powerful impetus to the twin bubbles of credit and house prices.

Tri-Party Repurchase Agreements (Repos)

In addition to commercial paper, another device used for short-term financing is the tri-party repurchase agreement, known as "repo." In a repo, a borrower arranges to "sell" U.S. Treasury securities, MBS, or other securities to the lender for cash, agreeing to buy the securities back at a specified date and price. (In reality, the securities are not sold to the lender, but simply posted as collateral.) Repos are typically of extremely short maturity, frequently only one day or one week, and are widely used by investment banks and other financial firms to raise funds. The amount by which the repurchase price exceeds the original price constitutes the interest payment on the loan. A large commercial bank such as JPMorgan Chase serves as the middleman in the deal, giving rise to the term "tri-party." This market grew from less than $400 billion in the early 1990s to more than $4,500 billion by the summer of 2008, making it a crucial source of the expansion of credit during the formation of the twin bubbles.

The lender in such an arrangement was perceived to be taking minimal risk in making the loan because the securities posted by the borrower as collateral—typically U.S. Treasury bonds and MBS—were believed to be virtually free of default risk. However, as the price of MBS declined in response to problems in subprime mortgages and other markets, a "run on the repo" took place as lenders withdrew from this market out of fear of not being repaid in full.

Countrywide Financial, an aggressive and rogue mortgage lender based in California, became a victim of the run on repos. Countrywide had become accustomed to borrowing in the overnight repo market to finance mortgage loans pending their sale to investment banks to be securitized. By mid-summer of 2007, lenders began to suspect that the value of the MBS that Countrywide was posting as collateral in the repo transactions was in doubt. In August, the intermediary bank in the tri-party arrangement told the New York Fed that, barring the posting of additional collateral by Countrywide, it would repay the lender the next day not in cash but in the MBS that Countrywide had put up as collateral. Tim Geithner, then-president of the New York Fed, realized such a development could lead to a highly contagious dumping of MBS. Geithner was able to mediate an acceptable collateral arrangement between the two parties. (Shortly thereafter, Bank of America took over the failing Countrywide firm.) At any rate, this event served as an early warning of the vulnerability of the repo market. And about six months later, problems with borrowing through repos helped sink the venerable investment bank, Bear Stearns. Within a year, as house prices and MBS prices fell, the annual volume of transactions in the repo market declined from $4500 billion to $2700 billion.

Structured Investment Vehicles and Conduits

Large global banks set up entities known as structured investment vehicles (SIVs) to make huge investments in CDOs and residential mortgage-backed securities. Taking advantage of upward-sloping yield curves, the SIVs borrowed short—typically in the form of commercial paper or repos—to purchase long-term mortgage-related securities. As long as they were able to borrow at the traditionally low rates available in the commercial paper and repo markets, and as long as the prices of the high-yielding MBS and CDOs in their portfolios remained stable, this activity was highly profitable. In normal times, combining the yield spread with high leverage provided handsome returns for the SIVs.

Capital requirements limit leverage and therefore reduce profitability in boom times. The overriding motive for banks to establish SIVs was to circumvent capital requirements and increase leverage. Those assets held in off-balance sheet SIVs—principally MBS, CDOs, and Treasury bonds—were not subject to capital requirements.[2] By the middle of 2007, it is estimated that global banks held approximately $1.5 trillion worth of MBS and CDOs in SIVs.

As the slow decline in house prices across the country began to accelerate in 2007, holders of MBS saw the handwriting on the wall. With house prices falling, the prices of MBS and related CDOs were sure to come down. Investors began dumping the MBS and CDOs, causing their prices to plummet. The money market mutual funds and other lenders that had financed the SIVs by purchasing their commercial paper soon recognized that this paper was risky—there was a significant likelihood that they might not get their money back. They refused to roll over the paper as it matured.

Most of these SIVs had credit lines with the banks that had created them. Banks had favored this arrangement because they collected fees from the SIVs. And it apparently had not occurred to them that the price of the mortgage-backed securities might ever fall significantly, or that the insurance contracts guaranteeing the mortgage-related securities might not be viable. Either out of fear of lawsuits, or because they felt their reputation was at stake, the banks took these SIVs back onto their balance sheets. The associated losses impaired the financial condition of many large banks.

Large global banks also created a mechanism to get newly issued mortgage loans off of their books pending securitization of the loans. These were known as conduits. Such loans were financed through commercial paper issued by the banks. These warehoused mortgage loans, which amounted to some $400 billion in 2007, were not subject to capital requirements because they were technically owned by the conduits, not by the banks. But as the prices of MBS and CDOs tanked, the conduits ran into the same problem as the SIVs—they could not find new buyers for their commercial paper as the paper matured. Lending depends on confidence and trust, and trust was beginning to evaporate as lenders feared their counterparties might be unable to make good on their debts. Inability to refinance maturing short-term debt drove the conduits out of business. This impaired the entire private securitization business, which essentially came to a halt in 2007, leaving only Fannie Mae and Freddie Mac as major players.

The Shadow Banking System Again

Issuers of commercial paper and repos can be considered part of the so-called "shadow banking system." This includes SIVs, conduits, hedge funds, and investment banks, among others. To obtain funds, traditional banks issue deposits that are insured by the Federal Deposit Insurance Corporation (FDIC). They also have access to loans from the Federal Reserve in the event liquidity dries up. They are thus covered by the federal "safety net." The shadow banks, rather than issuing deposits to obtain funds, issue securities that are not insured—commercial paper and repos, for example. The shadow banks do not have routine access to the Fed's discount window to obtain liquidity in a crisis, as banks do. The shadow banks are thus subject to considerably more liquidity risk than are traditional banks, as we learned in 2007 and 2008. The extent of this risk was ignored or widely underestimated prior to the crisis.

The shadow banking system, which grew very rapidly after 2000, generally resides outside the purview of the regulatory authorities. Being largely unregulated, shadow banks are typically more highly leveraged than commercial banks. The upside of high leverage is the opportunity to earn phenomenal profits in good times. The exceptionally low interest rates in place from 2002 to 2005 encouraged firms to take on more debt and increase leverage. The financial crisis stemmed in part from the increasing recognition of the upside benefits of leverage, combined with utter failure to consider the downside possibilities.

The downside of high leverage is that if a financial shock like a decline in house prices reduces capital, a highly leveraged firm must reduce assets more aggressively than a less-leveraged player. If the commercial banking system is leveraged 8/1 and if its capital is reduced by $200 billion, it must eventually reduce assets (mainly loans) by $1,600 billion to reach equilibrium and abide by capital requirements. If the shadow banking system is leveraged 20/1 and suffers equity loss of $200 billion, it may eventually reduce assets by as much as $4,000 billion to reattain equilibrium.

Falling house prices and the associated decline in value of mortgage-related securities triggered a major loss of capital in both the "regular" and "shadow" banking systems. This resulted in a large and costly process of deleveraging—liquidation of loans—that began in 2006. This process continued for several years, accounting in large part for the severe tightening of lending standards in recent times. Because the shadow banking system is more highly leveraged than the traditional banking sector, and because the share of the overall credit created by the shadow banking system increased sharply in the decade leading up to the Great Crisis, the bursting of the housing bubble in 2007 and 2008 had much larger economic consequences than would have been the case 10 or 20 years ago.

Exhibit 5-1

Auction-Rate Securities: The Shadow Banking System Run Amok

In 2007, Merrill Lynch and other major financial houses aggressively marketed an ostensibly attractive financial instrument to well-heeled clients who were in a position to put down cash of $25,000 or more. These "auction-rate securities" seemed too good to be true. This instrument, devised by financial engineers in the 1980s at the now-defunct Lehman Brothers investment bank, appeared to combine the attractive returns associated with long-term bonds with the liquidity of passbook savings accounts or money market mutual fund shares. When yields on money market instruments and savings accounts dropped to extremely low levels in 2008, issuance of auction-rate securities increased dramatically.

In buying an auction-rate security, purchasers would commit loans to a municipal organization, such as the Denver Airport Authority, on a long-term basis. In legal terms, the money was tied up for perhaps 20–30 years, as is the case with traditional bonds. However, at regular weekly or monthly intervals, the investment bank sponsoring the securities would hold an auction in which potential new investors would bid for the right to replace investors who wanted their money out. The interest rate determined in the bidding auction would be paid to all owners of these securities during the period until the following auction. This financial innovation appeared to offer benefits to savers in the form of high liquidity and attractive yields, and it offered lower borrowing costs to issuers of these securities than conventional bonds. The value of auction-rate securities outstanding ballooned to more than $350 billion in 2008.

How was this new instrument able to offer such attractive terms to both lenders and borrowers, thereby taking market share from traditional banks? Because auction-rate securities did not fall under the purview of the Federal Reserve or other regulators, their issuers gained important financial advantages not enjoyed by banks. Banks are subject to capital requirements and reserve requirements—regulations that reduce profitability. And they are charged fees by the FDIC for deposit insurance. None of these costs were incurred by the issuers of auction-rate securities.

In early 2008, as the financial crisis deepened and demand for liquidity surged, bidders for the auction-rate securities disappeared. Those who wanted out were denied. Instead, they faced the prospect of being tied up for decades until the securities reached maturity. When the first two or three auctions failed, the auction-rate system experienced a classic run as panicked security holders tried to get out. The contagion shut the entire system down. Today, the auction-rate security system is defunct. Fortunately for individual investors, the attorney general of New York stepped in, threatening sponsoring firms like Merrill Lynch with lawsuits. Merrill and most other sponsors backed off. They returned the cash to their clients and were left holding the bag.

The short-lived but explosive growth of auction-rate securities exemplifies the nature of the changing shadow banking system. It shows how new financial innovations have reduced the relative importance of traditional banks in the credit-generating process and challenged the Federal Reserve's ability to control the amount of credit outstanding in the nation's economy.

V. The Fall of the Dominoes

An indicator of the extent of fear in financial markets is the spread between yields on financial instruments that are considered to contain risk and those considered riskless. Figure 5-2 illustrates the spread between yields on AA commercial paper and U.S. Treasury bills during the most critical period of the financial crisis—mid-2007 through the end of 2008. Commercial paper is normally considered to have very low risk of default. U.S. Treasury bills are considered to be *totally* free of default risk. In normal times, this yield spread typically averages about 25 basis points, that is, 0.25 percentage points.

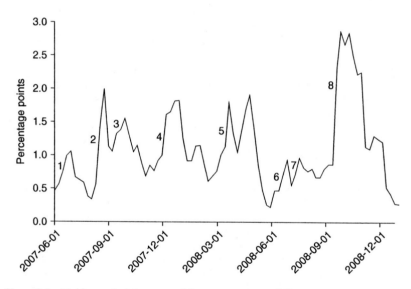

Figure 5-2   Yield spread: AA commercial paper vs. treasury bills, June 2007 to December 2008.

Source: Federal Reserve Bank of St. Louis, FRED database.

Notes:

1. June 23, 2007: Bear Stearns pledges $3.2 billion to bail out its hedge funds.
2. August 9–14, 2007: BNP Paribas and other European banks freeze redemption of investment funds by shareholders.
3. September 13, 2007: Northern Rock receives emergency loan from Bank of England.
4. November 27, 2007: Citigroup receives $7.5 billion capital injection from Abu Dhabi Investment Authority.
5. March 13–16, 2008: Bear Stearns losses lead to its takeover by JPMorgan.
6. June 16, 2008: Lehman Brothers reports $2.8 billion loss in second quarter.
7. July 11, 2008: IndyMac depositors stage run on bank.
8. September 15–25, 2008: Lehman files bankruptcy papers; Bank of America buys troubled Merrill Lynch; AIG downgraded by all three rating agencies; Primary Reserve Fund "breaks the buck"; Washington Mutual closed by Office of Thrift Supervision.

As the financial crisis unfolded, this spread increased, averaging 1.13 percentage points in 2008. The spread exhibited a series of spikes in 2007 and 2008 as alarming news events caused financial agents to dump commercial paper in favor of U.S. Treasury bills, the ultimate safe haven.[3] Emergency actions implemented by the Federal Reserve, the Treasury, or both, would ease fears for a time, returning the spread to a more normal level until the next crisis occurred. The figure illustrates several specific events that sent the spread sharply higher, including the downfall of the investment bank Bear Stearns in March 2008. The most unexpected and shocking event was the announcement of the bankruptcy of Lehman Brothers in September 2008. Immediately following the announcement, the commercial paper-Treasury bill yield spread jumped by approximately 2 percentage points as fear became rampant.

Mid-September 2008 goes down as one of the most cataclysmic periods in U.S. financial history. It ranks with Black Tuesday—October 29, 1929—as the most notorious financial episode. We will discuss the events of that period momentarily. First, we look at a series of crises leading up to the disasters of September 2008.

The Demise of Bear Stearns

When a couple of hedge funds of the renowned investment bank, Bear Stearns, failed in March 2007, this was an early but little-recognized signal of troubles to come. Bear's hedge funds had invested heavily in CDOs built from AAA-rated subprime MBS. For several years, the hedge funds had earned phenomenal returns, often exceeding 20 percent per year. But as rising subprime mortgage defaults triggered a decline in MBS prices, large banks that had made huge loans to the hedge funds got nervous and demanded more collateral. This forced Bear to dump some of their MBS and CDOs onto the market to pay down their bank debts. This action only further depressed the price of the MBS, thus exacerbating the problem and inducing the banks to demand even more collateral. Unable to comply, Bear's hedge funds were wiped out.

It was thought that Bear Stearns itself would weather the storm. However, by early 2008, Bear's problems had deepened significantly. House prices had by now fallen appreciably. Bear was heavily invested in subprime MBS, financing its position through repos and commercial paper. As the prices of these MBS fell, rumors spread that Bear Stearns might be insolvent. This triggered a liquidity crisis for Bear in March 2008 as money market mutual funds and other investors stopped buying its commercial paper.

Bear Stearns was the nation's fifth largest investment bank. In the Federal Reserve's view, a collapse of Bear would very likely cause major systemic problems, possibly even triggering a panic in world financial markets. For one thing, Bear had written CDS that insured banks and other institutions against losses on loans and MBS. If it failed, these CDS—with notional values (potential payoffs) in the trillions of dollars—would be rendered worthless, thus impairing numerous important firms. In addition, Bear had large debts to other financial institutions. Bear Stearns was believed to be too interconnected to fail. The Fed and Treasury agreed that the government could not let it.

At first, the Fed appeared to have a willing buyer in JPMorgan Chase. However, when Morgan's management team carefully examined Bear's books, it reported that Bear's problems were deeper than initially thought. JPMorgan Chase told the Federal Reserve it would have to take $30 billion of bad assets off of Bear's books to make the deal viable. The Fed and Treasury reached an agreement with JPMorgan Chase. The bank was to receive a collateralized loan of $30 billion from the Fed; however, JPMorgan Chase insisted the Fed loan be a nonrecourse loan. If the collateral taken by the Fed in support of the loan were to diminish in value, it would be the Fed's problem, not JPMorgan's. Thus, the Fed took on significant risk in making the loan to JPMorgan Chase. It had been forced to cross a line it had been reluctant to cross. Whether the Fed was conducting its traditional role of serving as a lender of last resort or in effect subsidizing and saving an insolvent institution was unclear. At any rate, JPMorgan Chase ended up paying $10 per share for Bear's stock, which had sold for $170 less than a year earlier. Thus, while Bear's creditors were saved by the Fed's intervention, shareholders were nearly wiped out.

Fannie Mae and Freddie Mac Again

Fannie Mae was created as a government organization during the Great Depression as part of Franklin D. Roosevelt's program to boost economic activity and provide mortgages at attractive rates to assist households in purchasing homes. Freddie Mac was established in 1970 to compete with Fannie Mae and enhance the efficiency of the mortgage market. These institutions make the United States almost unique among countries in providing this subsidy to homeowners. These firms, which were initially purely public institutions, later became hybrid public–private organizations.

During the late 1960s, the U.S. had escalated its involvement in the Vietnam War and federal budget deficits increased appreciably. These deficits were politically damaging to the Congress and the administration of President Lyndon B. Johnson, inhibiting implementation of his Great Society program. In a cynical political ploy, Fannie Mae was privatized in 1968 as a way to get the deficits associated with her operations off the federal government's books. Freddie Mac, established later, was similarly privatized. Fannie and Freddie were now GSEs—privately owned government-sponsored enterprises.

This meant that Fannie and Freddie now had a dual mission. The first was to continue to support the housing market with the purpose of increasing the flow of new mortgages, thereby subsidizing home ownership. The second and new mission was to earn maximum profits for their shareholders and bonuses for top management. In 1988, Fannie and Freddie were publicly listed and traded on the New York Stock Exchange. Fueled by continually increasing house prices, the companies prospered and Fannie's share price increased from around $2 per share in 1988 to about $65 per share by 2004. In this period, the dual missions seemed compatible.

Fannie and Freddie's GSE charters mandated that their activities be limited to purchasing and securitizing mortgages. Given that the size of the mortgage market is inherently limited and homeownership appeared to be approaching its natural limits by the early 2000s, the drive to boost profits meant that these firms would have to increase risk-taking. Given the unique nature of the GSEs, forces that normally inhibit risk-taking by purely private firms were blunted. Fannie and Freddie's bondholders felt protected from risk by the implicit government guarantee, while their stockholders stood to directly benefit from higher returns typically available to those willing to take greater risk. This absence of countervailing incentives, given the environment of enormous profits being made in the mortgage boom of the 2000s, tilted the behavior of Fannie and Freddie toward taking more risk.

This increased risk-taking took several forms. First, Fannie and Freddie sharply increased the size of their holdings of retained mortgages—those not securitized. These instruments were highly profitable relative to holdings of MBS because the spreads between returns on the mortgages and borrowing costs were typically around 2 percentage points—higher than those on MBS. Second, the GSEs boosted these spreads by shortening the maturity of their debt, thereby taking advantage of the upward-sloping yield curve. This meant, however, that they had to roll over a larger amount of debt each year, exposing themselves to increased liquidity risk. Third, the GSEs cut costs by not taking actions to fully hedge themselves against interest-rate risk. Finally, the GSEs took on increased credit risk to boost their expected returns. While they did not purchase individual subprime mortgages, they began purchasing senior tranches of securities built from subprime mortgages, stepping up these purchases sharply after 2003 as the housing boom entered its manic and final phase.

The risks taken by the highly leveraged GSEs left them vulnerable to any number of potential shocks. The subprime mortgage crisis provided the shock that toppled Fannie and Freddie. Given the requirement that the GSEs "mark to market"—that is, compute the value of their assets at market prices—the sharp decline in value of the subprime MBS on Fannie and Freddie's books resulted in severe erosion of their capital in 2007 and 2008. This threatened to result in a major liquidity crisis if investors began to refuse to refinance maturing debt.

China and other Asian countries that had purchased large amounts of the GSEs' bonds and MBS began raising questions about Fannie's and Freddie's financial viability. They wanted to know whether the guarantees would be honored. Fearful that the GSEs were about to encounter problems in rolling over their debt, Treasury secretary Hank Paulson publicly committed up to $200 billion of government funds in July 2008 to backstop the GSEs. A few months later, this figure was bumped to $400 billion. As the declining values of their mortgage-related securities pushed the GSEs toward insolvency, Fannie and Freddie were put in conservatorship in September 2008, essentially nationalized by the government.

The prices of the MBS on Fannie's and Freddie's books continued to decline; the negative net worth, and drain on the U.S. Treasury, reached $110 billion by the third quarter of 2009. At the end of 2009, President Barack Obama acknowledged the inevitable—the U.S. government commitment was open-ended. Together, Fannie and Freddie owned or guaranteed more than 30 million home loans worth some $5.5 trillion. They were now the only source of mortgage securitization, as private sector securitization had essentially shut down. In the near-term interests of the U.S. economy, the government had no alternative to backstopping these behemoths to keep them in business. The only question was their ultimate status. Would they be permanently nationalized, totally privatized with implicit guarantees stripped away, or given some intermediate status? Because the appropriate status of Fannie and Freddie is a highly contentious issue, the financial reform legislation implemented in July 2010 failed to address their future status. The subject is likely to be debated in Congress in 2011 or 2012.

Ironically, pending a decision about the ultimate fate of the GSEs, their role in the mortgage markets expanded significantly after their September 2008 takeover by the government. While the GSEs held or guaranteed about half of the total stock of $12 trillion of mortgages outstanding in 2008, they accounted for more than 75 percent of new mortgages issued in 2009 and 2010. Given the almost total drying up of private sector securitization of mortgages after 2007, together with severe tightening of standards by mortgage lenders, heavy involvement of the GSEs in the mortgage market was essential if that market was not to collapse and further add to the nation's economic woes.

Lehman Brothers, Merrill Lynch, AIG, and Reserve Primary Fund

Lehman Brothers was a large investment bank that had evolved from its beginnings in 1850 as a dry goods merchant. It had survived the Great Depression and more than 20 recessions over the years to become an enormous firm with more than $600 billion of debt and plenty of assets to cover the debt prior to the financial crisis. In the early 2000s, under the leadership of hard-charging CEO Dick Fuld, it became one of the largest firms participating in the securitization of subprime mortgages. Lehman was caught holding a very large portfolio of these securities as housing prices and mortgage-related security prices plummeted in 2008. It is not clear whether Lehman was unable to find buyers for the securities before it was too late or simply decided to hold onto them in the expectation that their prices would soon recover.

In 2004, in a serious policy error, the Securities and Exchange Commission had reduced capital requirements for investment banks. Lehman responded by ramping up leverage to 30/1. This meant it could be rendered insolvent by a write-down of assets of less than 4 percent. In addition to its large holdings of subprime residential MBS, Lehman had large holdings of commercial mortgages on its books, including many of dubious quality. Crucially, about half of Lehman's debt was short-term, consisting of commercial paper and repos. In combination with high leverage and an asset structure heavy in subprime MBS, the maturity structure of its debt made Lehman extremely vulnerable to liquidity problems. A firm can fail either because it is insolvent or because it cannot refinance maturing debt. Lehman was brought down by a "run"—an inability to roll over its debt as the persistent decline in U.S. house prices and mortgage-related instruments led investors to suspect the firm was approaching insolvency.

In September 2008, Lehman reported a loss of $2.8 billion and was forced to liquidate $6 billion of assets to meet a collateral call from JPMorgan Chase, its clearing bank. U.S. officials became aware that the firm was on the verge of failure. Fed chairman Bernanke, Federal Reserve Bank of New York president Tim Geithner, and Treasury secretary

Henry Paulson met to look at the government's options. Both Bernanke and Geithner expressed their view that a failure of Lehman would likely be contagious, possibly setting off a worldwide financial panic. They argued that Lehman should not be permitted to fail. Secretary Paulson, however, was feeling intense pressure from the Bush administration. The public was angry about the previous week's costly government takeover of Fannie and Freddie, as well as the recent bailout of Bear Stearns. Many analysts were worried about the moral hazard implications associated with repeated government bailouts of risk-taking firms. Perhaps it was time for the U.S. government to draw a line in the sand. Paulson appeared to rule out putting government money into Lehman. He let it be known that any action to save Lehman would have to be done through the private sector.

From Friday, September 12 through Sunday, September 14, Paulson, Bernanke, and Geithner struggled to find a buyer for Lehman. To raise funds to make a private takeover of Lehman palatable to potentially interested parties, Paulson convened top executives of ten of the largest banks for emergency weekend meetings at the New York Fed.[4] Under intense pressure from Paulson and Geithner, the bankers grudgingly agreed to come up with more than $35 billion to be used if needed. At first, it appeared that Paulson had interested buyers in Bank of America and Barclays, a venerable British bank.

Upon examining Lehman's books over the weekend, however, Bank of America officials discovered that the hole in Lehman's balance sheet was even worse than they had suspected. Lehman had overstated the value of real estate assets on its books. Bank of America withdrew, preferring instead to work out a last-minute deal to purchase the faltering Merrill Lynch. And Barclay's interest in buying Lehman was quashed by British regulatory authorities, who indicated they would not allow their country to be put at risk to bail out reckless American bankers. On Monday, September 15, 2008 Lehman filed for bankruptcy protection.

Like Lehman, Merrill Lynch also became heavily involved in subprime MBS and was highly leveraged. Also, like Lehman, Merrill was spiraling toward bankruptcy in September 2008. Bank of America had been courting Merrill for some time. With active encouragement from the government, Bank of America purchased Merrill on the same day that Lehman declared bankruptcy.

Meanwhile, AIG, the largest insurance company in the world, was also experiencing extreme problems. Giants like AIG had traditionally insured municipal bonds, thereby helping stabilize that market. After 2000, these insurance companies got into the business of insuring the higher-rated tranches of MBS, mainly through the instrument of credit default swaps. The same agencies that apply ratings to MBS—Standard and Poor's, Moody's, and Fitch—also rate the insurance companies. Many pension funds, banks, and other buyers of MBS and related instruments were required to limit themselves strictly to AAA-rated securities. As house prices continued to fall in 2008, the viability of the MBS came under question. If their ratings were to be downgraded, this would trigger forced selling and a self-reinforcing downward spiral in the security prices and associated increase in liabilities of the insurance companies.

Consistent with the antiregulatory sentiment of the times, the insurance companies were lightly regulated and held very little capital. If ratings of MBS were downgraded, the insurers would be on the hook for very large payments. Seeing this development coming, the rating agencies informed the insurers that they would have to raise capital or see their ratings downgraded, possibly resulting in a panic in the market for MBS.

AIG had written more than $400 billion in insurance policies in the form of CDS with numerous counterparties, and much of this insurance pertained to securities backed by subprime loans. As house prices and MBS prices continued to fall, AIG was forced to make good on its insurance. In the first half of 2008, AIG reported losses of more than $12 billion. With house prices continuing to fall, AIG was in a death spiral. On September 16, one day after the blockbuster Lehman and Merrill Lynch announcements, Standard and Poor's and Moody's downgraded AIG's credit rating. Because only top-rated insurance companies were permitted to issue CDS without depositing collateral, AIG was now required to post additional collateral with all of its counterparties. It was unable to do so.

Bernanke, Geithner, and Paulson agreed that, in combination with the previous day's bankruptcy of Lehman, the failure of AIG might very well tip the financial system into the abyss. It was now not difficult to envision a replay of the catastrophic Great Depression of the 1930s. All agreed that AIG had to be saved. Late in the day on September 16, the Federal Reserve announced it was creating a new credit facility in which AIG would be allowed to draw as much as $85 billion. The terms of the loan were justly and deliberately punitive—the interest rate on the loan was set to float at 8.5 percentage points above the London Inter-bank Borrowing Rate (LIBOR). In addition, in return for the loan, the U.S. government received warrants granting it nearly 80 percent ownership in AIG. As house prices and MBS prices continued falling, AIG was contractually required to honor its commitments under the terms of the CDS. The U.S. government was therefore forced to put additional money into AIG, with the ultimate bill approaching $200 billion.

By creating fear and placing further pressure on MBS prices, the downward spiral and ultimate failure of Lehman Brothers undoubtedly exacerbated AIG's problems and hastened the government bailout. Also, because numerous money market mutual funds (MMMFs) had purchased commercial paper issued by Lehman that was now worthless, these MMMFs came under pressure as well. Reserve Primary Fund, a large MMMF, "broke the buck" in October 2008. This meant that its total assets were insufficient to honor its commitment to redeem the shares at their face value of $1 per share. The firm was insolvent. Several other MMMFs experienced stress as shareholders withdrew their funds in favor of safe U.S. Treasury bills. To stem the tide and prevent further repercussions, the Federal Reserve stepped in and guaranteed MMMF shares.

VI. Conclusion

After rising more than 120 percent in a large sample of American cities during 2000–2005, house prices peaked in the spring of 2006 and began to decline. By June 2008, house prices across the nation were down more than 20 percent, on average. Millions of homeowners who had taken out high loan-to-value mortgages had been hit with a double whammy—their homes were significantly underwater, and many of them had experienced interest-rate resets on ARMs that sharply boosted their monthly payments. A highly pernicious cycle set in: mortgage delinquencies triggered foreclosures and forced home sales, causing price declines and begetting more delinquencies, force sales, and drops in prices.

Foreclosure is costly not only for the household involved, but also for the lending institution. Legal expenses are involved, and in the period in which the home is vacant, neglect and vandalism often result in significant depreciation in value. By the time the foreclosed home is finally sold, the proceeds often amount to only 50 percent of the mortgage balance. It appears that mortgage lenders would thus have a strong incentive to rework the terms of the loan to induce the owner to stay in the home, either by reducing the mortgage rate or writing down a portion of the principal. However, in the early 2000s, most originators of such loans did not have sufficient staff or expertise to revise the terms. More importantly, they typically had sold off these loans to be packaged with hundreds of others. Ownership of the bad mortgages was now dispersed among a large number of investors with varying degrees of claims on the income accruing from the bundle of mortgages. Because of these factors, efforts on the part of the Bush and Obama administrations to prevent massive foreclosures through renegotiation of mortgages met with very limited success. The initial slow stream of foreclosures became a river, totaling more than 6 million in the three-year period ending in early 2010.

Even though many of America's largest banks were impaired by the write-offs of mortgage-related instruments, the contraction of credit in the shadow banking system did more damage to the economy than the tightening of credit standards by traditional banks. The amount of total credit generated in the shadow banking system had reached parity with that of the traditional banking system by 2006. At this point, credit in the shadow market funded through repos, asset-backed commercial paper, auction-rate securities, and other instruments began declining sharply as massive deleveraging took place. The shadow banking system imploded. It shriveled up, becoming a "shadow" of its former self.

Many of those denied credit in the shadow banking world turned to traditional banks for credit. However, given their loss of capital, together with a natural tendency to become more conservative in reaction to financial shock, these banks were in no position to offset the contraction of credit in the shadow banking system. In fact, most banks tightened lending standards and the huge quantity of funds pumped into the banks by the Federal Reserve simply remained on banks' books as excess reserves. The severe tightening of overall credit conditions in the nation thus became one of the numerous avenues through which the financial crisis spilled over and created the longest and deepest economic contraction since the 1930s. We turn to that subject in chapter 6.

Chapter 6

The Great Crisis and Great Recession of 2007–2009

I. Introduction

In spite of monetary and fiscal stimulus of unprecedented magnitude implemented relatively quickly, the Great Crisis severely impacted U.S. economic activity during 2008, 2009, and beyond. By most conventional measures of cyclical activity, the period extending from December 2007 through June 2009 was the most severe economic contraction in the United States since the Great Depression of 1929–1933. The Depression, in which real gross domestic product (GDP) fell by 25 percent and the unemployment rate reached 25 percent, dwarfed anything in U.S. experience, before or after. But the 2007–2009 economic contraction, dubbed "The Great Recession," was the most severe of the ten post-1950 U.S. recessions. This chapter examines the ways in which the Great Crisis led to a severe contraction in aggregate expenditures, output, and employment, thereby exacting a very large price in terms of well-being of the nation.

II. Fundamental Macroeconomic Concepts

To understand the economic cost of the Great Crisis, it is essential to think about the output (and associated income) that was lost because of the crisis. Figure 6-1 illustrates the pattern of potential real GDP and actual real GDP in the period extending from the first quarter of 1960 through the first quarter of 2010. The potential real GDP line sketches the hypothetical level of real GDP that would be produced if the unemployment rate were always maintained at the full-employment level of real output. This unemployment rate is known as the natural rate of unemployment or NAIRU, an acronym standing for nonaccelerating inflation rate of unemployment, to be discussed shortly. Potential real GDP grows over time, owing principally to growth of the labor force and growth of productivity or output per hour of work. The U.S. economy was capable of producing twice as much output in 2010 as it was in 1980, and it did.

Because the data in the figure are plotted on a logarithmic scale, changes in the slope of the potential real GDP line indicate changes in the growth rate of potential real GDP. One can discern in the figure that this growth rate was relatively high from 1960 to the early 1970s. It then slowed down significantly until the mid-1990s, when it again increased for the better part of a decade. This pattern can be explained largely by the trends in productivity growth. Productivity growth averaged about 3 percent per year from the late 1940s through the early 1970s, slowed to an average annual rate of about 1.4 percent until the mid-1990s, and then jumped to about 3 percent for several years before slowing down again after 2003.

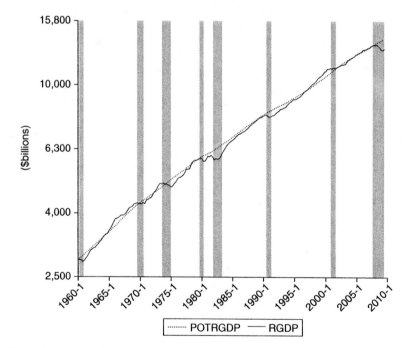

Figure 6-1   Potential and actual real GDP in the United States, 1960–2010.

Source: Federal Reserve Bank of St. Louis, FRED database.

Note: Shaded areas represent recessions.

Potential Real GDP and the Natural Unemployment Rate (NAIRU)

In the United States, the Department of Labor calculates the unemployment rate each month by querying a large sample of households via telephone survey about the current job status of all members of the household above age 16. The nation's unemployment rate is calculated as the percentage of the labor force counted as being unemployed. To be considered part of the labor force (approximately 155 million persons in late 2010), one must be counted either as employed or as unemployed. Everyone with a job (including part-time workers) is counted as employed. To be counted as unemployed, respondents must indicate that they are out of work and have been actively searching for work in the most recent 4 weeks.

At any given point in time, millions of workers who are normally employed and will soon again be employed are in transition between jobs. These individuals may have quit or been fired from one job and are searching for another. Other individuals are making their initial entry into the labor force, perhaps having recently graduated from high school or college. This pool of individuals out of work for short periods while conducting a normal search for a job can be categorized as frictionally unemployed. On the day the survey is taken, perhaps 2–3 percent of the labor force falls into the category of *frictional unemployment*, a normal manifestation of a dynamic labor market.[1]

In addition, at each point in time, a large number of individuals looking for work are simply not qualified for the jobs that are available. This is typically attributable to very low levels of education and inadequate job skills on the part of those seeking work. Millions of jobs are open alongside millions of unemployed individuals who lack the requisite skills for these jobs. Such workers are said to constitute *structural unemployment*, which, unlike frictional unemployment, is a serious national problem.[2]

The existence of frictional and structural unemployment means there is a realistic floor, far above zero, to the nation's unemployment rate at any point in time. Those in charge of monetary and fiscal policies cannot responsibly attempt to maintain the actual unemployment rate below this floor because escalating inflation would result. For example, even in the economic boom of the late 1990s—with its attendant sellers' market for labor services, in which qualified job applicants were receiving numerous offers—the nation's unemployment rate did not drop below 3.8 percent. And near the peak of the next business cycle, in 2007, the lowest unemployment rate achieved was 4.4 percent. The NAIRU is thus defined as the lowest unemployment rate that can be maintained over time without overheating the nation's economy and initiating an increase in the nation's ongoing or underlying rate of inflation. As the unemployment rate falls below the NAIRU, shortages of various types of skilled workers become increasingly prevalent. This leads to more rapid wage hikes in those sectors and therefore higher average wage and price-level inflation in the nation as a whole.

The NAIRU is a slippery concept because its level changes over time and cannot be precisely measured at any point in time. A widely quoted study indicates that the NAIRU level is highly uncertain—that is, the confidence interval surrounding the estimated NAIRU is quite large.[3] Economists simply don't know with a high degree of accuracy the ongoing level of the NAIRU. And it is not uncommon for conflicting forces operating on the NAIRU to make it difficult to even be confident of the direction that NAIRU will be moving in the near future.

Liberal economists, concerned about employment opportunities for the lower and middle classes, tend to argue that the level of NAIRU is relatively low. This implies that there is often ample room for monetary and fiscal policy stimulus to boost output and employment. Conservative economists tend to be inflation hawks and often argue that NAIRU is relatively high, thus emphasizing the inflation risks inherent in proposed economic stimulus programs. Thus, different estimates of NAIRU exist. The nonpartisan Congressional Budget Office (CBO) publishes quarterly estimates of NAIRU; Figure 6-2 illustrates the CBO NAIRU estimates from the first quarter of 1960 through the first quarter of 2010, juxtaposed against the actual unemployment rate over the same period.

Life would be greatly simplified for policymakers if they knew the current level of NAIRU and the direction it was moving. For example, if the Federal Reserve knew that the NAIRU was currently 5 percent and would remain relatively stable for the next three years, while the current unemployment rate was 10 percent, the Fed could be confident that strong monetary policy stimulus would be appropriate. Rising inflation in the ensuing three or four years would be highly unlikely barring a huge increase in oil prices, a severe drought, or other major exogenous supply shock. Unfortunately, the level of NAIRU is not only uncertain, but it varies over time in response to such factors as changing demographic forces, changing trends in productivity growth, and changing competition in labor and product markets.

Factors Influencing the NAIRU

Different age groups exhibit different average unemployment rates. For example, very young workers change jobs more frequently than older workers. Hence, younger workers show higher frictional unemployment

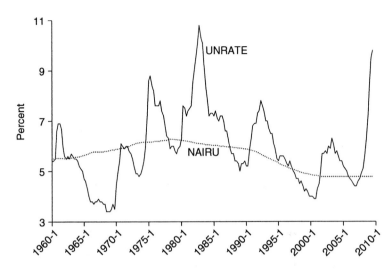

Figure 6-2   CBO estimates of NAIRU and actual unemployment rates, 1960–2010.
Source: Congressional Budget Office and Federal Reserve Bank of St. Louis, FRED database.

rates because a larger percentage of them are in between jobs at the times of the monthly employment surveys. Also, younger workers have not typically achieved the level of job skills of more experienced workers, and are therefore likely to exhibit higher rates of structural unemployment as well. Thus, unemployment rates are higher for 18-year-olds than for 40-year-olds. In the past 50 years, the unemployment rate for workers aged 16–24 averaged more than 10 percent while the corresponding rate for workers older than 45 averaged less than 5 percent.

As the baby boom generation, born during 1946–1964, began to move into the workforce in large numbers from the mid-1960s through the early 1980s, frictional and structural unemployment increased. Any given amount of economic stimulus, and thus inflation, was associated with a higher rate of unemployment. Alternatively stated, to achieve any given level of unemployment, a more stimulated economy with higher inflation was required. As a result, the NAIRU increased. Later, as these baby boomers moved into middle age after the mid-1980s, frictional and structural unemployment declined. Any given rate of inflation was associated with a lower unemployment rate. Therefore, NAIRU declined.

A second factor contributing to change in the NAIRU is known as the wage aspiration effect. There is a tendency among workers to aspire (and expect) to receive real pay increases in line with those realized in previous years. Workers feel entitled to experience rising living standards in line with the trend rate of the nation's productivity growth, as they have done in the past. And employers are inclined to grant such increases in real wages, a development that is compatible with firms and labor maintaining stable shares of the nation's income over time. If the trend growth of productivity unexpectedly declines, however, real wage hikes in line with those of the past are not compatible with the current inflation rate. Production costs rise more rapidly, inflation increases, and the nation requires a higher unemployment rate to remain in equilibrium. In this kind of a scenario, NAIRU increases. On the other hand, if productivity growth surges above the long-term trend, real wage growth in line with that of the past is compatible with a lower inflation rate, and NAIRU declines. This phenomenon helps account for a decline in the NAIRU after the early 1990s, as the trend of productivity accelerated during the information technology boom (review Figure 6-2).

In addition, increasingly competitive forces in labor and product markets have likely contributed to the decline in NAIRU in the past 30 years. The forces of globalization have exposed U.S. manufacturing and other sectors to additional competition. Increasing immigration of relatively unskilled workers, rising scope for outsourcing of U.S. jobs in the information technology age, declining penetration of the U.S. workforce by labor unions, and a falling level of the real value of the statutory minimum wage have restrained the wage increases of U.S. workers. All this has worked to hold down inflation and thereby contributed to a decline in the NAIRU. Together with deregulation of the airline, telecommunication, and other industries, these forces have contributed to enhanced competition in the U.S. economy. The level of NAIRU today is appreciably lower than it was some 25–30 years ago.

As indicated in Figure 6-2, the CBO estimates that NAIRU trended upward from 1960 to about 1980, declined slowly until the early 1990s, dropped sharply until around 2000, and then stabilized just below 5 percent during the most recent decade. Note that periods of severe recessions (1973–1975, 1981–1982, and 2007–2009) are associated with spikes in the actual unemployment rate, which surges far above the concurrent level of NAIRU during severe downturns. In periods of economic boom, especially the late 1960s and late 1990s, the nation's unemployment rate drops significantly below the NAIRU. With the exception of the late 1990s, in which extraordinary forces were at work, periods shown in Figure 6-2 in which the unemployment rate fell below NAIRU were periods of rising inflation.

III. Patterns of Actual Real GDP and Output Gaps

Returning now to Figure 6-1, note that actual real GDP, which is driven by fluctuations in the forces of aggregate demand and aggregate supply, exhibits far more variability than potential real GDP. Every nation, no matter how effectively its officials conduct monetary and fiscal policy, goes through the ups and downs of business cycles. This figure indicates that during the full 50-year period, the nation experienced two major booms in which actual output surged significantly above potential output for an extended period. This means in Figure 6-2 that the unemployment rate fell sharply below the NAIRU. The first episode occurred during the U.S. escalation of military expenditures in the Vietnam War after the mid-1960s. In this case, major increases in military expenditures at a time the economy was already near full employment pushed the unemployment rate as low as 3.3 percent by 1969, a rate far below the contemporary NAIRU. This excessive stimulus resulted in a sharp increase in the nation's inflation rate in the late 1960s.

The second lengthy economic boom occurred in the second half of the 1990s. In this instance, advances in information technology, the buildout of the Internet, and increasing globalization contributed to a virtuous economic cycle of high investment in new technology, rising productivity and corporate profits, and surging output growth that pushed the nation's unemployment rate as low as 3.8 percent in early 2000. This unemployment rate was considerably below consensus estimates of the nation's NAIRU. Normally, one would have expected the inflation rate to have increased. In this instance, however, the confluence of a series of fortuitous events—including surging productivity growth, strong appreciation of the U.S. dollar, sharply falling oil prices, and increasing competition provided by low-cost imports from China and other emerging nations—enabled this unique economic boom to be accompanied by declining inflation in spite of the falling rates of unemployment.[4]

Several periods of declining real GDP are visible in Figure 6-1 (recessions are indicated by shaded areas). Especially severe were the contractions of November 1973 to March 1975, July 1981 to November 1982, and the recent recession that extended from December 2007 until June 2009.[5]

As discussed in chapter 2, it is well established that economic contractions associated with major financial crises are typically more severe and prolonged than recessions that result from more normal recurring shocks to aggregate demand and supply. As documented in Table 6-1, the Great Recession was lengthier, and by several key measures more severe than any of the previous nine post-1950 U.S. recessions. Reflecting this recession, the S&P 500 stock market index fell by 55 percent in the period from October 2007 to March 2009, the largest percentage decline in stock prices since the 1929–1933 crash (Table 6-1).[6]

The table provides various criteria on which to judge the severity of recessions, and indicates the behavior of these variables during each of the ten cyclical contractions. Note that the duration of the 2007–2009 contraction encompassed 18 months, topping the severe 16-month recessions of 1973–1975 and 1981–1982. The peak-to-trough percentage contraction in real GDP during 2007–2009 measured 3.8 percent, ranking it more severe by this important indicator than any other post–World War II recession. Other indicators tending to verify that the 2007–2009 recession was the most severe postwar downturn include the 14.8 percent contraction of industrial production (exceeding the 13 percent decline in the 1973–1975 recession) and the 38 percent decline in corporate profits (topping the 27 percent decline in 1957–1958).

The unemployment rate often lags several months behind the changes in real GDP as firms are hesitant to add to their payrolls until they are convinced that a fledgling economic expansion will be sustained. This rate, which reached 10.2 percent in October 2009, before declining slightly in 2010, was a bit lower than the previous postwar peak unemployment rate—10.8 percent—reached at the end of the severe 1981–1982 recession. However, owing to the changing age composition of the labor force and other factors, the nation's NAIRU was much higher in the early 1980s (estimated to be 6.1 percent in the fourth quarter of 1982, according to the Congressional Budget Office) than in the recent period (4.8 percent by the CBO estimate in the fourth quarter of 2009).

Using CBO estimates of the NAIRU, the table indicates that the amount by which the nation's unemployment rate exceeded the NAIRU in the third quarter of 2009—5.4 percentage points—was the highest in the post-1950 period. In addition, the lowest rate of capacity utilization of any post-1950 recession, both in manufacturing (65 percent) and in overall industry (68 percent), was experienced in this recent contraction (not shown in table).

The actual number of people employed fell by more than 8.2 million from December 2007 through February 2010, an average of some 300,000 workers per month over this period. In the 15 years preceding the Great Recession, employment increased by more than 150,000 per month, on average. One measure of the enormous consequences of the financial crisis and the ensuing recession is that it cost the U.S. economy approximately 10.8 million jobs (450,000 per month × 24 months) in the two years commencing in December 2007.

Table 6-1 Indicators of Severity of Post-1950 Recessions

Cycle Peak	Trough	Duration (months)	% Decline Real GDP	Largest Output Gap (%)	% Decline Industrial Production	Peak Unemployment Rate (%)	Peak Unemployment Rate Minus (NAIRU) (%)	% Decline After-Tax Profits
July 1953	May 1954	10	-2.8	1.0	-9.1	6.1	0.7	-24
Aug 1957	Apr 1958	8	-3.7	4.8	-12.7	7.5	2.1	-27
Apr 1960	Feb 1961	10	-1.6	4.1	-8.6	7.1	1.6	-17
Dec 1969	Nov 1970	11	-1.0	2.2	-7.0	6.1	0.3	-18
Nov 1973	Mar 1975	16	-3.2	5.1	-13.0	9.0	2.8	-21
Jan 1980	Jul 1980	6	-2.2	3.8	-6.6	7.8	1.6	-18
July 1981	Nov 1982	16	-2.9	8.6	-9.3	10.8	4.7	-25
July 1990	Mar 1991	8	-1.4	3.4	-4.2	7.8	1.9	-1
Mar 2001	Nov 2001	10	-0.3	1.0	-6.1	6.0	1.2	-14
Dec 2007	Jun 2009	18	-3.8	7.0	-14.8	10.2	5.4	-38
Average		11.3	-2.3	4.1	-9.2	7.8	2.2	-20

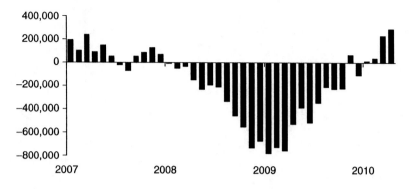

Figure 6-3 Change in U.S. total nonfarm employment, 2007–2010.
Source: Federal Reserve Bank of St. Louis, FRED database.

The monthly change in total U.S. nonfarm employment for the 40 months extending from January 2007 through April 2010 is shown in Figure 6-3. Note that, with exception of the tiny increase in November 2009, total employment declined in each month of 2008 and 2009. The monthly rate of decrease in employment peaked in January 2009 at 741,000 and averaged nearly 650,000 per month in the six-month period ending in April 2009.

Exhibit 6-1

The Phenomenon of the "Jobless Recovery"

Productivity growth is the overwhelming source of rising living standards over the long run. Improvements in technology, along with a better educated and trained workforce, boost productivity of the workforce and allow more output to be produced and enjoyed per person. This is the principal reason why the typical American worker today has nearly three times as much real income and purchasing power as did her grandparent some 50 years ago. Productivity growth is good.

However, for workers, increases in productivity can be a two-edged sword in times of high unemployment because rapid productivity growth means a firm can boost output appreciably in response to rising sales without hiring additional employees. The phenomenon of high productivity growth can result in jobless recoveries in the first year or two after the economy enters the expansion phase of the business cycle. For example, in the third and fourth quarters of 2009 (the first two quarters of the post-recession economic expansion), productivity growth of U.S. workers increased at an exceptional rate of more than 6 percent per year. This development was not due principally to better technology. It was the result of employers, with profits under severe pressure from a slack economy, taking steps to squeeze more output out of the average employee. Because real GDP increased at an annual rate of only about 3 percent during this time, employment declined sharply and the nation's unemployment rate increased from 8.6 percent in March 2009 to 10.1 percent just seven months later.

In the first eight recessions after World War II (those occurring prior to the 1990s), unemployment rates peaked within one or two months after the trough of the cycle, on average. However, in the expansions that followed the more recent recessions of 1990–91, 2001, and 2007–2009, employment continued to decline and unemployment to rise for several months after real output began to expand.

Why are employers reluctant to take on additional workers in the first year or two of an economic expansion? First, business confidence declines during recessions and management is initially wary about the vigor and durability of the incipient expansion. This was especially true in 2009 and the first half of 2010 because many analysts feared that the initial output gains that were fueled by temporary government stimulus programs such as "cash for clunkers" and the $8,000 first-time homebuyers tax credit might prove to be transitory. Analysts were fearful that private sector demand might fail to pick up the slack after the effects of the stimulus programs wore off (this fear turned out to be largely justified).

Profits of many U.S. companies increased in the second half of 2009 and early 2010 not because of revenue growth but because of aggressive cost-cutting measures that included reductions in payrolls. Employers simply learned to get more output out of fewer workers. Also, as the length of the average workweek had declined to 33 hours, employers found it more prudent and efficient to lengthen the workweek of existing workers rather than hiring and training new employees.

Again, this phenomenon is relatively new. In the case of the 1990–1991 recession, the unemployment rate peaked 11 months after the official (May 1991) end of the recession. Unemployment continued to rise for 5 months after the end of the 2001 recession. And employers shed payrolls for 7 of the first 8 months after the 2007–2009 recession ended.

IV. Impact of the Great Crisis on the Individual Components of Aggregate Demand

Like most of the ten post-1950 recessions, the 2007–2009 downturn was triggered by an adverse aggregate demand shock—a decline in aggregate spending. The initial shock was a sharp drop in private residential investment (residential construction) associated with the glut of houses for sale due to escalating mortgage defaults and foreclosures that commenced after the housing bubble began to deflate. The Great Recession was especially prolonged and deep because of the systemic, worldwide nature of the crisis, because the U.S. financial system became severely impaired, and because residential and nonresidential construction fell much more sharply than in typical downturns.

The components of aggregate expenditures or aggregate demand include consumption spending, investment expenditures, government purchases, and net exports of goods and services. The Great Crisis impaired the banking system and unleashed forces that adversely impacted consumption and investment expenditures. By reducing economic activity, the crisis and ensuing recession also severely impaired state and local government revenues and led to cutbacks in state-local government spending. In addition, a significant supply shock contributed to the recession as crude oil prices spiked briefly to $140 per barrel in the summer of 2008, temporarily increasing gasoline and home-heating oil prices.

The resultant combination of declining economic activity and rising unemployment then unleashed an adverse feedback loop that further impaired the banking sector and other components of the financial system.[7] Because the severe contraction of economic activity was a worldwide phenomenon, U.S. exports fell sharply. However, U.S. imports fell by an even larger amount, so the decline in the U.S. international trade deficit served to temper the contraction in aggregate demand for U.S. goods and services. Each of the four components of aggregate demand will be discussed in turn.

Consumption Expenditures

Consumption spending, after barreling ahead strongly during the 2001 recession and the ensuing expansion, declined sharply midway through the 2007–2009 recession. While it did not initiate the recession, the downward swing in consumption spending in the second half of 2008 totaled about $380 billion and contributed to the depth of the recession.

Consumption spending is heavily influenced by disposable income (take-home pay), along with wealth or net worth, consumer confidence, the level of interest rates, and the availability of credit from lending institutions. The nation experienced a very large increase in wealth in the quarter century leading up to the Great Crisis. Equity in the family home constitutes the single most important source of wealth of the typical U.S. household. The enormous appreciation in home prices in the 20-year period extending from the mid-1980s to the mid-2000s produced an aggregate gain in household wealth of some $10 trillion ($10,000 billion). In addition, the appreciation of stock prices that extended from the early 1980s through the end of the 1990s constituted the greatest bull market in U.S. history. In the period from 1982 through 1999, funds invested in the Standard & Poor's 500 stock market index, assuming reinvestment of dividends, provided a compounded average rate of return of 17 percent per year. One thousand dollars invested in the S&P 500 Index in 1982 had grown to more than $14,000 by the end of 1999. Stock market appreciation in this period resulted in a gain in wealth of more than $10 trillion, much of it in retirement accounts. The growth (and subsequent contraction) of wealth in the form of housing equity and stock market equity is illustrated in Figure 6-4.

As indicated, important determinants of consumption spending include disposable income, wealth, consumer confidence, the level of interest rates, and availability of credit from banks and other lending institutions. With the exception of (lower) interest rates, each of these forces worked to reduce consumption spending during 2008 and 2009. With the unemployment rate skyrocketing during 2008 and 2009, and with millions more potential workers not being counted as unemployed and others moving involuntarily to part-time employment or less remunerative full-time employment, aggregate U.S. disposable income began falling after the second quarter of 2008 and did not return to mid-2008 levels until the first quarter of 2010. This constrained consumption spending.[8]

Economists define the wealth effect as the impact that a $1 change in wealth has on consumption spending. Many households apparently decided that because of this gain in wealth in the years prior to the crisis,

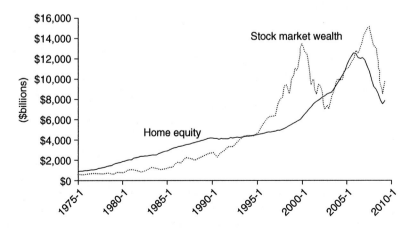

Figure 6-4   Stock market wealth and home equity wealth of U.S. households.
Source: Federal Reserve System, Flow of Funds Accounts.

saving out of current income was not as essential as in earlier times of more modest wealth. In addition, in the recent period commencing with the arrival of the new millennium, interest rates have been lower on average than in earlier periods. Economic theory indicates that lower interest rates reduce the incentive to save, thereby stimulating consumption spending. Lower interest rates also mean that monthly payments on loans for cars and other durable goods are lower, thus boosting affordability and expenditures.

House prices declined from their late 2005 peak to early 2010 by more than 30 percent in 20 large metropolitan areas and by more than 20 percent nationwide. The decline in wealth stemming from the decline in house and stock prices totaled more than $14 trillion ($14,000 billion) during the period from 2006 to early 2009, though stock prices rallied after hitting lows in March 2009. Econometric studies indicate a fairly wide difference among estimates of the magnitude of the wealth effect. However, a median of numerous estimates places the marginal propensity to consume wealth in the range of .03 to .05. In this event, holding constant other factors, a $14 trillion contraction in wealth may lead to a reduction in consumption spending of some $420 billion to $700 billion per year. In our $15,000 billion (GDP) economy, this represents some 2.8–4.7 percent of GDP.

Exhibit 6-2

The Wealth Effect: Houses versus Stocks

Economic theory suggests that consumption spending should be positively related to wealth. Total wealth or net worth of U.S. households reached $65 trillion ($65,000 billion) in 2007 before declining to approximately $51 trillion in March 2009 when stock prices were at their nadir. In aggregate, the largest and most variable forms of wealth owned by U.S. households are equity owned in the family home and in shares of stock. Consensus estimates of the marginal propensity to consume wealth cluster in the range of .03 to .05, although some estimates range far lower while others are significantly higher. If the marginal propensity to consume wealth is .04, this means a family whose house or retirement account depreciates by $50,000 will reduce expenditures on consumption goods by $2,000 per year, other things being equal.

Is the strength of the wealth effect the same whether an increase in wealth comes from appreciation of stock prices or an increase in the value of the family home? Economic theory is ambiguous on this issue. On the one hand, shares of stock are more liquid—they are easier to cash in to finance increased consumption than is the family home. This suggests the wealth effect could be larger for stocks than for houses. On the other hand, the typical individual holding most of his/her wealth in stocks is far wealthier than the average individual whose wealth derives predominantly from equity in the family home. The latter individual, having less wealth and more unsatisfied wants, is likely to consume a larger portion of any increment to wealth. Hence, in the aggregate, the wealth effect arising from house price appreciation may exceed that arising from higher stock prices.

Another consideration is that, notwithstanding the enormous run-up and subsequent decline in house prices in many U.S. cities since the end of the twentieth century, stock prices are typically more volatile and exhibit more downward flexibility than house prices. A gain in wealth through stock market appreciation may be regarded as more transitory than a similar gain in wealth earned through house appreciation, and therefore be less likely to induce an increase in consumption spending.

A recent study estimated that the wealth effect from changes in house prices is considerably stronger than that arising from changing values of stocks.[9] The authors estimate that households respond to a $10,000 increase in housing wealth by increasing consumption by about $170 after one quarter, and by about $900 after several years have elapsed. That is, the marginal propensity to consume wealth is estimated to be 1.7 percent in the short run, rising to 9 percent in the long run. This sluggish adaptation of spending to wealth may be attributed to the time it takes to change habits. The corresponding long-run increase in consumption resulting from a $10,000 gain in stock market wealth is estimated by the authors to be much lower, roughly $400, or 4 percent. These findings are consistent with the strong rise in consumption spending during the 2001 recession and the early portion of the ensuing expansion. In this period, stock prices fell dramatically while house prices increased strongly.

If in fact the wealth effect associated with changing house prices is as large as this study indicates, those in charge of monetary policy would be wise to take account of house prices in implementing interest rate policy. Had the Federal Reserve done so in the past, it would have kept interest rates higher that it did as the housing bubble developed during 2002–2006. In that scenario, the bubble in houses—and the ensuing crash and financial crisis—might have been at least partially attenuated.

Adding to the negative effects on consumption spending generated by the declines in disposable income and wealth, one must consider the adverse effects exerted by the severe tightening of lending standards by banks, the contraction in the value of collateral to support such loans, and the decline in consumer confidence. Consumer confidence, as measured by the University of Michigan, began to decline about one year before the recession started, and then plunged sharply in the early phase of the downturn. From July 2007 to June 2008 the index declined from

90.4 to 56.4, its lowest level since 1980. It remained significantly below its 25-year average in the fall of 2010.

Coupled with the fact that consumption expenditures make up more than two-thirds of aggregate expenditures, these negative forces impinging on consumption help explain why many economists feared the expansion that began in the summer of 2009 might turn out to be less robust than is typical. Consumption spending stood to be inhibited by heavily indebted and confidence-impaired households struggling to pay down debt, continue to make mortgage payments on their homes, and restore wealth lost through lower house and stock prices.[10]

Investment Expenditures

In the U.S. national income accounts, investment includes residential construction, nonresidential construction, expenditures on plant and equipment including software and technology, and the change in the nation's inventories. All four of these components declined sharply in the Great Recession and remained at low levels in the early portion of the ensuing recovery that began in the third quarter of 2009.

Residential construction, officially known as private residential fixed investment, began dropping rapidly approximately one year before the recession officially started in December 2007. This precipitous decline, illustrated in Figure 6-5, was the trigger that started the Great Recession. Note that the contraction in residential investment (homes, duplexes, apartments) was approximately $450 billion per year or 3 percent of GDP. New single-family housing starts declined from the peak-year number of 1,720,000 in 2005 to only 445,000 in 2009, a contraction of nearly 75 percent. This contraction dwarfed previous experience.

House prices began falling in late 2005—slowly at first and then more rapidly. By the end of 2009, nearly half of new homes built after 2003 were underwater, their market value having fallen below the balance on the mortgage. It was estimated that in October 2010 about 25–30 percent of all U.S. homeowners—some 15 million—were underwater. Home repossessions began to surge in 2008. A vicious cycle of falling house prices, repossessions, and forced sales begetting additional price declines, foreclosures, and forced sales quashed demand for new homes. Many contractors, unable to sell the new homes they had built during the height of the housing bubble, were driven out of business. Employment in the construction industry plunged.

The value of mortgage-backed bonds and related instruments issued in the United States, owned in massive quantities by many of the largest

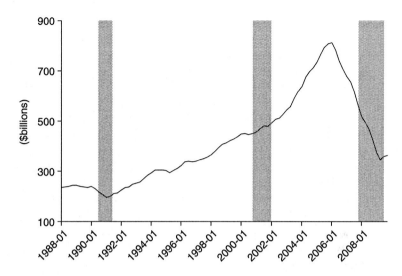

Figure 6-5   U.S. private residential fixed investment, 1988–2010.

Source: Federal Reserve Bank of St. Louis, FRED database.

Note: Shaded areas represent periods of recession.

U.S. and foreign banks, declined sharply in response to falling house prices. This eroded banks' capital positions, which, in turn, forced banks to reduce their lending in order to meet capital standards. The securitization of mortgages by private entities dried up almost completely after 2007, sharply curtailing lending available for housing. The prevailing posture of mortgage lenders toward prospective homebuyers swung from "anything goes" to unreasonably tight lending standards. The market for mortgage-backed bonds evaporated and the Federal Reserve was forced to step in to buy huge quantities of these instruments in 2009 and early 2010 in a bid to stabilize the financial system and resurrect the construction industry.

Shortly after the housing market crashed, nonresidential construction began to experience serious problems. As vacancy rates of commercial properties such as shopping malls, office buildings, and hotels increased in 2008 and 2009 in response to the ongoing recession and rising unemployment, prices of these properties began to decline. Expenditures on construction of commercial properties started dropping in the spring of 2008 and fell by more than $300 billion in an 18-month period. Many of the properties were financed by issuance of commercial mortgage-backed securities (CMBS). Some observers feared that banks could be facing a second round of major loan defaults--this time in the commercial sector, beginning in 2010.

Business investment in plant and equipment is heavily influenced by business confidence—the "animal spirits" of businesses in Keynes' terminology. With business profits declining by nearly 40 percent in the Great Recession, and with thousands of firms becoming severely impaired or insolvent, business confidence fell sharply. Given that most of the nation's businesses (including nearly all small businesses) rely on bank loans to finance investment expenditures, and given the severe tightening of bank lending standards in response to the reduction in bank capital at thousands of banks, one would expect to observe a contraction in investment spending on plant and equipment in 2008 and 2009. This is what happened.

Finally, given the pessimistic outlook for sales as the recession deepened in 2009, firms deliberately reduced their inventory stocks as part of their effort to cut expenses. A voluntary inventory contraction results in a decline in national output as firms reduce orders for new goods, and is counted as a decline in investment spending in the national income accounts. All told, gross private investment expenditures (including residential and nonresidential construction; plant, equipment, and software expenditures; and the change in the nation's aggregate inventories) declined by more than 30 percent or by some $800 billion per year during the Great Recession.

State and Local Government Purchases

Aggregate purchases of goods and services by state and local units of government are much larger than corresponding expenditures of the federal government. In 2009 and 2010, 48 of the 50 states were in deficit as tax receipts plunged sharply in the recession. At least 20 states experienced a contraction of revenues of more than 10 percent; California exhibited a budget shortfall of $25 billion in 2009, the largest of any state. The aggregate deficit of the 50 states was in excess of $125 billion, even after receiving some $200 billion in emergency assistance from the federal government in the $787 billion stimulus bill enacted in early 2009. Unlike the federal government, state and local units of government are essentially constrained in their expenditures by the amount of revenues on hand. In the first half of 2009, aggregate tax revenues of the 50 states had declined by more than 10 percent relative to the first half of 2008, forcing states to slash expenditures. Local units of government typically depend on property taxes and sales taxes. The decline in property values and sales tax revenues across the country also forced many local governments to cut expenditures accordingly.

Net Exports (Exports – Imports)

The Great Recession was worldwide in scope. Few developed or emerging nations escaped the devastation. Because of falling incomes abroad, U.S. exports dropped sharply after the middle of 2008. However, as the result of lower employment and income at home, U.S. imports declined by an even larger amount. Hence, the United States' trade deficit declined sharply after the middle of 2008. This $400 billion swing in the trade deficit served to cushion the U.S. downturn.

The phenomenon of the declining U.S. trade deficit may prove to be transitory. As soon as the recovery from the Great Recession gains strong momentum, U.S. imports may again begin to grow rapidly. An important problem is posed by China's reluctance to permit market forces to produce a significant appreciation of the Chinese currency (the renminbi) against the U.S. dollar. To do so would remove the substantial undervaluation of the Chinese currency—often estimated to be of an order of magnitude of 25 to 35 percent—which has facilitated a huge expansion of Chinese exports and powered China's tremendous economic growth in the past 15 years. China's persistent trade surpluses over the years (more than $400 billion in 2010) allowed it to accumulate more than $2.5 trillion of reserves of foreign currencies. This ammunition gives China sufficient power to finance an appreciable portion of the U.S. budget deficit each year and to strongly influence the dollar-renminbi exchange rate.[11]

V. Conclusion

Triggered by the bursting of the U.S. housing and credit bubbles and the associated decline in construction activity and severe damage to the U.S. banking and financial system, the U.S. economy in 2007–2009 experienced its most severe contraction since the Great Depression of 1929–1933. The Federal Reserve responded to the crisis, albeit somewhat belatedly, with unprecedented vigor—dropping its short-term interest rate target from 5.25 percent in summer 2007 to essentially zero by the end of 2008. The Fed also implemented an array of innovative actions in an attempt to prevent a collapse in the flow of credit in the U.S. financial system and a major depression. In addition, the U.S. Congress enacted a fiscal stimulus program of unprecedented magnitude (nearly $800 billion) in early 2009. Nevertheless, these actions failed to prevent the nation from experiencing double-digit unemployment and the largest contraction of real GDP, industrial production, corporate profits, and stock prices of any of the post–World War II recessions.

Given the large amount of slack in the U.S. economy at the beginning of 2011, only the most optimistic of observers believe the nation can expect a return to full employment before 2014 or 2015. Nevertheless, given the enormous increase in reserves injected into the banks by the Federal Reserve during the crisis, together with the huge federal budget deficits facing the nation during the next decade and beyond, many commentators fear that the stage may have been set for an era of high inflation. We will examine that argument in chapter 10. First, however, the modus operandi of Federal Reserve monetary policy will be outlined in chapter 7 and the performance of the Fed in the Great Depression will be contrasted with that in the recent Great Crisis (chapters 8 and 9).

Chapter 7

The Framework of Federal Reserve Monetary Control

I. Introduction

Regarding the financial crisis of the early 1930s, the Federal Reserve's behavior may most charitably be described as passive. While scholars disagree on whether the Fed can legitimately be considered responsible for the Great Depression, they agree that it failed to take significant steps to prevent it. The Fed was asleep at the switch and failed to react appropriately to the banking panics—the runs on banks. In a remarkable lapse of memory, key Federal Reserve officials apparently forgot why the institution was created fewer than 20 years earlier—to serve as a lender of last resort to the banking system in times of panic. In large part as a result of the Fed's failure to respond, the public's panic and the banks' reaction to it triggered a sharp contraction in the U.S. money supply. This in turn contributed strongly to a 25 percent decline in the U.S. price level over a period of less than four years. This enormous deflation of prices led to massive debt defaults by farmers, businesses, and homeowners, a development that took down more than 9,000 banks in a four-year period and was instrumental in the conversion of a recession into the Great Depression.

In contrast, in the Great Crisis of 2007–2009, the Federal Reserve acted in an extremely decisive fashion. It pumped a huge amount of funds into the nation's banking system, opened its lending facility full throttle, and implemented an array of innovative programs designed to compensate for numerous credit channels that had closed down. Through extraordinary measures, the Fed was able to engineer significant increases in the nation's money supply during and after the crisis, and was thus successful in preventing deflation of the nation's price level. Even though the

U.S. economy suffered a very severe recession in 2007–2009, the Federal Reserve under Ben Bernanke deserves credit for limiting the contraction of real gross domestic product (GDP) to about 15 percent of that experienced in the 1929–1933 catastrophe. The contrasting stories about Fed policy in the Great Depression and in the Great Crisis are narrated in detail in chapters 8 and 9.

This chapter presents a framework of analysis that explains the determination of a nation's money supply and the central bank's role in that process. This analytical framework will be used in chapter 8 to understand why the money supply collapsed in the Great Depression and to assess the Federal Reserve's policy errors and the extent of its culpability in the contraction of money supply and credit availability and onset of the episode of deflation that was instrumental in the nation's economic disaster. The framework will also be used in chapter 9 to show how the Bernanke Fed's Herculean efforts prevented a decline in the money supply that could have set off the deadly phenomenon of deflation.

II. The Federal Reserve Balance Sheet, Bank Reserves, and the Money Supply

To understand the Federal Reserve and how it wields its formidable power, one must understand its balance sheet, or at least a few of its key components. And one must understand how the Fed can change the magnitude and composition of this balance sheet. Table 7-1 lists the components of the balance sheet, together with their magnitudes in September 2007, just prior to the onset of the Great Crisis. In chapter 9, we study the enormous changes the Fed implemented in its balance sheet as it responded to the crisis.

Assets of the Fed—that is, items that the Fed owns and claims it has on other entities—include gold certificate and special drawing rights accounts (G), coins issued by the Treasury and held in the 12 Federal Reserve banks (Fca), loans to depository institutions (D), the Fed's critically important portfolio of U.S. Treasury and other securities (P), items in the process of collection (IPC), and assets denominated in foreign currency plus other Federal Reserve assets such as buildings and computers (OA).

Liabilities of the Federal Reserve are its debts or the claims outside entities have on the Fed. These debts include Federal Reserve notes, that is, the paper currency issued by the Fed (FRN); deposits at the Fed owned by depository institutions (Fb), the U.S. Treasury (Ft), and foreign entities such as the International Monetary Fund and World Bank (Ff);

Table 7-1 Consolidated Balance Sheet of the 12 Federal Reserve Banks (September 5, 2007)

Assets ($ billions)		Liabilities and Capital ($ billions)	
Gold Certificate Accounts (G)	11.04	Federal Reserve Notes (FRN)	778.66
Special Drawing Rights Accts (G)	2.20	Deposits	
Coins (Fca)	1.02	A. Banks (Fb)	11.29
Loans to Dep. Institutions (D)	1.34	B. U.S. Treasury (Ft)	4.49
U.S. Treasury Sec. (P)	814.64	C. Foreign and other (Ff)	0.34
Items in Process of Collection (IPC)	5.50	Deferred Avail. Items (DAI)	4.77
Assets Denominated in Foreign Currency and other Assets (OA)	39.32	Other Liabilities (OL)	41.16
		Total Liabilities	840.70
		Capital Accounts (CAP)	34.35
Total Assets	875.06	**Total Liabilities and Capital**	875.06

Source: http://www.federalreserve.gov/releases/h41

deferred availability items (*DAI*); and other liabilities like bills payable (*OL*). The capital accounts of the Federal Reserve (*CAP*) represent the owners' stake in the Fed. This capital is simply the difference between the Fed's total assets and its total liabilities; that is, capital is the Fed's net worth. Technically, the Fed is owned by commercial banks that are members of the Federal Reserve System.[1]

The first three items on the asset side of the balance sheet are relatively small and quite stable over time and can safely be ignored in our analysis of the money supply, as can "items in process of collection." This latter item, along with the corresponding "deferred availability items" on the liability side of the balance sheet, are technical items connected with the Fed's check-processing activities that give rise to Federal Reserve float. Assets denominated in foreign currencies consist of the Fed's stock of euros, yen, and other currencies held as ammunition for the purpose of attempting to stabilize the dollar exchange rate (by using these currencies to purchase dollars) in the event of a speculative run on the dollar.[2] The key Federal Reserve assets are its holdings of U.S. Treasury securities (*P*) and, especially in times of financial crisis, its loans to depository institutions (*D*).[3] Note that the Federal Reserve security portfolio (*P*) accounted for more than 90 percent of total Fed assets in 2007.

On the liability side of the Fed balance sheet, the Fed issues all the nation's paper currency today in the form of Federal Reserve notes (*FRN*), and this debt of the Fed is typically by far its largest liability. For purposes of understanding how the Fed influences economic activity, the key items on the liability side are the deposit accounts held by banks and other depository institutions (*Fb*). In particular, we will see that the Fed's enormous power derives largely from its authority to purchase U.S. Treasury securities (asset side) and to pay for these by crediting the deposit account at the Fed of the bank of the sellers of these securities (*Fb*). These sellers are typically government securities dealers. The Fed is wired electronically to 18 primary security dealer firms, which are large banks. When the Fed purchases securities from one of these dealers, it wires funds to this bank's account at the Fed. This action increases bank reserves in the form of *Fb* on a dollar-for-dollar basis. When the Fed changes *P*, *Fb* changes in lockstep.

Bank *reserves* are defined as the sum of cash residing in banks and banks' deposits at the Federal Reserve (*Fb*). Regulations governing depository institutions, known as *reserve requirements,* mandate that each bank must maintain reserves in an amount no less than a specified small percentage of the bank's checking account liabilities.[4] Reserves held by a bank above and beyond the required amount are known as *excess reserves.* Until 2008, the Fed was prevented by law from paying interest to banks on their reserves. The opportunity cost of holding excess reserves was essentially the interest rate banks could earn on loans and Treasury securities. Because the Fed now pays interest to banks on their excess reserves, the opportunity cost today is the difference between the yield a bank could earn on loans or securities and the interest rate paid by the Fed on excess reserves. Given the interest rate the Fed pays banks on excess reserves, an increase in bank loan rates and Treasury security yields induces banks to use a portion of their excess reserves to extend loans and purchase securities, both of which result in an increase in the nation's money supply.

The key point is that the Fed is capable of accurately controlling aggregate bank reserves. It can inject reserves and excess reserves into the banks in any amount it desires by purchasing assets, as it demonstrated in unprecedented fashion in 2008 and 2009 as it dramatically increased its balance sheet. In purchasing government securities and other assets, the Fed creates a disequilibrium in which banks are initially holding more excess reserves than they wish. Banks normally respond by increasing loans and purchasing Treasury securities, both of which increase the nation's money supply and reduce the level of short-term interest rates.

III. The Monetary Base

The monetary base, sometimes known as "high powered money," consists of the net liabilities of a monetary nature of the "monetary authorities"— the Federal Reserve and Treasury. The base can be viewed as the net liabilities of a consolidated joint Federal Reserve-Treasury balance sheet that could potentially be held as bank reserves. The Treasury issues the nation's coins, which constitute a minor portion of bank reserves and a minor portion of currency held by the public (Cp). The Federal Reserve issues the paper currency (Federal Reserve notes), which make up the predominant portion of Cp. Those Treasury coins and Federal Reserve notes that are held by banks count as reserves, as do the deposits banks maintain with the 12 district Federal Reserve banks (Fb). The monetary base can be written as follows:

$$B = R + Cp. \tag{7-1}$$

The monetary base (B) consists of bank reserves (R) and currency held by the public, that is, currency in circulation outside of the banks, the Federal Reserve, and Treasury (Cp).

The public determines Cp within the limits of its financial wealth (checking accounts, savings accounts, and so forth). If you go to your bank or ATM and withdraw $80 in cash from your checking account, Cp increases by $80.[5] If there is a large increase in demand for currency by the public, the signal is transmitted first to the banks, then to the Federal Reserve. As your bank runs short on currency to meet the increased public demand, it contacts its district Fed bank and requests a shipment of currency via armored truck. The Fed ships the currency, charging the bank for it by debiting the bank's deposit account at the Fed, Fb. As the Fed runs low on paper currency it prints up additional Federal Reserve notes. Hence, we see that the Fed prints Federal Reserve notes passively in response to the public's demand for it. This does not mean the Fed cannot control the money supply, $DDO + Cp$. It means only that the Cp portion of the money supply is determined by the public rather than the Fed.

Sources of the Monetary Base

Returning to equation 7-1, which defines the *uses* of the monetary base, indicating where it resides, we can write an expression for R (bank reserves) as follows:

$$R = Fb + Cb, \tag{7-2}$$

where Fb stands for bank deposits at the Federal Reserve and Cb represents cash held in the banks. Substituting this expression for R in equation 7-1, we get

$$B = Fb + Cb + Cp, \tag{7-3}$$

that is, the monetary base consists of bank deposits at the Fed (Fb), along with the cash held by the banks (Cb) and by the nonbank public (Cp). Now, if we return to the Federal Reserve balance sheet shown in Table 7-1, we can derive an expression for the key item Fb, bank deposits at the Federal Reserve, over which the Fed is capable of exerting very precise control. Given the basic accounting identity that total assets must equal total liabilities + capital, we can solve for Fb and obtain equation 7-4:

$$Fb = G + FCa + D + P + IPC + OA - FRN$$
$$- Ft - Ff - DAI - OL - CAP. \qquad (7\text{-}4)$$

Substituting this long expression for Fb into equation 7-3 to solve for the monetary base, we get

$$B = G + FCa + D + P + IPC + OA - FRN - Ft$$
$$- Ff - DAI - OL - CAP + Cb + Cp \qquad (7\text{-}5)$$

Next, defining TCu to be Treasury Currency outstanding (total value of coins issued by the Treasury) and TCa to be currency and coins held in the Treasury itself, consider the following identity:

$$FRN + TCu = FCa + TCa + Cb + Cp. \qquad (7\text{-}6)$$

This identity simply states that all the paper currency issued by the Fed (FRN) and coins issued by the Treasury (TCu) must be held in one of four places: the Federal Reserve (FCa), the Treasury (TCa), depository institutions (Cb), or as currency and coins held by the nonbank public (Cp). There is literally nowhere else this paper currency and these coins could be.[6] Rearranging equation 7-6, we get

$$TCu - Tca = Fca + Cb + Cp - FRN. \qquad (7\text{-}7)$$

Now, if we substitute into equation 7-5 the two terms on the left-hand side of equation 7-7 for the four terms on the right-hand side, and if we define Federal Reserve Float (Float) to be the difference between items in process of collection (IPC) and deferred availability items (DAI), we get our final expression for the monetary base:

$$B = P + D + G + Float + OA + TCu - Ft - Ff$$
$$- Tca - OL - CAP. \qquad (7\text{-}8)$$

This expression defines the *sources* of the monetary base—that is, it lists all the factors that influence the monetary base. The key point behind all these terms and equations is that the Federal Reserve has total control over P, its portfolio of securities, along with the authority to change this portfolio at will. The Fed security portfolio makes up the overwhelming portion of the base. Therefore, the Fed can dominate the size of the monetary base even though it has little or no control over many of the individual items that make up the base.

Defensive and Dynamic Aims of the Federal Reserve

Because several of these sources of the base change significantly each business day, the monetary base would fluctuate considerably if the Fed did not manipulate its portfolio of securities (P) to offset fluctuations in these factors. An especially important factor is Ft, U.S. Treasury deposits at the Fed. The Federal Reserve serves as the Treasury's bank—that is, the Treasury makes payments from its account at the Fed just as you make payments via your checking account in a bank. Each month, for example, the Treasury makes large payments to senior citizens receiving social security benefits. The Fed does this by drawing on its account at the Fed. As these social security checks are deposited in commercial banks and cleared by the Fed, the Fed debits the Treasury's account (Ft) and credits the recipient depository institution's account at the Fed (Fb). Other things being equal, this would sharply expand bank reserves, the monetary base, and the money supply.

In order to prevent this, the Fed keeps in daily contact with the Treasury about impending Treasury disbursements from its Federal Reserve account. In the above case, if the Treasury draws down its Federal Reserve account by $8 billion on a given day, the Fed would sell $8 billion of securities from its portfolio to accomplish its defensive aim. In this event, P in equation 7-8 would decline by $8 billion to offset the $8 billion of reserves and base created as Ft declines by $8 billion. In such transactions by the Fed, which occupy the predominant portion of its typical daily security transactions, the Fed fulfills its *defensive aim* of preventing various forces outside its control from producing undesired fluctuations in the monetary base and the nation's money supply. In this aim, the Fed defends the base to maintain the status quo. In a similar fashion, the Fed changes P to offset the potential change in reserves and base money caused by changes in float, Treasury currency outstanding, and other factors included on the right-hand side of equation 7-8.

In the Federal Reserve's *dynamic aim*, the Fed deliberately changes the monetary base to fulfill some specific objective. For example, suppose the economy gains strong positive momentum in 2013 and the declining unemployment rate begins to approach consensus estimates of the NAIRU. Suppose the contemporary federal funds rate is 2 percent and the Fed seeks to boost it to 3 percent, thereby increasing bank loan rates and yields on an array of financial instruments. The Fed would sell securities in the open market, reducing P. This action would reduce bank reserves and excess reserves, along with the monetary base. Because this action reduces the supply of excess reserves in the banks, the federal funds rate would begin rising. The Fed would continue selling securities (reducing P) until the federal funds rate reached the target level of 3 percent. This would increase other short-term interest rates and slow the growth of aggregate spending, consistent with the Fed's intention.

Recalling equation 7-1 ($B = R + Cp$), it is important to repeat that, even though the Fed cannot control Cp, it is capable of totally dominating R (bank reserves). It can therefore accurately control the size of the monetary base if it seeks to do so. In fractional reserve banking systems that exist in nations throughout the world today, the monetary base serves as the foundation that supports the larger monetary aggregates or measures of the nation's money supply, M1 and M2. M1 is defined as demand deposits and other checkable accounts in depository institutions (DDO) plus currency and coins held by the public (Cp). M2, a broader measure of money, includes M1 and certain other liquid assets owned by the public, like savings accounts and money market mutual fund shares (OLA). The relationship between the monetary base and these measures of the money supply is illustrated in Figure 7-1. Note that each dollar of monetary base normally supports more than one dollar of M1 and M2.

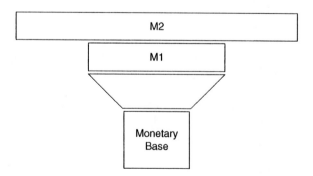

Figure 7-1   The monetary base and the monetary aggregates.

IV. The Money Supply Multiplier

The two measures of the money supply, M1 and M2, can be expressed as products of the monetary base (B) and corresponding money supply multipliers ($m1$ and $m2$), which reflect the magnification of base money into M1 and M2 inherent in a fractional reserve banking system. These relationships are expressed in the following equations:

$$M1 = m1 \times B \tag{7-9}$$

$$M2 = m2 \times B. \tag{7-10}$$

M1 and M2 are the narrow and broad measures of the nation's money supply, as defined above, and the variables $m1$ and $m2$ represent the narrow and broad money supply multipliers that link the base to M1 and M2, respectively. While the monetary base is subject to relatively accurate control by the Federal Reserve, the money supply multipliers are not. They are influenced by behavior of the public through its demand for currency, and by the behavior of banks through their willingness to hold excess reserves. The Fed significantly influences these multipliers only on the rare occasions that it changes the percentage reserve requirements for banks. In earlier periods in which the Fed was setting explicit targets for M1 and M2 growth, it sought to hit these targets by essentially forecasting the money supply multipliers and then putting the base at the level that, in conjunction with the expected multipliers, would come reasonably close to hitting the money supply targets. For example, if the Fed were shooting for an M1 target of $1,000 billion and expected the m1 money multiplier to be 2.5, it would take actions to place the monetary base as close as possible to $400 billion.

Returning to equations 7-9 and 7-10, we will let DDO represent aggregate demand deposits and other checkable deposits in banks. Because **M1 = DDO + Cp** and **M2 = DDO + Cp + OLA**, and because the monetary base consists of reserves plus currency held by the public (that is, $B = R + Cp$), we can write

$$m1 = (DDO + Cp) / (R + Cp) \tag{7-11}$$

and

$$m2 = (DDO + Cp + OLA) / (R + Cp). \tag{7-12}$$

Because bank reserves (R) can be divided into two components—required reserves (Rr) and excess reserves (Re); and because these two variables in turn can be expressed as some fraction (rr and re, respectively) of DDO, we can rewrite the above equations as

$$m1 = M1 / B = (DDO + Cp) / [(rr + re)DDO + Cp)] \qquad (7\text{-}13)$$

and

$$m2 = M2 / B = (DDO + Cp + OLA) / [(rr + re)DDO + Cp)]. \qquad (7\text{-}14)$$

Now, defining the public's preferred currency ratio or ratio of currency to checking accounts customarily maintained (k) as $k = Cp/DDO$, and dividing both numerator and denominator of the above equations by DDO, we obtain

$$m1 = (1 + k) / (rr + re + k) \qquad (7\text{-}15)$$

and

$$m2 = (1 + k + ola) / (rr + re + k), \qquad (7\text{-}16)$$

where ola represents the public's desired or customary ratio of other liquid assets included in M2 to DDO.

The size of the narrow money supply multiplier ($m1$) varies inversely with the magnitude of each of the underlying variables—k, rr, and re. An increase in k means that a larger portion of the monetary base is now held as currency (Cp) and a smaller portion is available as reserves ($Fb + Cb$). Because each dollar of reserves supports several dollars of DDO (and M1) while each dollar of Cp accounts for only one dollar of M1, the increase in k reduces the money supply multiplier. A withdrawal of currency reduces reserves, forcing banks to sell assets, thereby reducing the money supply. Similarly, an increase in rr means that, given the amount of their actual reserves, banks now face a disequilibrium in which they are holding fewer excess reserves than they wish. Banks therefore reduce loans and/or security holdings in an effort to reestablish their desired amount of excess reserves. This action by banks reduces the amount of the nation's DDO, M1, and M2. Finally, if banks become more conservative and decide to hold more excess reserves—that is, if re increases (as it did in the Great Crisis), banks again reduce loans and/or sell off securities. An increase in banks' desire to hold excess reserves, as manifested in an increase in re, reduces the money multipliers, along with M1 and M2.

Factors Influencing k, rr, and re

Equation 7-15 indicates that the narrow money supply multiplier (*m1*) depends on three variables: the currency ratio (*k*), the required reserve ratio (*rr*), and the banks' desired excess reserve ratio (*re*). Because currency held by the public responds entirely to the public's demand for it (within the limits of financial assets held by the public), we may regard *k* as being determined by the public based on the perceived costs and benefits of holding money in the form of currency versus holding checking accounts. The public's demand for currency and checkable deposits, in turn, depends on certain variables such as interest rates, income, confidence in the banks, and the state of financial technology. Other things equal, if banks increase the interest rate paid on checking accounts, *k* will decline as the public opts to hold less of its money in currency and more in checking accounts.[7] In a banking panic such as was experienced in the Great Depression, *k* increases as the public becomes fearful about the safety of their deposits. Periodic changes in financial technology also clearly influence the currency ratio. For example, the introduction and increasing use of debit cards tends to reduce the need to use currency, thereby pulling down *k*.

The variable *rr* is the weighted average reserve requirement, which is broadly determined by the Federal Reserve in setting these requirements. However, *rr* varies independently of Fed actions in the short run as the distribution of bank deposits among larger banks and smaller banks changes over time. This follows from the fact that a lower level of reserve requirements applies to demand deposits below a threshold level of approximately $55 million in each bank. Hence, when a check written by a customer of a large bank is deposited in a very small bank, aggregate required reserves and *rr* decline slightly. For this reason, clearing of checks across banks of different size introduces a small amount of variation in *rr*. Major changes in *rr* occur only when the Federal Reserve changes the percentage reserve requirements applicable to banks.[8]

The variable *re* is determined at the discretion of commercial bank management on the basis of the perceived costs and benefits of holding excess reserves. Banks deliberately hold excess reserves because they operate in an uncertain environment. For example, a bank does not know its final reserve position at the Fed (*Fb*) until the end of the day, after debits and credits to its Federal Reserve account from the check-clearing process have been determined. If the bank comes up short on reserves to meet the reserve requirement at the end of the day, there are costs involved. In this instance, a bank must borrow reserves or sell off assets to obtain reserves, both of which involve transactions costs.

Thus, there are both costs and benefits of holding excess reserves. The benefit is reduced exposure to the above-mentioned adjustment costs when a bank inadvertently comes up short on reserves. The cost is the interest income forgone by holding excess reserves. Banks make their decision on the optimal amount of excess reserves to hold on the basis of these costs and benefits. When interest rates fall, the (opportunity) cost of holding excess reserves declines and banks therefore deliberately hold more excess reserves. In order to increase holdings of excess reserves, banks reduce loans and sell off some of their Treasury securities. As the public writes checks to pay off bank loans and purchase securities that banks are selling, DDO, M1, and M2 decline. When the perceived risk to banks of granting loans increases, as clearly occurred during the Great Crisis, banks react by tightening lending standards and deliberately holding more excess reserves. If the Fed fails to offset this development by increasing the monetary base, the nation's money supply declines. This explains in part why the Federal Reserve massively increased its balance sheet and the monetary base in 2008 and 2009. The increase in the banks' willingness to hold excess reserves caused a sharp drop in the money multiplier. The Fed stepped in and increased the monetary base in a dramatic fashion to prevent a decline in M1 and M2.

In summary, considering the monetary framework expressed in the above equations, we see that the money supply is influenced by the public, bank behavior, and the Federal Reserve. The Fed is quite capable of accurately controlling the magnitude of the monetary base by altering its holdings of U.S. government securities (P). While changes in k, rr, and re help account for cyclical and short-term changes in the monetary aggregates, changes in the monetary base account for the predominant changes in M1 and M2 over long periods of time.

One can analyze the causes of the fluctuations in the $m1$ multiplier by examining the behavior of the three factors underlying this multiplier—that is, the currency ratio (k), the required reserve ratio (rr), and banks' desired excess reserve ratio (re). The patterns of k, rr, and re over the period from 1988 through 2007 are illustrated in Figure 7-2. The narrow money supply multiplier ($m1$) trended downward from the early 1990s until the Great Crisis. The overwhelming source of the decline in $m1$ in this period was the persistent upward trend in the currency ratio, k. Currency held by the public (Cp) increased from less than 40 percent of DDO (checking accounts) in 1988 to more than 100 percent in recent years.

Reductions in reserve requirements for banks implemented by the Federal Reserve in late 1990 and early 1992 show up in the figure as downward jogs in rr. These reductions were implemented in response to the 1990–1991 recession and to help banks strengthen their financial condition following banking crises in the 1980s. The level of bank excess reserves is normally so small—typically less than half of 1 percent of *DDO*—that *re* scarcely registers in the figure. However, in 2008 and 2009 (not shown in the figure, but analyzed in chapter 9) *re* increased enormously, becoming several times larger than *rr*, indeed even larger than *k!* In the Great Crisis, this huge buildup of bank excess reserves confounded the Federal Reserve's efforts to boost bank lending and reopen bank lines of credit for small businesses that often had no access to other sources of funds to conduct their operations.

During and immediately following the Great Crisis, the Federal Reserve would have preferred to have seen growth in bank lending and more rapid growth in the monetary aggregates than actually occurred. The tightening of lending standards by banks thwarted the desired expansion of bank loans. And, as previously discussed, the extremely low level of short-term interest rates made many banks willing to hold very large quantities of excess reserves.[9]

Hence, it appeared that the effectiveness of Fed policy was being hindered by a development approaching a *bankers' liquidity trap*, an occurrence reminiscent of the 1930s. In a bankers' liquidity trap, the central bank has great difficulty inducing an increase in bank lending and the money supply. The Fed can pump a large volume of reserves into the banks. However, if banks are unwilling to grant loans or if loan demand

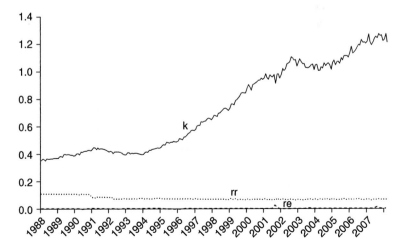

Figure 7-2 Behavior of factors underlying money multiplier (m1), 1988–2007.
Source: Federal Reserve Bank of St. Louis, FRED database.

by the public has declined sharply, and if interest rates are so low that buying Treasury securities is not profitable for banks, the link between the monetary base and the money supply is severely bent or possibly even broken. In the extreme polar case, a doubling of the monetary base by the central bank through massive purchases of government securities would reduce the money supply multiplier by 50 percent as all of the additional reserves would simply be held by banks as excess reserves, thus leaving the money supply unchanged. We will examine the issue of Federal Reserve policy in a low interest-rate environment in more depth in chapter 9.

V. Tools of Federal Reserve Policy

The Federal Reserve has three general tools that it can use to influence bank lending, interest rates, and the monetary aggregates (M1 and M2). These tools include open market operations, discount window policy, and changing the level of reserve requirements. By far the most important tool in the past 60 years has been open market operations, although discount window policy also became very important during the Great Crisis. Open market operations and discount window policy derive their influence primarily by impacting bank reserves and the monetary base, while a change in reserve requirements derives its influence entirely by changing the money supply multiplier. We will briefly examine each of these instruments of Fed policy.

Open Market Operations

The Federal Reserve buys and sells U.S. government securities through a network of security dealers to influence bank reserves and the monetary base. Because such transactions typically have only indirect and minor effects on the money multipliers, M1 and M2 normally respond strongly to open market operations that directly alter the monetary base. Let us assume that, in response to signs of an incipient recession, the Fed purchases $1,600 million of Treasury bonds from dealers. The changes in the balance sheets of the Fed and the aggregate commercial banking system are as follows:

Federal Reserve System		*Commercial Banking System*	
Assets	Liabilities	Assets	Liabilities
U. S. Gov't Sec + $1600 m	Dep. of dealer bank + $1600 m	Dep. at Fed + $1600 m	DDO (dealer firm) + $1600 m

The Fed has acquired $1,600 million of assets in the form of U.S. Treasury securities, paying for them by crediting (via electronic impulse) the dealer's bank's deposit account at the Fed (Fb, an asset of the dealer's bank and a liability of the Fed). As a direct result, bank reserves and monetary base have each increased by the amount of the transaction—$1,600 million, and both M1 and M2 have increased by the same amount. This demonstrates that the Fed has fingertip control over the monetary base—each dollar of assets the Fed purchases creates one dollar of reserves and monetary base.[10]

In the event the Federal Reserve sells Treasury securities to a dealer, the Fed collects payment from the dealer's bank by debiting that bank's deposit account at the Fed (Fb). The dealer's bank then collects from the dealer by debiting the dealer's checking account. In this scenario, the above t-accounts would show negative signs across the board. Aggregate bank reserves and the monetary base would decline by the amount of the Fed transaction.

Remember that we have a fractional reserve system in which each bank is required to back only a small fraction of its deposit liabilities with reserves (cash and deposits at the Fed). Assume the percentage reserve requirement in the above t-account transaction is 10 percent. In this instance, the Fed injected $1,600 million of reserves into the banking system but required reserves increase by only $160 million (10% × $1,600 million). This means that of the $1,600 million of new reserves, $1,440 million are excess reserves. Banks are likely to lend the bulk of them out in order to accommodate loan demand, earn interest income, and boost profits.

As banks use their excess reserves to increase their loans, two things happen. First, the supply of loans in the banking system increases, thus reducing interest rates on loans. Second, as banks increase loans, they create demand deposits for the borrowers, thereby boosting M1 and M2. Given the 10 percent reserve requirement, the initial $1,440 million of excess reserves injected into the banking system can support a much larger amount of additional *DDO* in the system beyond the $1,600 million directly created in the above t-account. Thus, the Fed's injection of reserves touches off a multiple expansion of deposits in the banking system, encompassed in our money supply multipliers, *m1* and *m2*. M1 and M2 increase by multiples of the $1,600 million expansion in reserves.

Under normal conditions, the Fed confines its open market transactions to the U.S. government securities market. However, in the Great Crisis, the Fed began buying huge quantities of mortgage-backed securities (MBS). Following the failure of Lehman Brothers in September 2008, the MBS market froze up as trading came to a halt. This had severe consequences not only for large banks caught holding these MBS and related instruments, but also for the nation's economy. In an effort to reduce long-term interest rates and get credit flowing again in the depressed mortgage market, the Fed committed itself to purchasing up to $1,250 billion of MBS. This program injected a huge amount of reserves into the U.S. banking system and dramatically increased the monetary base, a result consistent with the Fed's overriding objective of stimulating bank lending and economic activity.

Discount Window Policy

Since the inception of the Federal Reserve System in 1913, banks have been permitted to borrow reserves directly from the Federal Reserve "discount window."[11] Discount window policy involves both determining the conditions under which banks are permitted to borrow from the Fed, and setting the *discount rate*—the interest rate that the Fed charges banks that avail themselves of this short-term source of funds. Traditionally, the criterion for legitimate bank borrowing was that a bank could borrow for "need" but not for "profit." This was interpreted to mean that if a bank inadvertently came up short on reserves at the end of the day because of unexpected developments, it could call the Fed and request (and expect to be granted) a loan that would allow the bank to meet the reserve requirement. It was not considered legitimate to borrow from the Fed at its relatively low discount rate and then turn around and use the funds to grant new loans or purchase securities featuring a higher rate.

When a bank requests and is granted a loan from the Fed, the Fed credits the bank's reserve account by the amount of the loan. Hence, bank reserves and the monetary base increase by the amount of the discount loan, as indicated in equation 7-8. Suppose, in a given week, banks collectively increase borrowing at the discount window by $400 million. The t-account implications are as follows:

Federal Reserve System		*Commercial Banking System*	
Assets	Liabilities	Assets	Liabilities
Discount loans + $400 m	Dep. of bks. +$400 m	Dep. at Fed + $400 m	Borrowings + $400 m

In this event, the transaction exerts its monetary influence solely by increasing the monetary base (B). Aggregate reserves have increased by $400 million but there is no change in the money multiplier. However, if the Fed were to surprise markets by announcing an *unexpected* increase in the discount rate, this would likely be interpreted by banks as an indication that the Fed was signaling it was implementing a more restrictive policy stance.

Banks in this case would tend to deliberately increase their precautionary holdings of excess reserves. This increase in re reduces the size of the money supply multiplier. Given the size of the monetary base, an unexpected hike in the discount rate would therefore result in a reduction of M1 and M2 as banks tighten lending standards and reduce loans. In terms of equations 7-15 and 7-16, re increases and the multipliers ($m1$ and $m2$) decrease.

On the other hand, an unanticipated reduction in the discount rate would likely be taken by bankers as a signal that the Fed is moving toward a more expansionary policy, including likely forthcoming injection of additional reserves into the banking system through open market purchases of securities. In this event banks would ease lending standards somewhat and deliberately use some of their excess reserves to expand loans and purchase Treasury securities. Both of these activities tend to reduce interest rates and increase M1 and M2.

In the early (pre–World War II) years of the Federal Reserve, changing the discount rate was the principal instrument of Fed policy. In the half century immediately preceding the Great Crisis, discount policy was considered to be a relatively minor tool of policy. Only a tiny portion of the monetary base was the product of Fed loans to banks (review the balance sheet in Table 7-1). However, beginning in 2008, the Fed massively expanded its discount window loans and used innovative measures to induce banks to borrow from the Fed. Hence, unlike the Fed balance sheet shown above for 2007, its balance sheet for the following couple of years showed a sharply elevated volume of bank borrowing from the Fed. We will examine this development in more detail in chapter 9.

Changes in Reserve Requirements

The Board of Governors of the Federal Reserve has the authority to change the percentage reserve requirements applicable to banks (within statutory limits set by Congress). Unlike open market operations, a change in reserve requirements derives its impact not by changing the monetary base but by changing the money multiplier. If the Fed raises the reserve requirements, bank reserves are initially unchanged (as is the base). However, required reserves increase and excess reserves decline, possibly even becoming negative. In either case, with banks initially holding fewer excess reserves than they desire, they react by tightening lending standards, reducing loans, and selling off securities. Such actions reduce DDO as bank borrowers write checks to pay off loans and dealers write checks to banks to purchase the securities banks are liquidating. In terms of our money multiplier expressions in equations 7-15 and 7-16, rr increases and this reduces the money multipliers, $m1$ and $m2$. Unless the monetary base is increased, M1 and M2 decline.

Compared to open market operations, this tool is blunt and is therefore seldom used. The last time reserve requirements were significantly changed was in the early 1990s. Banks had taken a big hit following the banking crises and associated bad loan write-offs of the late 1980s and early 1990s. Reserve requirements are essentially a form of tax on banks that limits bank profitability. To provide relief and help bolster the financial condition of the nation's banks, the Fed reduced the reserve requirement applicable to all *DDO* above the threshold from 12 percent to 10 percent in 1992. Since that date this instrument has not been used.

For purposes of monetary control, the tool of open market operations is superior to changing reserve requirements. Open market operations is a more sensitive, accurate, and flexible tool in which the Fed can conveniently change course as needed. The reserve requirement tool is largely redundant. Most economists advocate determining an optimal level of reserve requirements and leaving them unchanged at that level except in rare cases of emergency.[12]

VI. Conclusion

In this chapter, we have outlined the factors that influence the level and growth of the nation's money supply, M1 and M2. These measures of the money supply can be viewed as the product of the monetary base and a corresponding multiplier that links the monetary base to the money supply in the nation. While the Federal Reserve is capable of accurately controlling the monetary base, it cannot control the money supply multipliers, which are determined by the behavior of the public and banks. If the Fed is in a passive mode and does not deliberately attempt to control the monetary aggregates, fluctuations in the money multipliers triggered by the public and banks will bring about changes in M1 and M2. As we will see in the next chapter, this is exactly what happened in the Great Depression of the early 1930s. In that episode, onset of fear on the part of both the public and the banks, induced by cascading waves of bank failures, triggered a sharp decline in the money supply multipliers as both the currency and excess reserves ratio(k and re) increased sharply. Because the Fed failed to compensate by sharply increasing bank reserves and the monetary base, this behavior of the public and banks led to major contractions in M1 and M2. These developments contributed strongly to the decline in the price level and the massive contraction of the nation's output and employment in the Great Depression. This story is told in some detail in the next chapter.

Chapter 8

Federal Reserve Policy in the Great Depression

I. Introduction

Students of U.S. economic history agree that Americans living during 1929 to 1933 experienced the biggest economic catastrophe in the history of the nation. The terror visited upon families by the disaster cannot be expressed in numbers. However, an impression of the severity of the Great Depression can be gained by examining a handful of pertinent facts. From the fall of 1929 to the spring of 1933, the nation's nominal gross domestic product (GDP) fell nearly 50 percent. Real GDP declined by 30 percent and industrial production fell in half. This decline in real GDP was more than seven times the magnitude of the contraction experienced during the Great Recession of 2007–2009, the most severe U.S. downturn since the Great Depression. Table 8-1 indicates some of the salient indicators of macroeconomic conditions in the United States from 1928 to 1938.

In the Great Depression, the nation's unemployment rate surged from around 3 percent to 25 percent. Stock prices lost more than 85 percent of their value, with each $100 of market value in 1929 collapsing to less than $15 at the bottom of the crash in 1933. Cumulative bank failures totaled more than 9,500 in this period, with 4,000 banks failing in 1933 alone. Given the absence of federal insurance of bank deposits, the bank failures impaired the life's savings of millions of families. The nation's money supply fell by approximately 30 percent and the price level declined by 25 percent.

This deflation of the nation's price level triggered a huge wave of foreclosures of farmers, homeowners, and business firms. At the time Franklin D. Roosevelt was inaugurated president of the United States on March 4, 1933, farm foreclosures were running at the rate of 20,000

Table 8-1   Key Macroeconomic Indicators from 1928 to 1938

Year	Nominal GNP ($ billions)	Real GNP ($ billions)	Unemployment Rate (percent)	Stock Prices*	Bank Failures	Consumer Price Index
1928	$98.2	$98.2	4.2%	153	498	100.0
1929	104.4	104.4	3.2	201	659	100.0
1930	91.1	95.1	8.7	161	1350	97.4
1931	76.3	89.5	15.9	100	2293	88.7
1932	58.5	76.4	23.6	36	1453	79.7
1933	56.0	74.2	24.9	79	4000	75.4
1934	65.0	80.8	21.7	78	57	78.0
1935	72.5	91.4	20.1	80	34	80.1
1936	82.7	100.9	16.9	112	44	80.9
1937	90.8	109.1	14.3	120	59	83.8
1938	85.2	103.2	19.0	80	54	82.3

Sources: U.S. Department of Commerce, *Historical Statistics of the United States*; Board of Governors of the Federal Reserve System, *Banking and Monetary Statistics* (Washington, DC: National Capital Press, 1943).
Note: *Index of common stock prices for June of each year; 1935 to 1939 = 100.

per month and aggregate corporate profits of the nation's business firms were negative. The overwhelming majority of Americans experienced a substantial decline in their standard of living during the 1930s. The nation's unemployment rate averaged 18 percent during the entire decade of the 1930s and did not decline below 10 percent until 1941.

Before discussing the specific events of the Great Depression, it is instructive to review the general pattern of developments that typifies the formation of bubbles that often precede major crises like the Great Depression and the recent Great Crisis. In the case of stock market bubbles in the 1920s and 1990s and the 2002–2006 housing bubble, rapid expansion of credit developed alongside (and facilitated) the development of the bubbles. This sets the stage for a later bust.

As discussed in chapter 2, events follow a typical pattern. First, an economic upswing occurs in the nation, initially grounded in favorable economic fundamentals. Inflation remains low for a time, allowing the central bank to maintain interest rates at low levels. Easy credit terms and rising confidence join forces to create appreciation in the prices of such assets as stocks, land, and houses. Lenders and borrowers become increasingly confident about economic prospects. After a period of time, increasingly high-risk ventures come to be funded as the volume of credit increases and its quality declines. These developments often spring from important technological breakthroughs that create potentially profitable business ventures. Eventually, expectations become fanciful and herd psychology takes hold.

Asset valuations become unhinged from reality. Then some event such as tightening of credit by the central bank bursts the bubble. The economy is left with an overhang of investment projects of dubious viability in place, heavily indebted firms and households, and distressed banks.

Abetted by low inflation and easy credit conditions set by the Federal Reserve, the nation's output and profits grew robustly in the 1920s. Yet inflation remained nonexistent. Bank credit expanded strongly, fueled by financial sector innovations that facilitated purchases of durable goods by the masses of homeowners. Excesses started to become evident, first in the real estate boom in Florida in the mid-1920s, and later in the stock market bubble of the late 1920s. Price-earnings ratios of stocks increased fivefold on average, reaching then-unprecedented levels. High rollers were getting rich and others wanted in on the action. Times were ripe for emergence of scam artists in the United States and Europe, including Charles Ponzi (Florida), Clarence Hatry (London), and Ivan Krueger (Stockholm). Finally, the stock market crash of October 1929 popped the bubble.

This chapter discusses the worldwide nature of the Great Depression and examines various explanations of its causes, including the role of price deflation in contributing to the extraordinary depth and duration of the economic contraction. The chapter also analyzes the sources of contraction in the monetary aggregates (M1 and M2) and looks at alternative viewpoints about the role played by the Federal Reserve in the economic catastrophe. Different hypotheses that may account for the Fed's inept response to the severe economic contraction are presented. The chapter concludes by examining the forces that ended the Great Depression.

II. The Worldwide Nature of the Great Depression

The Great Depression was worldwide in scope. None of the major industrial nations escaped the disaster. Not only the United States, but also Germany, Canada, France, Italy, the Netherlands, and at least five other industrial countries suffered contractions of more than 30 percent in industrial production. The U.K., Japan, Sweden, and New Zealand experienced milder output contractions in the neighborhood of 15 to 20 percent. The depression was the most severe in the United States and Germany, where industrial production fell more than 50 percent.

Scholars believe the contraction in economic activity was deeper in the United States than in most other countries because of the magnitude of the preceding bubble in U.S. stock and real estate prices, along with the nature of U.S. banking. Important factors include the huge increase in U.S. farm indebtedness during World War I and the unique structure of the U.S. banking industry. Unlike other nations which had a small number of relatively large and well-diversified banks, the United States had more than 20,000 small and independently owned banks with poorly diversified asset structures. Assets of thousands of these banks were dominated by agriculture-related loans. The collapse of more than 9,000 of these banks in the early 1930s, owing initially to distress in the agriculture sector, meant that the monetary contraction in the United States was more severe than in other nations.

As will be discussed in the next section, the causes of the Great Depression are complex. Most scholars believe the *initial* U.S. downturn in 1929 was caused by restrictive Federal Reserve measures taken in 1928 and 1929 to combat increasing speculative activity in the growing stock market bubble. Federal Reserve actions pushed up nominal and real short-term interest rates. The real commercial paper rate jumped from less than 6 percent in the fourth quarter of 1927 to more than 9 percent one year later. Interest-sensitive expenditures quickly declined as building permit applications dropped 20 percent in 1929 relative to peak 1928 levels. Also, U.S. exports began falling in 1928 as Germany and a few other nations entered downturns before the United States. Contrary to popular belief, the U.S. economic contraction began several months prior to the October 1929 stock market crash.

Powerful forces transmit business cycles across national borders. A decline in European output and income feeds back to the United States, pulling down U.S. exports. And declining U.S. economic activity reduces European exports to the United States. Although there is disagreement in the literature on the details, an important chain of causation suggests that the U.S. downturn contributed strongly to the worldwide depression through two mechanisms. First, declining U.S. income reduced demand for foreign goods. More importantly, higher U.S. interest rates were transmitted to the rest of the world through the gold standard mechanism. In the gold standard, foreign nations were authorized to convert their holdings of foreign currency reserves into gold in the United States on demand. Because gold stocks held by foreign nations were already low, the Federal Reserve's interest rate hikes in 1928 and 1929 forced other nations to boost their own interest rates in an effort to prevent an outflow of financial capital and gold to the United States. In fact, because the United States' commitment to the maintenance of the gold standard was perceived to be stronger than that of other nations, foreign central banks likely had to boost their interest rates even more than the U.S. hikes to prevent an outflow of financial capital and gold. As it turned out, those countries that were first to abandon the shackles of the gold standard in the early 1930s were typically the first to emerge from the Great Depression.

III. Causes of the Great Depression

What caused the Great Depression? What was the Federal Reserve's role in this disaster? Can it legitimately be held accountable for the Great Depression, or was it an innocent bystander, powerless to halt the cascading events that contributed to the vicious cycle of downward movements in the economy? This section presents alternative answers to these questions. Also, the role of banking panics in accounting for the contraction of credit and the onslaught of bank failures is discussed.

Nonmonetarist Explanations

In explaining the causes of the Great Depression, economists emphasize the negative shocks to aggregate demand for goods and services.[1] The severe decline in aggregate demand reduced the nation's real output and price level, setting in motion the deadly phenomenon of deflation. Some scholars emphasize the negative shocks that originated from nonmonetary forces. For example, the huge construction boom of the 1920s made a decrease in building activity almost inevitable in the 1930s.[2] Gross investment spending on business plant, equipment, and structures declined from $14 billion in 1929 to less than $3 billion in 1933. Net investment—the change in the nation's capital stock—was actually *negative* in 1933, as depreciation and obsolescence exceeded gross investment expenditures. The stock market crash and the associated decline in wealth and consumer confidence played an important part in depressing both consumption and investment spending. It is not clear that these events stemmed principally from monetary causes.

The infamous Smoot-Hawley Tariff Act of 1930 initiated a global movement toward economic nationalism that helped account for a massive contraction in the volume of international trade in nations around the world. U.S. exports plummeted and massive unemployment developed in export industries worldwide. Also, fiscal policy turned contractionary in the 1930s. The Revenue Act of 1932 increased taxes at a time of massive unemployment. Nonmonetarist economists argue that these forces were largely unrelated to monetary forces or the conduct of Federal Reserve policy.[3]

Furthermore, economists traditionally claimed that monetary policy was actually very "easy" in the 1930s. Short-term interest rates—the rates the Federal Reserve is capable of accurately controlling—were generally quite low. The Treasury bill rate, which stood at 4.7 percent in August 1929, declined to 3.0 percent in December 1929 and to 1.9 percent in June 1930. Except for a spike to around 2.5 percent that lasted from December 1931 to April 1932, this yield remained below 1 percent throughout the remainder of the 1930s.

Monetarist Explanations

Economists of monetarist persuasion disagree with the above diagnosis of the causes of the Great Depression. They lay the blame squarely on monetary forces and Federal Reserve policy. In this view, the collapse of the money supply and banking system was responsible for converting a typical economic downturn into a massive economic collapse. The monetary contraction, in this theory, was triggered by banking panics and a series of blunders committed by the Federal Reserve. For failing to serve as a lender of last resort during a series of banking panics and committing numerous other important mistakes, monetarists hold the Fed accountable for the precipitous contraction in M1 and M2 that followed the banking panics. In this view, the contraction of the money supply led to the disastrous episode of deflation. Deflation set in motion the widespread defaults on household, farm, and business debts that led to waves of bank failures and the denial of credit to legitimate bank customers.

Bank Failures and the Run on Banks

To gain a perspective on the Great Depression of the 1930s, it is important to look first at the experience of American banks during the 1920s. The 1920s were a time of general prosperity in the U.S. economy. As indicated, a building boom took place, in part as a result of low interest rates and natural optimism that followed the victorious conclusion of World War I. Electrification of homes, mass production of automobiles, construction of roads and highways, and emergence of telecommunication in the form of widespread purchases of radios contributed to rising prosperity, as did strong purchases of durable goods by households in the second half of the decade.

However, the 1920s were a time of great stress in the agriculture sector. Agriculture played a larger role in the U.S. economy in those times than it does today. A much larger proportion of families made their living by farming. While the period from the 1880s until World War I had been a "golden age" for agriculture, in the beginning years of the 1920s, crop prices declined by approximately 50 percent. While these prices recovered for a time, the 1920s generally witnessed falling agricultural prices and farm distress throughout the world. Farm profits fell along-side falling crop prices, pulling down farm values. Thousands of farmers who had purchased land with borrowed money in the decade prior to the 1920s lost their properties through farm foreclosures in the 1920s. This process continued in the Great Depression.

In 1925, the nation had some 28,000 banks, most of them located in small towns and rural areas. The decline in agricultural prices and the rise in farm foreclosures weakened the balance sheets of thousands of rural banks that had extended loans to farmers, implement dealers, and other firms tied closely to the agricultural economy. An average of nearly 500 banks failed per year in the 1920s, most of them in agricultural regions of the country, especially the Great Plains.[4]

Banking Panics in the Early 1930s

Nearly 6,000 banks were suspended in the decade of the 1920s, but these bank failures did not set off general panics in which customers of other banks rush to withdraw their deposits in cash. The bank failures of the early 1930s were another story. These bank suspensions initiated a series of banking panics, which came in four waves. The first occurred in October 1930 when a series of bank closings in the Midwest and South touched off a relatively mild run on banks. The second wave came in December 1930, immediately following the failure of the Bank of the United States. This was the largest bank ever to fail in the nation. Given its name, many people mistakenly assumed the bank was run by the U.S. government, adding to the sense of fear and ensuing pandemonium. This crisis subsided in the early part of 1931.

However, in May 1931, a major Austrian bank—the Credit Anstalt—failed, shocking depositors throughout the world. Shortly thereafter, in September, England announced its decision to go off the gold standard. This led to expectations of an impending devaluation of the U.S. dollar. Anticipating a scramble by foreign nations to convert their dollar holdings into gold at the U.S. Treasury, the Federal Reserve Bank of New York took aggressive action. In two quick steps in October, it jumped its discount rate from 1.5 percent to 3.5 percent—at a time when the U.S. unemployment rate exceeded 15 percent.[5] These events in the spring and late summer of 1931 account for the third run on U.S. banks that occurred in early fall of that year.

The final destructive crisis came in early 1933, following nearly four years of price level deflation, widespread defaults by debtors, and thousands of bank closings. Given the massive unemployment, weakened condition of banks, and uncertainty about the wisdom and mettle of incoming president Franklin D. Roosevelt (FDR), fear was pervasive. In February, following failure of negotiations between Ford Motor Company and the Union Guardian Trust Company of Detroit to save that bank, the governor of Michigan announced a statewide closing of banks. This touched off a banking panic, which spread first to several contiguous states and then to other regions. On March 6, FDR's third day in office, a national banking "holiday" was declared as all banks were closed for a week.[6] The Roosevelt administration informed the public that all banks would be inspected, and only "sound" banks would be allowed to reopen.[7] Importantly, Congress established the Federal Deposit Insurance Corporation (FDIC) at this time to provide nationwide insurance of bank deposits.

In the view of some scholars, these two events marked the beginning of the end of the Great Depression. In any event, while 9,755 banks failed during 1929–1933, fewer than 60 banks failed each year in the remainder of the decade of the 1930s. As we will note, the initial banking panics played a key role in the severe contraction of bank loans and the monetary aggregates (M1 and M2) in the early 1930s. The bank failures and sharp decline in the nation's money supply contributed appreciably to the severe deflation of the nation's price level during the Great Depression.

IV. Deflation: Its Measurement and Role

It is important to understand the instrumental role deflation played in the disaster of the 1930s. Deflation is a highly pernicious phenomenon in the most common case in which falling prices are caused by declining aggregate demand. It may also occur when unexpectedly rapid productivity growth lowers production costs, thus increasing aggregate supply. While the latter form of deflation may be accompanied by increasing living standards, deflation caused by severely depressed expenditures is always associated with falling output, employment, and living standards.

Most episodes of severe deflation in U.S. history have been accompanied by depression. The reason that deflation is so damaging is that falling prices mean that (nominal) incomes must fall on average, while payments owed on debts already in place do not decline. Assume, for example, that a farmer or homeowner has a $100,000 mortgage debt to a bank, collateralized by the farm or house, respectively. Assume the interest rate on the loan is 6 percent, so that interest payments of $6,000 per year are owed to the bank (total payments owed are typically larger than this because such loans are normally amortized). Assume also that the net income after taxes of the farmer or homeowner is $40,000 per year. Now suppose that the nation's price level falls by 50 percent—that is, it falls in half. Other things being equal, this means aggregate nominal national income also falls by half. Given this fact, the farmer's and homeowner's incomes are extremely unlikely to remain at $40,000. The farmer's income falls because the price of his crops declines sharply, and the homeowner's income falls because the prices received (and revenues earned) by her employer decline sharply. Unfortunately, both individuals still owe $6,000 in interest each year on their debts.

This inevitably leads to defaults on debt. If the farmer's income falls to $20,000 as the prices of his crops plummet, it will be very difficult for him to meet the mortgage payments on the farm. As a result of deflation, his interest payments have risen from 15 to 30 percent of his disposable income. This example makes clear why sustained deflation is associated with widespread debt defaults, bankruptcies, severe unemployment, and surging bank failures.[8] The bank seizes the farm or house, but the value of these assets has declined sharply, typically in line with the decline in the nation's price level. The bank loss on the loan means bank capital has declined. Severe losses on loans result in bank failures.

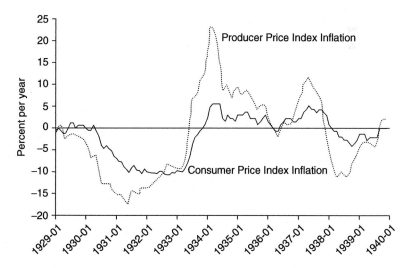

Figure 8-1   Inflation rates of U.S. consumer and producer prices, 1929–1939.
Source: Federal Reserve Bank of St. Louis, FRED database.

Figure 8-1 illustrates the U.S. inflation rate, as measured by the producer price index and consumer price index in the period extending from 1929 through 1939.

Because the producer price index (PPI) measures wholesale prices, changes in the PPI tend strongly to be followed by changes in prices of goods and services at the retail level, as measured by the consumer price index (CPI). Note that the producer price index began declining in the early part of 1929, and consumer prices followed suit about one year later. The rate of deflation of producer prices increased from the beginning of 1929 until 1931, when the rate of decline of the PPI exceeded 15 percent per year for several months. Producer price inflation remained negative until June 1933.[9] Consumer prices began dropping in February 1930 and reached a maximum deflation rate of about 10 percent per year from the fall of 1931 until the spring of 1933. It is no coincidence that the rate of farm, home, and business foreclosures and bank failures declined sharply after 1933 as the long period of deflation came to an end.

Deflation is both a cause and a consequence of economic depression. It is a *cause* of depression because it brings on widespread debt defaults, business bankruptcies, and bank failures. These developments lead to reduced consumption and investment expenditures, resulting in lower national output and employment. The debt defaults impair bank capital and induce severe tightening of lending standards by banks, deepening and lengthening the downturn. Deflation is a *consequence* of depression because the associated falling demand for goods and services forces firms to reduce prices in order to sell their products.

Deflation, once firmly established, tends to become a self-perpetuating cycle. This occurs as expectations of falling prices cause individuals and firms to postpone purchases in anticipation of better deals later. More importantly, development of expectations of deflation means that real interest rates exceed nominal rates. The *ex ante* real rate—the difference between the nominal interest rate and expected inflation—influences decisions about investment and consumption expenditures. If expected deflation is prevalent, even if a central bank lowers the nominal interest rate to zero, the real rate may be too high in an environment of widespread pessimism to induce a sufficient amount of investment and consumption expenditures to boost output and employment. This circumstance is known as the *zero-bound problem*—the problem caused by the fact that a central bank cannot push nominal interest rates below zero. The central bank may lose traction and be unable to extricate the economy from depression.

Table 8-2   Measures of U.S. Inflation Rates from 1930 to 1933 (Percent per year)

	1930	1931	1932	1933	Total
Consumer Price Index	−2.6%	−9.0%	−10.1%	−5.4%	−27.1%
Producer Price Index	−9.1	−15.7	−10.7	+1.3	−34.2
GDP Deflator	−2.6	−9.1	−10.2	−2.2	−24.1
Personal Consumption Expenditure Deflator	−3.1	−10.6	−11.7	−4.0	−29.4

Source: Historical Statistics of the United States and Economic Reports of the President.

To demonstrate the pervasiveness of deflation in the Great Depression, Table 8-2 indicates the rate of change of four different measures of the nation's price level in the four critical years of 1930, 1931, 1932, and 1933.

V. The Collapse of the U.S. Money Supply

Banking panics, bank failures, declining money supply, and price level deflation are interconnected factors that account for the extraordinary depth and duration of the Great Depression. From December 1929 to June 1933, M1 and M2 declined by 27 and 34 percent, respectively. The right-hand column of Table 8-2 indicates similar declines in the nation's price level. Table 8-3 indicates the magnitude of M1, the monetary base, and the money supply multiplier (m1), together with the variables underlying the multiplier, in June of each year from 1929 through 1934.

Causes of the Contraction in M1 and M2

Note that while M1 decreased sharply from 1929 to 1933, the monetary base (B) did not. From June 1929 to June 1933, the base increased by about 13 percent. It was higher throughout 1932 and 1933 than at any point in 1928 or 1929. Because the money supply multipliers (m1 and m2) are simply the ratios of M1 and M2 to the monetary base, respectively, this implies that the proximate cause of the collapse of M1 and M2 was the severe contraction in the corresponding multipliers, m1 and m2. The table indicates that m1 declined 40 percent from 1929 to 1934.

Table 8-3 shows the pattern of the three variables that determine the narrow money multiplier, m1. These factors are k (the currency/DDO ratio), rr (the weighted average required reserve ratio), and re (the banks' desired excess reserves/DDO ratio). The general forces underlying each of these variables were discussed in chapter 7.

Table 8-3   Monetary Variables During the Great Depression

	M1 $ billions	B $ billions	m1	k	rr	re
June 1929	26.2	6.82	3.84	.161	.104	.001
June 1930	25.1	6.62	3.79	.155	.110	.000
June 1931	23.5	6.92	3.40	.184	.116	.004
June 1932	20.2	7.39	2.73	.296	.116	.010
June 1933	19.2	7.72	2.49	.330	.126	.033
June 1934	21.4	9.21	2.32	.279	.126	.104

Source: Board of Governors of Federal Reserve System, *Banking and Monetary Statistics* (Washington, DC: National Capital Press, 1943).

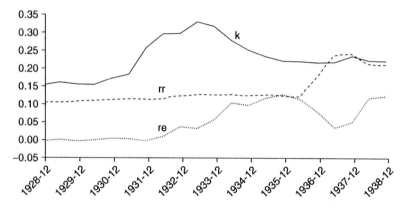

Figure 8-2   Behavior of money supply multiplier determinants, 1928–1938.

Source: Board of Governors of the Federal Reserve System, *Banking and Monetary Statistics, 1914–1941* (Washington, DC: National Capital Press, 1943).

Note that the narrow (m1) money supply multiplier declined very modestly from the middle of 1929 to the middle of 1930. It then declined sharply (39 percent) in the four years ending in mid-1934. The patterns exhibited by the three determinants of the money multiplier (k, rr, and re) are revealed in the table and are illustrated in Figure 8-2.

The collapse of the m1 money supply multiplier was initiated by the series of banking panics, during which the currency ratio (k) increased from 16 percent at the end of 1929 to 33 percent in June 1933. Given that bank deposits were not insured and hundreds of banks were failing each week, it is not surprising that the public withdrew large amounts of currency from their deposits in banks. As banks became increasingly cautious owing to defaulting loans, fear of additional runs, and the

Federal Reserve's failure to respond, they began to increase their holdings of excess reserves in 1932. As illustrated in Figure 8-2, as the banking panic subsided in 1933 and 1934 and the currency ratio declined, banks continued to build up their excess reserves—that is, *re* increased. Note in the figure that at one point in late 1935, excess reserves held by banks even exceeded their required reserves. Banks were holding twice as many reserves as were required.

The sharp increases in *k* and *re* account overwhelmingly for the decline in the narrow and broad money supply multipliers (and in M1 and M2) from 1929 to 1933. Note also the slight upward trend in rr, the weighted average reserve requirement. In the 1920s and 1930s, reserve requirements were considerably higher for larger city banks than for smaller rural banks throughout the country. The more rapid growth of the larger city banks owing to increasing urbanization gradually pulled up rr over time. This longer-term trend was further stimulated in the Great Depression as sophisticated depositors moved their funds into larger banks on the basis of the (correct) perception that these city banks were more diversified, safer, and less likely to fail. The sharp increases in rr in 1936 and 1937 were due to increases in reserve requirements implemented by the Federal Reserve, intended to mop up excess reserves in the banks.[10]

VI. Differing Interpretations of the Facts of the 1930s

Table 8-3 and Figure 8-2 indicate the facts about the elements that accounted for the sharp contraction of M1 and M2. Economists differ in the interpretation of these facts. One can find distinguished economists—even Nobel Laureates—who strongly disagree with each other about the Federal Reserve's role in the debacle of the 1930s. Some of these views are now presented.

The Original View of Keynes: You Can't Push on a String

The most influential early interpretation of the Great Depression—that advanced by the Fed itself and espoused by the great British economist, John Maynard Keynes—was generally accepted in the 30 years immediately following the depression. In this Keynesian view, the Federal Reserve instituted a policy of easy money soon after the economy turned down. However, powerful forces beyond the Fed's control prevented it from averting the collapse of the money supply and the ensuing contraction of output and the nation's price level. Yields on short-term securities—the rates that the central bank is responsible for—fell from 4 percent in October 1929 at the time the stock market began its long decline, to less than 1 percent by mid-1932. The Federal Reserve Bank of New York reduced its discount rate eight times, from 6 percent in October 1929 to 1.5 percent in mid-1931, before raising this rate sharply in September 1931 in response to international considerations previously discussed. Figure 8-3 shows the pattern of the Fed's discount rate, along with short-term and long-term U.S. Treasury security yields during this period.

Between December 1929 and December 1932, the monetary base—indisputably subject to Federal Reserve control—increased by approximately 14 percent. Excess reserves began piling up in the banks after the middle of 1932—normally an indicator of monetary ease—and reached massive levels by 1934. In the conventional early view, these facts suggest that the Fed's policy actions were certainly not restrictive, and the Fed was therefore absolved from responsibility for the Great Depression. It is suggested that "you cannot push on a string." The interest rate is clearly bounded by zero and once the central bank pushes short-term interest rates close to that limit and provides banks with ample excess reserves, it is alleged to be out of ammunition. If the public is unwilling to borrow from banks (or if banks are unwilling to lend) and if short-term security yields are so low that banks find it not worthwhile to buy these securities, there is nothing further the Fed can do. It cannot force banks to make loans or purchase securities.

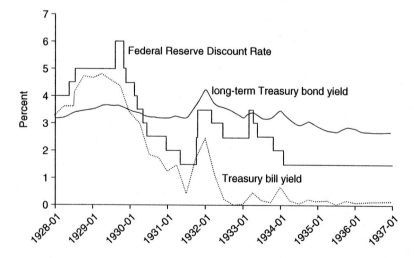

Figure 8-3 Treasury security yields and Federal Reserve discount rate, 1928–1936.

Source: Board of Governors of Federal Reserve System, *Banking and Monetary Statistics, 1914–1941* (Washington, DC: National Capital Press, 1943).

Because short-term yields had reached extraordinarily low levels by 1932, bank demand for excess reserves was alleged to have become perfectly elastic with respect to the interest rate, an hypothesis known as a *bank liquidity trap*.[11] In this view, any additional excess reserves supplied to the banks by the central bank would simply be held by the banks rather than being loaned or invested in securities. The alleged existence of a banker's liquidity trap is a point of contention among economists with differing interpretations of the Fed's role in the 1930s fiasco.

In this view, the link between the monetary base and the money supply, if not totally severed, had been badly bent. The Fed allegedly lost ability to increase the money supply because banks had become unwilling to use additional reserves supplied to them by the Federal Reserve to expand loans or purchase securities, either of which would have boosted M1 and M2. Banks did not lend either because they were apprehensive about the viability of prospective borrowers or because such borrowers had disappeared because of extreme pessimism about economic prospects. Banks did not buy securities because of the low yields. In this extreme case, the money supply multiplier moves in inverse proportion to changes in the monetary base engineered by the central bank. Had the Fed aggressively purchased securities and further increased bank reserves and the monetary base, the money supply multiplier would have fallen even more as more excess reserves simply piled up in the banks.[12]

Thus, the situation was alleged to be beyond the Fed's control. The Fed did all it could, but only strong fiscal stimulus—tax cuts and/or increased government expenditures—could have extricated the nation from depression. In this Keynesian view, monetary policy was impotent. "You can't push on a string."

The Monetarist View: The Fed was not Pushing

Milton Friedman, the most famous monetarist economist, co-authored with Anna Schwartz in 1963 the highly influential book, *A Monetary History of the United States, 1867–1960*. This work challenged the Keynesian view of the Great Depression. Friedman and other monetarists argue that Fed policy in the early 1930s was definitely not expansionary. In fact, they believe it was highly restrictive. In their view, a typical business cycle contraction was converted into a catastrophe by banking panics and a series of Federal Reserve policy errors.

For example, the Fed raised its discount rate from 3.5 to 5 percent in three steps in February, April, and July 1928 in response to stock market speculation, even though price-level inflation was nowhere in sight. Other important alleged errors include permitting bank reserves to fall during the banking panics, raising the discount rate dramatically in October 1931, using open market security sales to sterilize the potential expansionary effect of gold inflows on the monetary base, and doubling reserve requirements in 1936 and 1937. Many economists are convinced the nation would have experienced only a normal recession had the Fed implemented aggressive stimulative policy actions in 1930 and 1931.

What evidence can monetarists marshal to challenge the traditional view that monetary policy was in an expansionary mode in the early 1930s? Several arguments appear compelling. First, while the monetary base (B) did increase in the Great Depression, the base consists of both bank reserves (R) and currency held by the public (Cp). While Cp increased dramatically in the panic, the Fed passively allowed R to decline by 18 percent between October 1929 and April 1933—the interval when the damage was done. Thus, the behavior of the monetary base is highly misleading because an increasing portion of it was unavailable to banks for the purpose of extending credit. The Fed should have recognized this fact and pumped reserves into the banks through open market purchases of securities.

Early interpretations argued that low short-term interest rates are indicative of "easy money." But monetarists contend this inference is invalid in a period of deflation like the early 1930s. Focus should have been on *real* rather than *nominal* interest rates. Table 8-2 indicates that several price indexes confirm very significant deflation of prices in the early 1930s. In fact, each of these indexes declined at an average rate of more than 6 percent per year from 1930 to 1933. Therefore, while nominal interest rates were very low, real or inflation-adjusted rates were extremely high in this period. In addition, a flight to quality on the part of security buyers after 1931 created an abnormally high level of demand for safe, short-term securities. This abnormal demand for Treasury securities, not Federal Reserve policy actions, contributed to the remarkably low level of their yields in the early 1930s.[13]

While it is true that little scope remained for the Fed to push down nominal short-term yields much further, monetarists assert that it could have implemented aggressive actions to arrest the ongoing deflation of the nation's price level, thereby preventing the disastrously high real interest rates.

Monetarists also point out that the Federal Reserve sharply tightened its discount window policy in the early 1930s. The incentive for a bank to borrow reserves at the Fed is not a function of the discount rate per se but rather of the difference between the discount rate and short-term money market yields. A bank short of reserves does not find the discount window an attractive source of funds if the discount rate significantly exceeds the yield the bank is earning on its short-term securities.

If the discount rate is an ostensibly low 1 percent but the bank is earning 0.2 percent on Treasury bills, the rational response of a bank short on reserves is to sell off Treasury bills rather than borrow at the discount window. While selling Treasury bills increases an individual bank's reserves, it does not increase reserves of the aggregate banking system. Note in Figure 8-3 the huge gap by which the discount rate exceeded the Treasury bill yield throughout the 1930s, especially after the discount rate hikes in fall 1931. This gap is indicative of a restrictive discount window policy and helps explain why banks were not using it to obtain reserves during the Great Depression.

In 1931, the Fed responded to England's abandonment of the gold standard by raising the discount rate sharply at a time when the unemployment rate stood near 15 percent. The Fed also took a tightfisted attitude toward lending to banks. In a bizarre move, the Fed sent a letter to banks admonishing them that it was inappropriate for banks to increase their use of the discount window. Faced with a national panic caused by increasing bank failures, the Federal Reserve apparently forgot that banks collectively can obtain reserves only if the central bank accommodates their needs, either via the discount window or through open market security purchases.[14] The Fed should have reduced the discount rate to zero, opened access to the window, and encouraged banks to borrow until the panic subsided. Instead, the Fed's actions only aggravated the panic.

Monetarists also challenge the alleged existence of a bankers' liquidity trap—that is, the hypothesis that bank lending would not have increased even if the Fed had poured more reserves into the banking system. Instead, monetarists assert that, rather than being horizontal, the bank demand curve for excess reserves was moderately steep but had shifted sharply rightward. This increase in bank demand for excess reserves was said to be due to bankers' fear that further runs might take place and that, based on recent experience, the Federal Reserve could not be counted on to supply banks with additional reserves if that happened.

In this interpretation, the excess reserves in the banks were not "excessive" or superfluous but were deliberately held as precautionary balances because bankers had recently been badly burned by banking panics and the wrongheaded Fed response to them. Had the Fed recognized that there had been a discrete rightward shift in the bank demand curve for excess reserves, it would have supplied banks with sufficient excess reserves to satisfy that demand. In this view, banks would have then resumed lending. It was not lack of loan demand that explains the sharp decline in bank lending in the early 1930s. Instead, banks were allegedly turning away willing and legitimate borrowers because the banks wanted to hold more excess reserves to protect themselves.

Table 8-4   Evidence of Restrictive Monetary Policy in the 1930s

Year	M1 ($ billions)*	M2 ($ billions)*	Bank Reserves ($ billions)*	Inflation Rate (%)	Real T-Bill Yield (%)†	Discount Rate Minus T-Bill Yield (%)‡
1929	26.3	46.0	3.20	0	+4.5	+0.2
1930	25.3	45.3	3.22	−2.5	+4.7	+0.6
1931	23.8	42.6	3.26	−8.8	+10.0	+0.9
1932	20.3	34.5	2.87	−10.3	+11.1	+2.1
1933	19.2	30.1	2.96	−5.1	+5.4	+2.2
1934	21.2	33.1	4.69	+3.4	−3.1	+1.4
1935	25.1	38.0	5.92	+2.5	−2.4	+1.4
1936	29.5	43.2	6.76	+1.0	−0.9	+1.3
1937	30.6	45.2	7.93	+3.6	−3.1	+0.9
1938	29.2	44.1	9.11	−1.9	+2.0	+1.0

Source: Milton Friedman and Anna J. Schwartz, *A Monetary History of the United States, 1867–1960* (Princeton, NJ: Princeton University Press, 1963, Appendix Tables A-1 and A-2).
*Averages of monthly figures for May, June, and July.
†Average monthly T-Bill yield minus CPI inflation rate.
‡New York Fed discount rate minus rate minus T-bill yield in June.

Table 8-4 summarizes the evidence supporting the view that monetary policy was restrictive in the early 1930s. Note first the sharp contraction in M1 and M2 from 1929 to 1933. Because monetarists believe that a central bank is responsible for the nation's money supply, they view this contraction as prima facie evidence of the Fed's ineptitude in the 1930s. Second, note the contraction of bank reserves in the early 1930s. Because the Federal Reserve is capable of accurately controlling aggregate bank reserves, this is an indication that the Fed either may have been negligent in conducting monetary policy or was a willing accomplice in the reductions of bank reserves, M1, and M2. Note also the extremely high level of real interest rates in 1931 and 1932 (the real T-bill column), which contributed to the massive foreclosures of farmers, homeowners, and small businesses. Finally, notice the large magnitude by which the Fed's discount rate exceeded the Treasury bill yield after 1931. All of these indicators suggest to monetarists that monetary policy was "tight" during 1929–1933.

VII. What Ended the Great Depression?

After reaching the trough of the depression in the spring of 1933, real GDP rebounded strongly, increasing at an average annual rate of nearly

10 percent during the following four years. In spite of several fiscal initiatives implemented in the Roosevelt administration's first year in office in an effort to boost employment, many economists attribute the 1933–1937 economic expansion to monetary forces rather than fiscal stimulus.[15] From mid-1933 to mid-1937, the nation's money supply increased at a rapid rate of 10 percent per year and the unemployment rate declined from 25 percent to around 14 percent.

What was the source of the monetary expansion? The money supply multiplier was stable from the middle of 1933 to mid-1936, as the effect of a declining currency ratio (k)—due to increasing confidence in banks and the implementation of federal deposit insurance—was offset by an increase in the excess reserve ratio (re). However, the monetary base increased steadily and strongly for several years beginning in mid-1933. This can be attributed to the January 1934 devaluation of the U.S. dollar, along with political instability in Europe after 1932 that led to a sustained capital (and gold) flight to the United States. An increase in the U.S. gold stock, unless neutralized by open market security sales by the Fed, increases the monetary base, M1 and M2. This monetary expansion was instrumental in causing deflation to give way to inflation in 1933, as indicated in Figure 8-1. The increasing inflation meant that real interest rates were falling, thus stimulating investment and consumption expenditures.

Unfortunately, the economic recovery from the Great Depression was interrupted by a severe recession in 1937–1938, caused in large part by the unwarranted increase in reserve requirements. The unemployment rate jumped to 19 percent by the end of 1938. Not until the massive and sustained fiscal stimulus associated with the preparation for the U.S. entry into World War II did the unemployment rate go below 10 percent. By then it was 1941, and the long economic nightmare was over.

Exhibit 8-1

Understanding the Federal Reserve's Thinking in the Great Depression

An objective student of the Fed's actions during the Great Depression might legitimately conclude that either the Fed conducted a tight policy in the midst of a downward economic spiral or sat back and passively watched the U.S. financial system and economy collapse. How can one account for the failure of the Fed to act appropriately in the 1930s? Several potential explanations exist.

One view asserts that the Fed was fooled by its own flawed strategy—its propensity to focus on the wrong indicators of its policy posture. In looking at low short-term yields, the low discount rate, and burgeoning excess reserves after mid-1932, the Federal Reserve incorrectly inferred that its policies were expansionary. Also, beginning in the 1920s, because banks were believed to be very reluctant to borrow at the Fed's discount window, the Fed viewed a large amount of such borrowing as a sign that money was tight. Hence, when such bank borrowing fell sharply following the 1929 stock market crash, the Fed took this to mean that money was "easy," rather than as an indication that the crash had made banks more conservative and cautious about borrowing. This theory can explain why the Fed did not aggressively purchase securities in the open market during the depression—it incorrectly believed it was already in an expansionary mode. The Fed's attention was riveted on *nominal* interest rates, excess reserves, and discount window borrowing rather than *real* interest rates, total bank reserves, and declining money supply. Some critics charge that the Fed was incompetent, its collective intellectual capital diminished by the 1928 death of Benjamin Strong, Federal Reserve leader in the 1920s.

A second view emphasizes the inherent conflict between the Fed's dual roles of stabilizing economic activity and ensuring safety and soundness of the nation's banks. In the early 1930s, because of very low loan demand by the public and/or very high risk aversion on the part of banks, banks engaged in a major reallocation of earning assets from loans to Treasury securities. Interest earned on these securities became a key determinant of bank profits. In early 1932, under Congressional pressure, the Fed finally began to engage in serious open market purchases of government securities to increase bank reserves. As yields plunged to extremely low levels (see Figure 8-3), the Fed quickly abandoned its short-lived expansionary program, allegedly out of fear of further impairing the depressed banks' financial condition. The Fed became concerned that interest rates were too low for banks to earn reasonable profits.

A third interpretation involves the gold standard. Until federal legislation enacted in 1932 allowed Federal Reserve holdings of Treasury securities to also be counted as collateral, each of the 12 Federal Reserve banks was required to hold gold in the amount of no less than 40 percent of Federal Reserve notes (paper currency) issued. In the early 1930s, "free gold"—gold held in excess of this collateral requirement—was precariously low at several Federal Reserve banks. When foreign nations began converting their dollar holdings into gold at the U.S. Treasury in late September and October 1931 following England's abandonment of the gold standard, the Federal Reserve banks dramatically increased their discount rates in an effort to reverse the ongoing outflow of financial capital and gold from the United States. Some students of the subject believe the Fed was heavily constrained by international economic conditions and the gold standard, and was thus limited in its ability to react to domestic economic conditions. This view of Fed policy has received increasing support among scholars in recent years in spite of Friedman and Schwartz's claim that the gold backing requirement did not significantly constrain the Federal Reserve.

Chapter 9

The Federal Reserve's Response to the Great Crisis

I. Introduction

Federal Reserve policy in the Great Depression of the early 1930s was analyzed in chapter 8 and was found to be very poorly conceived and conducted. Serious errors committed by the Fed include permitting bank reserves to decline significantly during banking panics, sharply raising interest rates in 1931 after Britain abandoned the gold standard, sterilizing gold inflows that would otherwise have expanded bank reserves and the monetary base, abruptly reversing course in mid-1932 after implementing a short-lived expansionary policy of open market security purchases, and doubling reserve requirements in 1936 and 1937. In this chapter, the Fed's policy during the Great Crisis of 2007–2009 and its aftermath is analyzed.

In many ways the challenges that confronted the Federal Reserve during the Great Crisis were more daunting than those of the 1930s. The recent crisis had the potential to do even more damage to the nation's economy. First, the series of financial innovations that gave us collateralized debt obligations, credit default swaps, and other poorly understood and dangerous instruments did not have an analogous counterpart in the 1930s. And a regulatory framework appropriate for the new financial technology was not in place. Second, the rapid expansion of the largely unregulated shadow banking system made the recent crisis more complicated and challenging. Third, given that two bubbles burst (housing and stock markets) at the beginning of the recent crisis, and that ownership of stocks and houses was more widespread in 2007 than in 1929, the pervasiveness of loss of wealth was relatively greater. Fourth, given the globalization movement of recent decades, the degree of interconnectedness among nations is much greater today than in earlier times. For example, U.S. imports increased from less than 4 percent of GDP in the late 1920s to more than 15 percent in recent years. The influence of declining economic activity in the United States on other nations (and the reverse feedback on the United States) is stronger today than in earlier times. And capital flows across nations loom much larger today. This meant that it was even more essential in the Great Crisis for central banks around the world to coordinate their responses.

Federal Reserve chairman Bernanke admits that he and his Federal Reserve colleagues were blindsided by the crisis, underestimating the interconnectedness and fragility of the various elements of the financial system. Nevertheless, the creativity and forcefulness with which the Bernanke-led Federal Reserve reacted to the crisis once it reached full force in fall 2008 stands in contrast to the passive Fed behavior in the Great Depression. In September 2007, two months before the Great Recession officially began, the Fed began reducing interest rates. While hindsight indicates the Fed should have reacted more strongly in the months immediately preceding the September 2008 Lehman Brothers collapse, it did then unleash an unprecedented number and variety of initiatives to prevent a meltdown of the financial system and an economic contraction that could potentially have been more severe than the catastrophe of the early 1930s.

One of the early signs of the financial tsunami that was to wreak havoc on economies throughout the world and challenge the most creative of central bankers occurred on August 9, 2007. On that date BNP Paribas, a Paris-based bank and one of the world's largest, announced that it was freezing three of its investment funds to forestall an impending run by shareholders. Within a week, several other European banks followed BNP Paribas' example. These banks moved to prevent shareholders from withdrawing their accounts because the banks could not place a specific value on the subprime mortgage-backed securities (MBS) owned by their investment funds. It was not clear whether these funds were solvent because trading in the mortgage-backed bonds had ceased, making it impossible to know the value of the bonds.

BNP Paribas may not have been in appreciably different straits than many other large banks. Rather, it was simply the first to publicly acknowledge the uncertain value of its MBS. Market observers quickly recognized that this meant that it was impossible to know whether several of the largest U.S. banks that held large portfolios of mortgage-related instruments were solvent. Among other things, this meant that banks that normally engaged routinely in lending to other banks in the interbank markets perceived that such loans were now quite risky because their prospective counterparties—other banks seeking to borrow—might be unable to make good on the loans. Hence, the critically important interbank markets virtually shut down.

Acutely aware of the implications of the BNP Paribas announcement for the demand for liquidity in financial markets, the Federal Reserve immediately issued a statement indicating that it stood ready to provide liquidity through the discount window. One week later, the Fed announced it was lowering its discount rate to reduce the normal spread between the discount rate and the federal funds rate (FFR) target from 1 to 0.5 percentage points. When banks still balked at using the discount window to obtain liquidity, the Fed in December 2007 initiated a new auction-loan program designed to encourage banks to avail themselves of credit through the Federal Reserve. A few weeks later, when the Bank of England announced that it was making an emergency loan to the troubled Northern Rock Bank, the Federal Reserve dropped its discount rate and federal funds rate target by 50 basis points. After a series of reductions, the Fed had reduced the FFR target to 3 percent by the end of January 2008. By April, the rate was at 2 percent, and by December 2008 the Fed had dropped the FFR target rate to the lowest rate on record—a range of 0–0.25 percent. The FFR target remained at that level during all of 2009 and 2010.

This chapter examines Federal Reserve policy during 2007–2010. It discusses Federal Reserve critics' argument that the Fed failed to fully realize the impending implications of the crisis prior to the September 2008 collapse of Lehman Brothers and was therefore insufficiently aggressive in reducing interest rates in 2008. The money supply mechanics triggered by the financial crisis, ensuing bank behavior, and the Federal Reserve response are examined. We will see how the Federal Reserve's unprecedented expansion of bank reserves and the monetary base—implemented through a huge expansion of the Fed's balance sheet after August 2008—prevented a contraction in the nation's money supply. In contrast to the experience of the early 1930s, M1 and M2 increased in 2008, 2009, and 2010. Several innovative actions implemented by the Fed to provide emergency liquidity to the financial system as it began to shut down in fall 2008 are analyzed. Finally, the measures the Fed employed in 2009 and 2010 in an effort to reduce mortgage rates and other long-term interest rates--measures known as "quantitative easing"—are discussed.

II. Criticism of the Fed's Interest Rate Policy in 2008

Critics of the Federal Reserve charge that, as the crucial year 2008 unfolded and the crisis deepened, the Fed was initially slow to recognize the impending severity of the financial crisis and its implications for economic activity. In this view, the Fed failed to reduce short-term interest rates as fast as was warranted by rapidly deteriorating circumstances.[1] Figure 9-1 shows the federal funds target rate over the course of calendar year 2008.

In two steps in January 2008, the Federal Open Market Committee (FOMC), the key policy-making group of the Federal Reserve, voted to reduce the federal funds target rate from 4.25 percent to 3 percent. On March 18, two days after Bear Stearns' collapse and takeover by JPMorgan, the Fed dropped the rate by another 75 basis points to 2.25 percent. At the April 30 FOMC meeting, the federal funds target rate was reduced another 25 basis points, to 2 percent. The Fed then maintained this target rate at 2 percent for more than five months before finally moving by unanimous vote to cut the rate to 1.5 percent on October 8. With the aid of hindsight it is clear that, as the financial crisis deepened during 2008, the Fed (and the overwhelming majority of economists) underestimated the powerful impact the crisis would have on economic activity. In spite of mounting evidence of spreading economic weakness, the Fed maintained its FFR target fixed at 2 percent during three consecutive FOMC meetings (June 25, August 5, and September 16), before finally dropping the rate by 50 basis points on October 8. In retrospect, it is clear that the Fed was excessively concerned about inflation and insufficiently cognizant of the forces working to reduce output and employment.

Federal Reserve documents indicate the Fed was sensitive to the risks of both falling output and rising inflation, but it is clear that discussion at these FOMC meetings placed excessive weight on the risk that

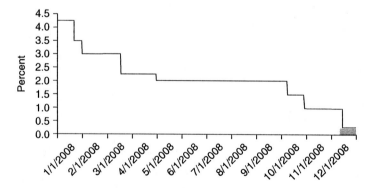

Figure 9-1   Federal funds rate target in 2008.

Source: Federal Reserve Bank of St. Louis, FRED database.

inflation would rise significantly. The following are excerpts from the statements that the Fed released immediately following these three key meetings at which the members of the FOMC voted to maintain the federal funds rate constant at 2 percent[2]:

June 25, 2008. "…labor markets have softened further and financial markets remain under considerable stress. Tight credit conditions, the ongoing housing contraction, and the rise of energy prices are likely to weigh on economic growth over the next few quarters…Although downside risks to growth remain, they appear to have diminished somewhat, and the upside risks to inflation and inflation expectations have increased."

August 5, 2008. "…labor markets have softened further and financial markets remain under considerable stress. Tight credit conditions, the ongoing housing contraction, and elevated energy prices are likely to weigh on growth over the next few quarters…Although downside risks to growth remain, the upside risks to inflation are also of significant concern to the Committee."

September 16, 2008. "Strains in financial markets have increased significantly and labor markets have weakened further…Inflation has been high, spurred by earlier increases in the prices of energy and other commodities…The downside risks to growth and the upside risks to inflation are both of significant concern to the Committee."

In the recorded minutes of the September 16 meeting, the conflict inherent in the Federal Reserve's dual mandate to maintain both high employment and price stability was reflected in the sentiments of FOMC members:

> …economic activity decelerated considerably in recent months. The labor market deteriorated further in August as private payrolls declined and the unemployment rate moved markedly higher. Industrial output was little changed in July, but fell sharply in August. Consumer spending weakened noticeably in recent months. Meanwhile, residential investment continued to decline steeply through midyear…On the inflation front, overall consumer prices rose rapidly for a third straight month in July but then edged down in August because of a sharp drop in energy prices…inflation risks appeared to have diminished in response to the declines in the prices of energy and other commodities, the recent strengthening of the dollar, and the outlook for somewhat greater slack…However, the possibility that core inflation would not moderate as anticipated was still a significant concern."

The nation's contemporary unemployment rate was known by FOMC members (and the public) to be 5.4 percent, 5.8 percent, and 6.1 percent at the times of the June 25, August 5, and September 16 meetings, respectively. This suggested that monetary easing would be appropriate. However, energy prices had been rising sharply for more than a year, with the price of crude oil moving from about $55 per barrel in January 2007 to more than $130 in June and July 2008. In the 2008 summer travel season, gasoline prices surged above $4 per gallon in many parts of the country. The 12-month CPI inflation rate in the first half of 2008 exceeded 4 percent per year and moved above 5 percent in July and August. The Fed was concerned that the dramatic increase in energy prices would feed through to pull up the critically important core inflation rate, which was running at an annual rate of about 2.5 percent in the summer of 2008. The direction of this core inflation rate was being driven by two opposing forces: the increasing slack in product and labor markets, which was working to pull down the core rate, and the sharp increase in energy prices, which was working to pull up the rate.

With the aid of hindsight, it is clear that the Fed underestimated the role of economic slack in pulling down core inflation and failed to recognize the transitory nature of the increase in crude oil prices through the summer of 2008.[3] By the end of 2008, oil prices were to decline to $40 per barrel and the nation's unemployment rate was to rise from its July level of 5.8 to 7.4 percent (and to 9.4 percent in May 2009).

Figure 9-2 shows the course of inflation during 2008 and 2009, as indicated by the 12-month rate of change of most economists' preferred measures—the personal consumption expenditures (PCE) deflator and the *core* PCE deflator. The latter measure strips out the effects of relatively volatile energy and food prices from the PCE and is therefore more representative of the underlying rate of inflation that is likely more influential in determining the critically important medium and longer-term inflation expectations.

At the time of the August 5 FOMC meeting, the PCE and Core PCE price indexes had risen at rates of 4.5 and 2.6 percent over the preceding 12 months, respectively. The Fed believed that there was a significant risk that persistence of relatively high actual PCE inflation might become embedded in core inflation. This development, in turn, could boost inflation expectations, thereby raising the cost of eventually bringing down inflation. As it turned out, by December 2008, the 12-month rate of change of the PCE and core PCE declined to 0.6 and 1.8 percent, respectively. And by July 2009, the corresponding rates declined to *negative* 0.9 and positive 1.3 percent, respectively. The combination of rapidly expanding economic slack and rapidly declining energy prices had, by the end of 2008, reduced the inflation rate well below the level preferred by the Federal Reserve.[4] Deflation had emerged as a more serious

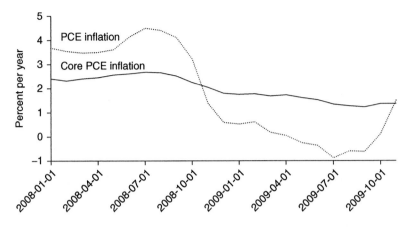

Figure 9-2   Inflation rates of PCE and core PCE price indexes in 2008 and 2009.
Source: Federal Reserve Bank of St. Louis, FRED Database.

threat than unacceptably high inflation. Had the Fed been blessed with accurate foresight, it would have lowered its federal funds rate target more quickly and more aggressively in 2008.

III. The Money Mechanics of the Crisis

Recall from the previous chapter that the money supply multipliers that link the monetary base to M1 and M2 collapsed in the early 1930s. The initiating force was the panic-induced withdrawal of currency from depository institutions by the public in response to bank failures. This was followed by increased bank demand for excess reserves as banks tightened lending standards in response to reduced capital and increased uncertainty about their forthcoming needs for, and availability of, liquidity. The large decline in the money multiplier, combined with the very modest increase in the monetary base, accounts for the 30 percent contraction in the U.S. money supply in the early 1930s.

As is characteristic in severe financial crises when demand for liquidity surges, the money multiplier fell sharply in the Great Crisis—this time by more than 40 percent, an even larger decline than in the Great Depression. The collapse in the narrow (m1) money supply multiplier is illustrated in Figure 9-3.

What caused this massive contraction in m1? Consider the three proximate determinants of the money multiplier: k (the public's desired currency/demand deposits ratio), rr (the weighted required reserves/ demand deposits ratio), and re (banks' desired excess reserves/demand deposits

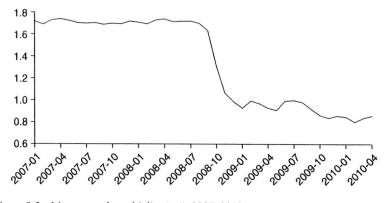

Figure 9-3   Money supply multiplier (m1), 2007–2010.
Source: Federal Reserve Bank of St. Louis, FRED database

ratio). In the recent crisis, the existence of deposit insurance helps account for the fact that the currency ratio (k) did not increase—in fact, it trended downward in 2008 and 2009. The weighted average reserve requirement, rr, was stable. However, re—the ratio of bank excess reserves to checkable deposits in depository institutions—increased dramatically as banks severely tightened lending standards and hoarded liquidity at a time when declining yields made purchasing Treasury bills increasingly unattractive. Figure 9-4 shows the behavior of k, rr, and re over the course of the 2007–2010 period.

The figure indicates that that the behavior of re accounts for virtually the entire contraction of the multiplier. Excess reserves of depository institutions increased from the normal level of less than one percent of checkable deposits in depository institutions (DDO) in August 2008 to more than 100 percent in January 2009. Potentially, this contraction in the multiplier could have caused a severe decline in the nation's money supply, likely resulting in price level deflation and a major depression. Unlike in the 1930s, however, the Federal Reserve massively increased the monetary base, approximately doubling it in a period of 8 months beginning in August 2008. Figure 9-5 indicates the behavior of the base, M1, and M2 in the period extending from 2006 through the spring of 2010. Over the course of 2008 and 2009, M1 and M2 increased at average annual rates of approximately 11 and 7 percent, respectively.

The huge increase in the monetary base after August 2008 is attributable to the enormous increase in reserves injected into the banks by

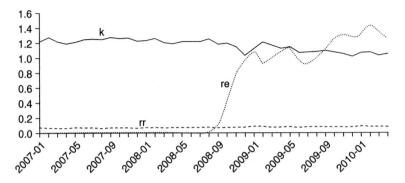

Figure 9-4   Behavior of factors underlying money multiplier (m1), 2007–2010.
Source: Calculated from data in FRED database.

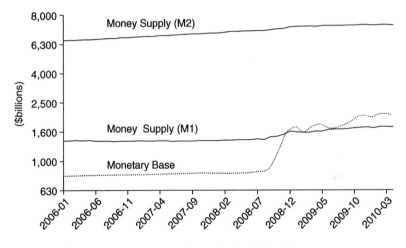

Figure 9-5   Growth of monetary base, M1, and M2, 2006–2010.
Source: Calculated from data in FRED database.

the Federal Reserve as it dramatically increased the size of its balance sheet. Total reserves in the banking system increased more than 13-fold in the 4-month period extending from July to November 2008 and more than 25-fold from July 2008 through the end of 2009. Almost all of the additional reserves were in the form of excess reserves because aggregate bank deposits (hence required reserves) increased by a relatively small amount. This rate of increase in reserves and excess reserves dwarf anything in the previous history of the Federal Reserve. The dramatic increase in reserves was the direct result of the enormous increase in the balance sheet of the Federal Reserve.

The Expansion of Federal Reserve Balance Sheet

Starting in September 2008, the Fed undertook an expansion of its balance sheet of unprecedented magnitude and speed. In part, this was intended to expand reserves and the monetary base and prevent a contraction of M1 and M2. Given the tightening of bank lending standards and the increased bank demand for excess reserves, the expansion of the base was needed to offset the contraction in the money supply multipliers (m1 and m2). In large part, the initial expansion of the Fed's balance sheet was intended to accommodate the exploding demand for liquidity in the financial system as perceived counterparty risk surged and normal channels of financial intermediation atrophied or shut down entirely.

To gain an idea about the expansion of the Fed's balance sheet, consider Table 9-1, which shows the various items on the balance sheet on December 12, 2007 and two years later, on December 9, 2009. First, note that total assets of the Fed increased dramatically, from approximately $885 billion to $2,190 billion, an increase of nearly 150 percent.[5]

Secondly, note the change in the *composition* of the Federal Reserve balance sheet. The Fed's portfolio of Treasury securities, which traditionally makes up more than 90 percent of total Federal Reserve assets, actually decreased over the two-year period and accounted for only 35 percent of the Fed's total assets at the end of 2009. The initial source of the expanded balance sheet lies principally in various types of loans extended by the Federal Reserve to provide temporary liquidity pending reopening of several blocked lines of credit. Somewhat later, acquisition by the Federal Reserve of such nontraditional assets as mortgage-backed bonds and securities issued by Fannie Mae and Freddie Mac and other entities took center stage as several of the temporary liquidity measures were phased down by the Fed.

To understand how the Federal Reserve was able to increase bank reserves and the monetary base so much, we review the sources of the monetary base, as indicated in equation 9-1 (previously discussed in chapter 7).

$$B = P + D + G + Float + OA + TCu - Ft - Ff$$
$$- Tca - OL - CAP \qquad (9\text{-}1)$$

In this equation B, P, and D represent the monetary base, the Federal Reserve portfolio of securities, and Federal Reserve loans to depository

Table 9-1   Federal Reserve Balance Sheets in 2007 and 2009 ($ billions)

Assets		Liabilities	
December 12, 2007			
Gold Certificates and SDR Accounts	13.24	Federal Reserve Notes	782.51
		Deposits	
Coin	1.21	A. Depository Inst.	13.89
Treasury Securities	822.49	B. U.S. Treasury	4.33
Federal Agency Sec.	0	C. Other	0.39
Mortgage-backed bonds	0	Other Liabilities	47.1
Term Auction Credit	0	Total Liabilities	848.22
Loans	4.55	Capital Accounts	36.88
Other Assets	43.61		
Total Assets	885.10	Total Lia + Capital	885.10
December 9, 2009			
Gold Certificates and SDR Accounts	16.24	Federal Reserve Notes	883.20
		Deposits	
Coin	2.04	A. Depository Inst.	1,106.67
Treasury Securities	776.55	B. U.S. Treasury	70.36
Federal Agency Sec.	156.15	C. Other	4.08
Mortgage – backed bonds	854.31	Other Liabilities	73.50
Term Auction Credit	85.83	Total Liabilities	2,137.81
Other Loans	84.30	Capital Accounts	52.16
Other Assets	214.55		
Total Assets	2,189.97	Total Lia + Capital	2,189.97

Source: http://www.federalreserve.gov/releases/h41

institutions, respectively. The other nine sources of the base played a relatively minor role in the growth of the base during 2008 and 2009. The initial (2008) expansion of the base resulted from the extremely large increase in D, Fed loans to the financial industry. This was followed, beginning in 2009, by massive acquisition by the Fed of mortgage-backed bonds, federal agency securities, and long-term Treasury securities, all of which are encompassed in P, the Federal Reserve security portfolio.

These *sources* of the doubling of the monetary base are found on the asset side of the Fed balance sheet. The *uses* of the enlarged base, or the manner in which the larger base was manifest, lies in the form of depository institution deposits at the Fed, shown on the liability side of the Fed's balance sheet in Table 9-1. Uses of the base include R and Cp (bank reserves and currency held by the public). In this connection, note in the two Fed balance sheets the enormous (80-fold) increase in depository institution deposits at the Federal Reserve. This item, along with cash in banks, constitutes bank reserves. Currency in the hands of the public increased somewhat in 2008 and 2009. But the overwhelming increase in the monetary base shows up as larger bank reserves in the form of bank deposits at the Federal Reserve that the Fed deliberately injected into the system by increasing its security holdings and loans to depository institutions.

Exhibit 9.1

Avoiding the Mistakes of 1937: Removing Those Excess Reserves

The dramatic increase in the magnitude of the Federal Reserve balance sheet and the 25-fold increase in reserves residing in the U.S. banking system in the 16 months extending from August 2008 to December 2009 is unprecedented in U.S. history. Nothing remotely comparable has ever happened before. Some professional economists, as well as numerous pundits, expressed concern that if banks were to use their excess reserves to extend loans and purchase Treasury securities, the U.S. money supply would surge, as would the likelihood of severe inflation. (This issue is examined in chapter 10.)

Accordingly, as the economy showed increasing evidence of recovery from severe recession in the second half of 2009 and first half of 2010, conservative economists admonished the Federal Reserve to begin withdrawing these reserves from banks. Liberal economists and the Obama administration advocated that the Fed maintain the status quo. A pertinent historical episode to study in this connection is the decision of the Federal Reserve in 1936 and 1937 to sharply increase reserve requirements.

During the latter phases of the Great Depression of 1929–1933, banks began accumulating excess reserves in relatively large quantities. In part, this was due to absence of strong loan demand and the extremely low level of short-term interest rates prevailing after the middle of 1932 as Treasury bill yields hovered in a range of 0 to 0.5 percent. The opportunity cost of holding excess reserves was nil. However, the build-up of excess reserves was also in part a defensive measure by banks to protect themselves from potential further bank runs by depositors. Given that thousands of banks had failed, those that survived understandably became very cautious.

Following the economic trough reached in early 1933, the economy staged a strong recovery during the next few years. Real output grew at nearly double-digit annual rates from the early part of 1933 until early 1937. This recovery was due in large part to low interest rates and monetary expansion fueled by gold inflows to the United States and projection of an optimistic outlook and an array of job-creating projects initiated by President Franklin D. Roosevelt (FDR) in the first year after assuming the presidency in March 1933. A clearly announced FDR priority was to "reflate," that is, to put a stop to the deflation of the price level and get prices back up to pre-Depression (1929) levels. This goal was pursued through monetary expansion, maintenance of very low interest rates, the devaluation of the U.S. dollar in early 1934, and by the numerous expansionary fiscal initiatives implemented in 1933 and 1934.

By the middle of 1936, the economy had recovered considerably from the depths of the Depression. Some commentators were worried about the possibility of an inflationary economic boom even though the unemployment rate was still above 13 percent. The Federal Reserve became concerned about the abnormally large amount of excess reserves in the banking system, viewing the excess reserves as "excessive" or superfluous reserves that might lead to an inflationary expansion of bank lending. The alternative explanation is that having been badly burned by the banking panics of the early 1930s and the Fed's failure to react appropriately to these crises, the banks had deliberately built up the excess reserves as a defensive backstop against potential future problems. In this interpretation, the excess reserves were not "excessive," nor were they likely to lead to inflation.

In a bid to eliminate the excess reserves, the Federal Reserve doubled the reserve requirement in three steps in 1936 and 1937. Economists today almost uniformly believe that was a terrible mistake, as banks reacted by tightening lending standards in an effort to re-establish their desired amount of excess reserves. The money supply decreased, interest rates rose, and the economy fell into a severe recession in 1937 and 1938. To make things worse, fiscal policy also turned contractionary in 1937. Income and capital gains tax rates were boosted, the government began collecting social security taxes for the first time, and a 1936 bonus program for World War I veterans expired. The unemployment rate soared to 18 percent in 1938.

As noted, the banking system was again awash in excess reserves in 2009 and 2010. Fed chairman Ben Bernanke, a long-time student of Federal Reserve policy in the 1930s, was determined not to repeat the mistakes made more than 70 years earlier. He was well aware of the need to eventually withdraw the excess reserves. However, given his awareness of Fed policy mistakes in the 1930s, his instincts led him to place higher priority on avoiding the risk of a double-dip recession and the possible onset of deflation than on avoiding the risk of higher inflation. This helps explains why the Fed was unwilling to abruptly remove those excess reserves in the early post-crisis environment of late-2009 and 2010.

Table 9-2   Changing Federal Reserve Asset Structure, 2008–2009 ($ billions)

Date	Treasury Securities*	Mortgage Backed Bonds	Term Auction Credit	Other Loans	Total Assets
12/27/2007	797.1	0	20.0	4.5	894.3
4/14/2008	615.6	0	125.0	27.9	880.7
9/03/2008	588.7	0	150.0	19.1	905.7
9/17/2008	577.8	0	150.0	121.3	996.1
9/24/2008	572.6	0	150.0	262.3	1,214.4
10/15/2008	570.7	0	263.1	441.4	1,772.4
10/29/2008	570.1	0	301.4	369.8	1,970.7
11/12/2008	569.4	0	415.3	316.1	2,214.5
4/08/2009	564.7	236.7	467.3	115.2	2,090.0
8/08/2009	813.4	542.9	233.6	105.7	1,992.2
12/30/2009	936.5	908.3	75.9	89.7	2,237.3

Source: http://www.federalreserve.gov/releases/h41
*This includes holdings of federal agency securities.

IV. Federal Reserve Measures to Increase Liquidity

This section analyzes the key changes in the Fed's balance sheet implemented during the Great Crisis, in the order in which they occurred. Table 9-2, by indicating changes in the Fed's asset structure, provides insight into the timing and magnitude of the various Federal Reserve initiatives implemented in 2008 and 2009.

Note that from late 2007 through the early part of 2009 the Fed's portfolio of Treasury securities and federal agency securities, traditionally the predominant portion of Fed assets, actually declined even though its total assets more than doubled. The discrepancy is accounted for mainly by the items in the table designated as "term auction credit" and "other loans." In mid-September 2008, Treasury secretary Henry Paulson, New York Fed Bank president Timothy Geithner, and Federal Reserve chairman Ben Bernanke were unsuccessful in brokering a deal to save Lehman Brothers, the floundering investment bank.[6] The announcement of Lehman's bankruptcy filing on September 15 was immediately followed by two additional shocking announcements: the shotgun wedding of the severely wounded Merrill Lynch and Bank of America and the bailout and takeover of the failing American Insurance Group (AIG) by the U.S. government. Within two days, the money market mutual fund Reserve Primary Fund had "broken the buck" and other money market funds were coming under heavy pressure, as was the commercial paper market.

The Federal Reserve quickly moved to institute half a dozen emergency measures to maintain the flow of credit in severely clogged markets as it struggled mightily to prevent a meltdown of the entire financial system. These innovations are listed under "term auction credit" and "other loans" in Table 9-2.

Note that the sum of term auction credit and other Federal Reserve loans increased from about $169 billion on September 3, 2008 to $731 billion some 10 weeks later (November 12). Altogether, the total amount of credit created through the various liquidity facilities increased from less than $1 billion in early December 2007 to a peak of more than $1,500 billion in December 2008, before declining steadily to a level of less than $200 billion in January 2010. Three of the most important of these Federal Reserve liquidity initiatives were the term auction credit facility (TAF), foreign central bank liquidity swaps (SWPs), and the commercial paper funding facility (CPFF). The timeline and evolution of the magnitude of these programs are illustrated in Figure 9-6. A few of the most important of these temporary Federal Reserve lending programs will be discussed.

The Term Auction Facility (TAF)

In normal times, the Federal Reserve is able to get funds into banks that have the most productive use for the funds through open market operations. The reserves initially created in the primary dealer banks by the Fed's open market purchases of securities get distributed efficiently

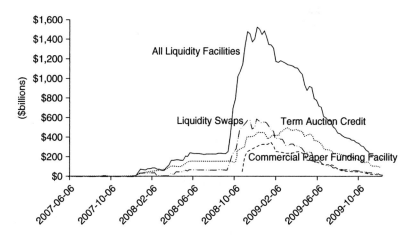

Figure 9-6 Federal Reserve liquidity initiatives, 2007–2009.
Source: Federal Reserve System.

through interbank funding markets and other avenues to banks that have sound use for these funds. However, when the interbank markets malfunctioned in the early stages of the financial crisis owing to great uncertainty about the financial condition of the banks seeking to borrow in these markets, this avenue of monetary transmission was severely impaired. This problem was particularly severe in term markets—those involving interbank loans for more than a day or two. Because many banks were shut off from access to funds in the interbank market, the Federal Reserve stood ready to lend to banks at the discount window. Unfortunately, however, this traditional channel failed to solve the liquidity problem during the financial crisis.

Historically, banks have been reluctant to borrow at the Federal Reserve discount window. This is thought to be due to existence of a "stigma"—a negative reputation effect that knowledge of such borrowing may unleash in the financial community. Financial market participants might wonder why a bank in good financial condition would need to borrow from the Federal Reserve, and might therefore view use of the Fed's discount window as a signal that the bank could be in trouble. Especially in the environment of fear that permeated financial markets during the Great Crisis, many banks believed it would be counterproductive to risk making use of the discount window. Especially if there were other signs that a bank was not in robust financial condition, it could trigger a potentially deadly run on the bank in the form of a withdrawal of funds by corporations and other customers with large deposits in excess of the FDIC insurance limit (initially $100,000 and later increased to $250,000). Largely because of this fear, in spite of a reduced discount rate and Federal Reserve pleas for banks to avail themselves of credit at the window, few banks were willing to do so. For this reason, the Fed announced creation of the term auction facility (TAF) on December 12, 2007. The first auction was to be held five days later.

Traditional use of the discount window involved overnight borrowing by depository institutions at a specific administered interest rate set by the Fed—the discount rate. In the TAF, the Fed auctioned off rights for banks to borrow on a collateralized basis for an extended period (28 days or 84 days) a limited amount of funds at a competitive interest rate determined in the auction process. The auctions were held every two weeks and the Federal Reserve set a specific limit on the aggregate amount of funds to be loaned. The early auctions were typically fully subscribed, that is, accepted bids exhausted the quota of loans available. Most of the auctions after the end of 2008, as the program was winding down, were not fully subscribed.[7]

Implementation of the TAF apparently solved the stigma problem and the associated unwillingness of banks to borrow from the Fed. This may have been due in part to the relative anonymity of the TAF participants owing to the large number of participants in the auctions.[8] It also may have been due in part to the fact that the settlement date—the date the borrowing bank received access to the funds—was three days after the auction. This meant that troubled banks that needed immediate credit owing to crisis conditions would be unable to immediately avail themselves of the requisite funds through TAF.[9]

The Federal Reserve viewed TAF as having certain advantages over the traditional discount window in times of crisis. First, the auctions would enable the Fed to determine when and how much liquidity was injected into the financial system. Second, the stigma associated with banks' use of the discount window would be largely overcome. Finally, the auction format would enable the Fed to allocate funds to a larger number of sound financial institutions. This wider dispersion of funds across borrowing banks was particularly important in view of the poorly functioning interbank markets during the crisis.

The first TAF auction took place in December 2007. It was fully subscribed at $20 billion. Table 9-2 indicates the amount of TAF credit subscribed at various dates. The offerings were gradually increased to $150 billion by late May 2008 and remained at that level until shortly after the failure of Lehman Brothers in September 2008. The magnitude of the auctions then increased dramatically as interbank lending markets seized up, with the amount subscribed peaking at nearly $500 billion in March 2009. After that date, bank borrowing through TAF steadily declined, reaching $76 billion in late December 2009. The TAF program was successful in increasing liquidity in the financial system, and was terminated in early 2010.

Liquidity Swap Lines or Reciprocal Currency Arrangements (SWPs)

Foreign banks with major funding obligations in U.S. dollars, like U.S. banks, experienced strong need for liquidity in the financial crisis. This need spilled over into the U.S. federal funds market near the end of 2007, creating instability in that market. In the liquidity swaps facility, the Federal Reserve worked with 14 foreign central banks (especially prominent borrowers were the European Central Bank and the Bank of Japan) to establish the swap lines. In these arrangements, the Fed loans dollars to foreign central banks, which, in turn, offer loans to banks in their respective countries. Because the foreign central banks, rather than privately owned foreign commercial banks, are the Fed's counterparties in these loans, credit risk to the Federal Reserve is negligible. Further reducing the credit risk to the Federal Reserve is the fact that the Fed concurrently receives foreign currency equivalent (at the current exchange rate) to the amount of the dollar loan granted in exchange for the loan.

As indicated in Figure 9-6, the magnitude of these dollar loans was relatively small until the Lehman Brothers collapse of September 2008. It then increased dramatically, reaching a peak of more than $580 billion in December 2008. In 2009 these lines declined steadily and the program was terminated in early 2010. However, the Fed reopened this facility in May 2010 as the burgeoning sovereign debt crisis in Greece, Ireland, and other euro-zone countries threatened to plunge Europe and perhaps even the United States back into recession.

Commercial Paper Funding Facility (CPFF)

The interconnectedness of financial markets was vividly demonstrated when Lehman Brothers filed bankruptcy papers in mid-September 2008. The Reserve Primary Fund, a large U.S. money market mutual fund with more than $60 billion of total assets, owned more than $700 million of commercial paper issued by Lehman. The bankruptcy of Lehman Brothers meant the commercial paper it had issued was worthless. The resulting write-down of Reserve Primary Fund's assets forced the firm to "break the buck." This meant that Reserve Primary Fund was unable to honor the commitment to redeem each share upon demand by the shareholders at the face value of $1.[10] Within one day after Lehman's bankruptcy, shareholders attempted to withdraw nearly $25 billion from the Reserve Primary Fund. Less than half of this was actually paid.

The announcement that Primary Reserve Fund was insolvent and had "broken the buck" provoked a run on other money market mutual funds in the United States. Fearing the worst, people began to sell their money market mutual fund shares and park the cash in insured certificates of deposit in banks. The run on MMMFs, in turn, forced these funds to liquidate assets, including large amounts of commercial paper. This severely disrupted the commercial paper market. Yields spiked on this paper, including the paper issued by top-rated corporations. Previous holders of commercial paper sold this paper and placed the funds in ultrasafe U.S. Treasury bills. This caused the "spread"—the difference between the yield on AA-rated commercial paper and U.S. Treasury bills to widen sharply. This spread, which averaged 0.28 percentage points during the more tranquil period from 2004 through 2006 and 0.75 percentage points in 2007, shot up to nearly 3 percentage points shortly after Lehman collapsed.

Because the commercial paper market is a critically important market through which major corporations finance inventories, payrolls, and other needs, the Federal Reserve realized it was imperative to prevent a shutdown of the commercial paper market. This was particularly true in light of the fact that banks—an alternative source of funds for large corporations as well as small businesses—had severely tightened credit availability.

In the CPFF, the Federal Reserve agreed to grant 3-month loans to high-quality corporations at an interest rate somewhat above normal market rates. To align incentives properly and to prevent abuse of this facility, the Fed also charged a significant up-front fee. As indicated in Figure 9-6, use of the CPFF accelerated rapidly after the Lehman collapse, reaching a peak of $350 billion in January 2009. It then rapidly declined to around $15 billion in December 2009. The program was terminated in early 2010. Given the fact that the spreads between commercial paper rates and other money market rates returned from abnormally high levels in October 2008 to normal levels by mid-2009, this program may be considered to have been successful.

Primary Dealer Credit Facility (PDCF)

In conducting open market operations, the Federal Reserve buys and sells securities through designated banks and brokers-dealers known as primary dealers.[11] These firms play an important role in providing liquidity in the massive and critically important U.S. government securities markets. Several markets in which these dealers finance their huge inventories of government securities became impaired during the crisis, with adverse implications for markets in which these dealers were instrumental. The Fed created the PDCF in an effort to maintain orderly functioning of U.S. financial markets.

In the PDCF, the Federal Reserve provided collateralized overnight loans to the primary dealers. The PDCF began lending on March 17, 2008, around the time of the Bear-Stearns crisis. The amount of PDCF loans increased to about $38 billion by early April and then rapidly declined as markets stabilized. PDCF loans then surged to $148 billion in the immediate aftermath of the Lehman crisis of September 2008. After May 2009, borrowing in this facility was nil, and the facility was terminated in early 2010.

Term Asset-Backed Securities Loan Facility (TALF)

As discussed in chapters 4 and 5, credit card loans, student loans, auto loans, and other types of loans have been securitized in recent decades—bundled into large blocks known as asset-back securities that are sold to large investors like pension funds, life insurance companies, and foreign entities. This advance in financial technology has resulted in more credit being made available to households, students, car buyers, and others on more favorable terms than would have otherwise prevailed. During the Great Crisis, however, strong investor resistance to these asset-backed securities resulted in a large increase in the yield spread on AAA-rated asset-backed securities relative to Treasury bonds, and a massive reduction in new issuance of these instruments. This, in turn, threatened to severely curtail availability of credit to households, students, car buyers, and small firms.

TALF was initiated in November 2008 as the Fed agreed to make available up to $200 billion of loans of one-year maturity to issuers of these securities. These loans are collateralized by the market value of the AAA-rated asset-backed securities. The TALF expanded rather steadily from less than $1 billion in March 2009 to more than $47 billion by the end of that year. Given continuing problems in asset-backed securities markets, this liquidity program, unlike most others, was still in operation in October, 2010.

Asset-Backed Commercial Paper and Money Market Mutual Fund Facility (AMLF)

At the time the Fed created the CPFF following the demise of Lehman Brothers and Reserve Primary Fund in fall 2008, it also established the asset-backed commercial paper and money market mutual fund facility (AMLF). The purpose of AMLF is to grant loans to U.S. depository institutions for the purpose of buying high-quality asset-backed commercial paper from money market mutual funds. This was intended to serve two purposes: to stabilize the important commercial paper market and to assist money market funds in meeting redemption demands from shareholders by boosting demand for the commercial paper that the MMMFs were being forced to unload. Loans to banks in this market increased from $22 billion in the third week of September 2008 to $151 billion less than a month later. It declined to less than $1 billion by August 2009 and has been negligible since then.

V. Federal Reserve Initiatives to Reduce Long-Term Interest Rates

The Federal Reserve is capable of exerting dominant influence over short-term interest rates, but has less influence on long-term interest rates such as mortgage rates and corporate and government bond yields. As the recession deepened by the beginning of 2009, with the Fed having already set its FFR target at 0–0.25 percent, one of the Federal Reserve's new initiatives was to aggressively work to push down long-term interest rates. If successful, such measures would stimulate expenditures by firms and households. Investment expenditures by business firms on plant, equipment, and research and development depend in part on long-term interest rates, especially yields on long-term corporate bonds. If the Fed could lower such yields through direct intervention in long-term debt markets and other measures, this would stimulate investment spending.

If the Fed could bring down mortgage rates, this would help households and boost economic activity through several channels. First, by lowering monthly payments on new mortgages, it would stimulate new demand in the housing market and thereby help end the vicious cycle of falling house prices, home foreclosures and repossessions, liquidation of houses, and further declines in home prices. And millions of existing homeowners might be able to refinance mortgages at lower rates. The reduced monthly mortgage payments would not only allow more households to make their payments and avoid foreclosure, but also free up cash for households to spend on other needs, thus boosting economic activity in nonhousing sectors.

Economic theory indicates that current long-term interest rates are strongly influenced by current expectations of short-term interest rates that will prevail in the future. For example, the yield on a 20-year bond is closely related to the average of the current yield on a one-year bond and the yields currently expected to prevail on one-year bonds over the course of the ensuing 19 years.[12] This means if the Federal Reserve is able to influence the public's current expectations of *future* short-term interest rates, it can influence *current* long-term rates such as mortgage rates and corporate bond yields. This explains the Fed's motive for including in each of the publicly issued directives of the FOMC during 2009 and 2010 the statement that it expects to "maintain very low short-term rates for an extended period." This helps keep long-term interest rates as low as possible while the housing market and economy are severely depressed.

More importantly, the Federal Reserve took the unprecedented step in early 2009 of committing itself by the early part of 2010 to buying, in a relatively short period, up to $1,250 billion of mortgage-backed bonds as well as $500 billion of long-term Treasury securities and bonds issued by federal agencies. This constituted an enormous magnitude of bond purchases, far exceeding any previous purchases or sales of securities by a central bank anywhere in the world. The mortgage-backed securities (MBS) market has evolved over the past 30 years as a crucial mechanism for financing home construction. As house prices fell sharply in recent years, the value of these MBS and instruments derived from them declined and the private market for them essentially shut down. Private-sector purchases of these bonds slowed dramatically, potentially inflicting severe damage to prospects for revival of the housing market and construction industry. In buying huge blocks of these MBS, the Fed sought not only to hold down mortgage rates, but also to get this important market functioning again.

Figure 9-7 illustrates the changing composition of securities owned by the Federal Reserve in 2009 and early 2010. Note the huge increase in Federal Reserve holdings of MBS, as well as federal agency bonds and longer-term Treasury securities, that commenced in early 2009.

Massive purchases of mortgage-backed bonds and other long-term bonds by the Fed, together with its efforts to lower the public's expectations of short-term interest rates in the near and medium term, appears to have been successful. The 30-year conventional mortgage rate fell from an average of 5.4 percent in June 2009 to 4.9 percent in December and to 4.5 percent in July 2010. Also, the spread between the conventional mortgage rate and the 20-year U.S. Treasury bond yield narrowed appreciably after the Fed commenced buying MBS in early 2009. A 2010 study estimates that this Federal Reserve program, by reducing the stock of these long-term assets available in the market, and by improving

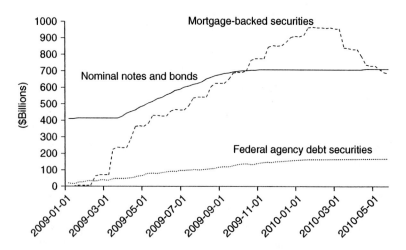

Figure 9-7   Federal Reserve holdings of long-term debt instruments.
Source: Federal Reserve System.

liquidity, reduced yields on MBS by some 50–100 basis points.[13] Because of the perceived success of the Fed program of long-term asset purchases, and because the U.S. economy slowed appreciably in the second half of 2010, it became widely anticipated in fall 2010 that the Fed would initiate a second round of "quantitative easing" in the final month or two of 2010.

VI. Conclusion

Hints of impending problems for the United States and other countries began to emerge as house prices declined significantly in 2006. A year later, these problems began to come home to roost as very large-scale debt instruments built from individual home mortgages began to decline sharply in value. At this point, virtually no one—including Nobel laureates and leaders of central banks around the world— anticipated how severe the consequences for homeowners, workers, and financial institutions would turn out to be. No one imagined that more than 8 million U.S. jobs would be lost by the end of 2009, that millions would lose their homes, and that nearly all 50 U.S. states and numerous foreign nations would be forced to impose draconian budget cuts.

The Federal Reserve began reducing short-term interest rates a couple of months before the U.S. recession officially began in December 2007. By the end of 2008 the Fed had dropped its short-term interest rate target to its lowest level in history—0 to 0.25 percent. However, "Monday-morning quarterbacks" are correct in charging that the Fed was initially behind the curve. It is now clear that it would have been helpful had the Fed reduced short-term interest rates more quickly and even more aggressively than it did. Accordingly, a tough grader might assign a grade of B minus to the conduct of Federal Reserve policy in the year immediately preceding the collapse of Lehman Brothers, a grade far higher than that received by the Fed for its horrendous performance during the Great Depression.

However, beginning in the fall of 2008 as the crisis reached full bore, Federal Reserve policy can only be described as innovative, timely, and aggressive. Indeed, Fed policy was brilliantly conducted. As borrowers and lenders became increasingly fearful, and normal channels of financial intermediation began to shut down, the Bernanke-led Federal Reserve stepped up very quickly and aggressively to implement a multitude of new initiatives to keep the credit flowing. Bernanke helped coordinate the actions of leading central banks around the world as policies were implemented to combat the crisis. As inevitably happens in severe crises, heightened caution on the part of banks and the public caused the money supply multipliers to contract severely in the fall of 2008. The Fed stepped in with aggressive lending programs, followed by heavy purchases of mortgage-backed bonds, federal agency securities, and Treasury bonds to dramatically increase bank reserves and the monetary base to prevent a potentially destructive contraction of the U.S. money supply. Deflation of the nation's price level was averted.

The Federal Reserve is culpable, especially in the latter years of Chairman Alan Greenspan's term that ended in 2006, for maintaining interest rates too low, and especially for eschewing measures to rein in the wildly egregious developments in the mortgage markets. However, its performance in the period since the crisis reached full force in September 2008 deserves very high marks.

Chapter 10

The Federal Reserve's Exit Strategy and the Threat of Inflation

I. Introduction

The National Bureau of Economic Research ultimately dated the end of the Great Recession at June 2009. Nevertheless, the nation's unemployment rate stubbornly remained between 9 and 10 percent for at least the next 16 months, the highest rate in a quarter century. About 8 million fewer Americans held jobs in October 2010 than in December 2007. Despite the considerable slack remaining in the U.S. economy, economists debated whether the Fed was overdue in unwinding its policy of extraordinary stimulus. While some economists worried about deflation, others feared the stage was set for an era of high inflation. The unprecedented expansion of the Federal Reserve's balance sheet during 2008–2010 had more than doubled the monetary base and multiplied bank reserves by a factor of 25. Excess reserves in the banks increased from less than $2 billion at the beginning of 2008 to more than $950 billion in October, 2010.

As Milton Friedman famously stated, "inflation is always and everywhere a monetary phenomenon." While M1 and M2 increased only at relatively modest rates in the period extending from the beginning of 2008 to the fall of 2010, many feared that as banks restored their diminished capital and regained confidence, the huge quantity of excess reserves could lead to an explosive increase in bank lending. This would ignite unprecedented growth of the money supply, potentially unleashing severe inflation.

Some critics of the extraordinarily expansionary Federal Reserve policy seemed to believe that there is a mechanical relationship between money growth and inflation, irrespective of the amount of unemployment and idle industrial capacity in the economy. Other critics acknowledged that this view is fallacious, yet worried that once the U.S. economy regained solid forward momentum and unemployment declined appreciably, the Federal Reserve would find it difficult—perhaps in large part because of political forces—to withdraw or isolate the excess reserves with sufficient speed to prevent a serious bout of inflation down the road. Given the considerable uncertainty about future conditions, they feared that the Fed would err in the direction of too much stimulus. In part, this fear stemmed from the knowledge that Chairman Ben Bernanke, a keen student of Federal Reserve policy in the Great Depression, was determined not to repeat the errors of the 1930s. One of those errors was the decision in 1936 to eliminate the burgeoning excess reserves through a major hike in reserve requirements. Economists believe this decision was instrumental in nipping the ongoing economic recovery from the Great Depression and triggering a severe recession in 1937–1938.

This chapter examines the prospects that the course of inflation in the 2010–2020 decade will be appreciably higher than the 2.5 percent average annual rate experienced during 1995–2010. The alternative methods the Fed has at its disposal to prevent such a rise in inflation—by draining the excess reserves from the banking system at the appropriate time or inducing banks to continue to hold these balances rather than using them to expand loans—will also be evaluated.

II. Okun's Law and the Prospects for Higher Inflation

A useful way to think about the outlook for inflation over a forthcoming three- or four-year period is to focus on the likely evolution of the gap between actual and potential real GDP, or the corresponding gap between the actual unemployment rate and the nonaccelerating inflation rate of unemployment (NAIRU). Conventional economic theory indicates that the degree of inflationary pressure in a market economy is fundamentally related to the extent of excess capacity in product markets and the degree of slack in labor markets. When excess industrial capacity is high and the unemployment rate is far above the NAIRU, market forces normally dictate that upward pressure on wages and prices is nil. Barring significant adverse supply shocks, firms are typically not facing significantly rising costs of production. And in instances in which costs do rise, firms experience difficulty in passing these higher costs on to the consumer through higher prices. In circumstances of substantial economic slack, the nation's underlying inflation rate typically declines.

Conversely, as the economy gains strength and approaches full employment of labor resources and full utilization of industrial capacity, wage and price level pressures increasingly assert themselves. Wages and other production costs are rising, and market demand is sufficiently strong that firms are increasingly able to make price hikes stick.

The difference version of Okun's law provides a useful method for evaluating whether the economic expansion that began in mid-2009, fueled by powerful monetary and fiscal stimulus, would soon lead to increased inflationary pressures by eliminating the gap between actual and potential GDP. This is expressed in equation 10-1.[1]

Change in URATE = alpha + beta (% change in RGDP)   (10-1)

In this equation, URATE represents the nation's unemployment rate and RGDP stands for real GDP. This form of Okun's law indicates that the change in the nation's unemployment rate over the course of one year depends on the growth rate of real GDP. The parameters alpha and beta spell out the details of this relationship. The equation indicates that if there is no change in real GDP over a 12-month period, the unemployment rate will increase by an amount indicated by alpha. Alpha is positive owing to the fact that the labor force grows over time and if real GDP remains constant, there will be no net additional jobs for the new entrants to the labor force. Unemployment will increase. Furthermore, even if the labor force remains constant over time, productivity or output per hour of work trends consistently upward owing to improving technology and other forces. This means that if real GDP remains constant, unemployment will rise over time because fewer workers are needed to produce the given level of output. In this instance, firms will lay off workers and unemployment will increase.

In essence, to maintain the unemployment rate at any given level, real GDP must increase by roughly the sum of the labor force and productivity growth rates. If the labor force grows 1 percent per year and productivity grows 2 percent per year, real GDP must grow 3 percent annually to keep the unemployment rate constant. Real GDP growth in excess of 3 percent will result in a declining unemployment rate, on average; growth at rates below 3 percent will be accompanied by an increasing rate of unemployment.

One may interpret the parameter beta as indicating the effect that each one percentage point difference in the growth rate of real GDP has on the unemployment rate. If beta is 0.40, the equation indicates that had the growth rate of real GDP been higher by one percentage point, the unemployment rate would have been lower by 0.40 percentage points after one year. Beta is sometimes referred to as "Okun's coefficient."

We can estimate the growth rate of real GDP required to keep the unemployment rate constant by setting the change in URATE equal to zero and solving for the requisite growth rate of real GDP. By doing so, our answer is minus alpha/beta. Beta is negative because higher output growth is associated with a lower rate of unemployment. Hence, alpha/beta is a positive number and if alpha is 1.20 and beta is negative 0.40, real GDP growth of 3 percent per year would keep the unemployment rate constant over time.

If we study the actual historical relationship between real GDP growth and the change in the nation's unemployment rate, we can estimate the size of alpha and beta. Figure 10-1 shows the percentage change in U.S. real GDP relative to four quarters earlier for each of the 241 quarters extending from 1950:1 to 2010:1, along with the change in the unemployment rate over the same one-year period.

The point plotted in the extreme right-hand (southeast) part of the figure indicates that in the four quarters ending in the fourth quarter of 1950, real GDP grew at the phenomenal annual rate of about 13 percent and the unemployment rate declined by 2.3 percentage points (from 6.6 to 4.3 percent). At the other (northwest) extreme part of the figure, real GDP declined at an annual rate of 3.8 percent in the year extending from

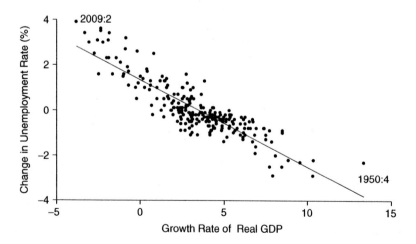

Figure 10-1 Annual rate of output growth and change in unemployment rate, 1950–2010.

Source: Federal Reserve Bank of St. Louis, FRED database.

2008:2 to 2009:2, and the unemployment rate jumped by 3.9 percentage points over this period (from 5.6 to 9.5 percent).

The regression line fitted through these points is shown in the figure and is indicated in equation 10-2.

$$\text{Change in URATE} = 1.34 - .385 \text{ (\% change in RGDP)} \qquad (10\text{-}2)$$
$$R^2 = .76$$

Both the constant term (1.34) and the slope term or Okun's coefficient (–.385) are statistically significant at very rigorous levels, and visual inspection of the figure indicates that there is a close relationship between the nation's growth rate and changes in its unemployment rate, as indicated by the R^2 of .76. The equation also indicates that, on average over this 60-year period, if real output remained constant for a year, the nation's unemployment rate increased by 1.34 percentage points in the same period. In addition, we can solve for the growth rate required to maintain the unemployment rate constant during this long period, on average. Setting the change in URATE equal to zero and solving for the requisite growth rate of RGDP, we get 1.34/.385, or 3.48 percent. This is the the point measured on the horizontal axis of Figure 10-1 where the fitted regression line intersects a horizontal line drawn through the origin. In this 60-year period, when real output increased more rapidly than 3.48 percent per year, the unemployment rate typically declined. When output increased more slowly, the nation's unemployment rate increased, on average.

This relationship between real output and unemployment changes over time in response to changes in the trend of productivity growth, labor force growth, and other factors. For example, if we examine the relationship between 1983:1 and 2009:3, the following regression is obtained:[2]

$$\text{Change in URATE} = 1.37 - .465 \text{ (\% change in Real GDP)} \qquad (10\text{-}3)$$
$$R^2 = .77$$

From this equation, one can infer that a constant real output maintained over four quarters was associated with an increase in the unemployment rate of nearly 1.4 percentage points, on average. Given the estimate of Okun's coefficient of negative .465, the output growth rate required to maintain the unemployment rate constant in this period was 1.37/.465, or 2.95 percent per year, on average. These equations prepare us for evaluating the threat of inflation in the early years following the Great Recession.

III. Prospects for Inflation: The Optimistic View

Given the nation's unemployment rate of 9.6 percent in September 2010 as a starting point, it is useful to think about the implications of the findings reported in equation 10-3 for the likely unemployment rate two, three, and four years after that date, that is, in September 2012, 2013, and 2014. This, in turn, makes it possible to form a judgment about the risk of higher inflation in those years. It seems unlikely, for example, that severe and sustained inflation is likely to coexist with an unemployment rate appreciably above 6 percent. To further organize thinking about this issue, consider that the annual output growth rates of real GDP growth in the first year, first two years, and first three years of the nine postrecession expansions since 1950 (prior to the Great Recession) averaged 4.9, 4.3, and 4.0 percent, respectively. Before the 1990s, early years of economic expansions were typically quite robust, with business cycles tending to exhibit V-shaped patterns.[3] The recoveries from the two most recent recessions preceding the 2007–2009 downturn were relatively anemic, however. Average annual output growth in the first three years following the 1990–1991 and 2001 recessions averaged only 3.2 percent and 2.4 percent, respectively. These instances became known as "jobless recoveries" because output growth was not sufficiently strong in the early years of the expansions to appreciably reduce the unemployment rate.

An examination of Table 6-1 (p. 101) suggests that the previous recessions most similar in severity to the recent Great Recession were the contractions of 1973–1975 and 1981–1982. The latter recession is considered to be the most severe post–World War II downturn prior to the Great Recession. Following the 1981–1982 recession, real GDP expanded at a very solid 5.2 percent average annual growth rate in the ensuing three years. However, given the damage done by the Great Crisis to the nation's wealth, banking system, and credit machinery, few economists expect the United States to recover from the Great Recession at such rapid rates.

Residential construction will likely be subdued for some years following the Great Recession due to the large numbers of homes facing foreclosure or in arrears on mortgage payments. Nonresidential construction also faces problems. Consumption spending will be constrained by the need for households to step up savings to restore wealth lost due to the decline in home prices and retirement accounts. Another important factor is bank lending (including shadow-bank lending), which declined persistently through 2009 and 2010 as the process of deleveraging continued. Additional fiscal stimulus beyond the $787 billion program enacted in early 2009 is limited by political forces stemming from the enormous budget deficits facing the United States.[4] The European sovereign debt crisis that erupted in 2010 led to imposition of severe austerity programs in Britain and numerous euro-currency nations, auguring adversely for U.S. exports in the coming years. In contrast to the 5.6 percent real GDP growth experienced in the first year of recovery from the 1981–1982 recession, the U.S. real GDP expanded at an annual average rate of only 3.0 percent in the first year following the Great Recession, that is, from mid-2009 to mid-2010. And even this meager performance was boosted by several temporary fiscal measures that have been terminated, including a tax credit for new home purchases and the "cash for clunkers" program.

Using equation 10-3 as our framework of analysis, assume that real GDP grows 4 percent annually from September 2010 to September 2013. According to the equation, the unemployment rate would decline by 0.49 percentage points per year, or a total of approximately 1.5 percentage points over the three-year period. This means that in September 2013 the nation's unemployment rate would stand at 8.1 percent. In this scenario, the unemployment rate would still be 7.6 percent in September 2014 and 7.1 percent in September 2015. Even in the unlikely event the economy were to expand at the robust rate of 5 percent annually, equation 10-3 suggests that the unemployment rate would decline by 2.9 percentage points over three years, leaving the rate at 6.7 percent in September 2013. Few economists expect the NAIRU to be that high any time soon, or the economy to grow in such robust fashion.

The upshot is that, given the enormous amount of apparent excess capacity prevailing in the U.S. economy, inflation optimists believe it is difficult to imagine demand in product markets pushing firmly against capacity and laying the groundwork for a major increase in the nation's inflation rate before 2014 or 2015. This suggests that fears of a near or medium-term upsurge of inflation are likely misplaced. Indeed, viewed from the perspective of fall 2010, an increasing number of economists were viewing deflation as a more likely outcome than significantly higher inflation.

IV. Prospects for Inflation: The Pessimistic View

Some noted economists as well as numerous pundits believe that inflation is headed sharply higher in the years ahead. Some analysts believe the Congressional Budget Office (CBO) estimates of potential real GDP and the NAIRU are flawed, overstating the size of the output gap—that is, the amount by which potential GDP exceeds actual GDP. If so, the

Fed might inadvertently maintain its policy of stimulus too long, thus committing a policy error that unleashes higher inflation. Others believe that worldwide political forces will dictate higher inflation as the most practical remedy for the dilemma stemming from the vast buildup of public and private-sector debt in the past decade in the United States, Britain, euro-currency nations, and many other countries. In this view, the Fed may either be a willing accomplice or be pressured to acquiesce in a forthcoming rise in inflation that will be deliberately fostered to ease the burden of debt. The monetary tinder is in place (in the form of enormous excess reserves) for a massive increase in the money supply in the near future, and many fear the Fed will inevitably err in the direction of being slow to implement restraint.

Differing Estimates of Potential GDP and the NAIRU

Some critics point out that the CBO estimates of potential GDP are higher than some alternative estimates, and the CBO estimates of the NAIRU are correspondingly relatively low. Hence, the CBO estimates of the magnitude of the output gap of recent years are larger than several other estimates. A recent survey of published work on estimating potential GDP indicates that while the nonpartisan CBO output gap estimate for the first quarter of 2009 was negative 6.2 percent, other estimates ranged from negative 4.9 percent to as low as negative 2 percent.[5] These figures suggest that solid economic growth after 2010 would likely result in the economy reaching capacity output and full employment much sooner than the CBO estimates would indicate.

Economists attempt to estimate potential GDP by using economic and statistical models. The CBO uses a framework that estimates both the future productivity of the labor force and the size of the labor force at full employment. These two estimates lead to the CBO estimate of potential GDP. To derive its estimate of workers' future productivity, the CBO employs such factors as education and experience of workers, along with available capital and technology. These forces are uncertain and therefore so are estimates of potential GDP.

The CBO methodology leads to estimates of potential GDP that are characterized by inertia—they trend upward rather smoothly and do not fluctuate sharply in the short run. Alternative approaches to estimating potential GDP assume that its determinants—productivity growth and labor force growth—are constantly in flux. In this view, potential GDP exhibits considerable short-run variability—its growth rate changes markedly over time and its *level* may even decline at times. For example, the huge energy price shocks of the 1970s likely reduced the nation's effective capital stock by rendering part of it obsolete. Because capital goods are energy-intensive, sharply higher energy prices signal firms to substitute labor for capital. This reduction in the capital/labor ratio lowers the productivity of workers. In this way, the energy shock lowered the level of potential GDP and the magnitude of the negative output gap.[6]

It seems intuitively plausible that severe financial crises like the 2007–2009 blockbuster reduce not only actual GDP but also potential GDP. There are several forces at work. One factor is that severe financial impairment of thousands of firms along with the banking sector leads to a major cutback in the willingness and/or ability of firms to invest in new equipment as well as research and development. The process of financial intermediation may be sufficiently impaired that firms are unable to fund prospective investment projects. For example, most medium and small firms do not have access to the direct credit markets in which large corporations obtain funds by issuing bonds and other debt instruments directly to those with surplus funds. Instead, small firms rely on bank loans. During and after periods of crisis, banks severely tighten lending standards even in the face of extraordinary efforts by the Federal Reserve to make funds available to banks at very low interest rates.[7]

Large corporations that do have access to direct credit markets may be deterred from borrowing in times of crisis by appreciably higher bond yields resulting from elevated risk premiums in corporate bond yields relative to safer government bonds. These factors help account for the contraction in business investment in plant and equipment during the crisis of 2007–2009. A reduction in investment spending slows the growth of the nation's capital stock and tends to reduce productivity growth. This reduces the growth of potential GDP, and in extreme instances may even cause it to decline.

Also, unemployment increases sharply both in magnitude and in duration in the aftermath of financial crises. Work habits, skills, and motivation of unemployed workers tend to atrophy in such circumstances and the potential future productivity of these unemployed workers may decline. In the fall of 2010, the long-term unemployment rate—those continuously out of work for more than 26 weeks—was nearly double the rate experienced at the low point of the severe 1981–1982 recession. This also could lead to a sharp slowdown in the growth rate of potential GDP, and perhaps even a decline in its level.

Lastly, the huge expansion of housing construction during the bubble years means that excessive resources were allocated to that sector. It may take several years for these resources to be reallocated to other sectors of the economy. This structural problem suggests that potential GDP may have been reduced and the NAIRU may have been elevated by the collapse of the housing bubble. In fact, this analysis can be extended to the U.S. financial sector, which also became bloated during the housing and credit bubbles, as a disproportionate share of the nation's brightest and most ambitious students were lured into Wall Street careers by the enormous salary prospects. Following the collapse of the twin bubbles and the demise of large investment banks, it is likely that economic forces are leading to a significant contraction in the financial industry.

These forces suggest that the CBO estimates of potential GDP may be too high and the corresponding estimates of the NAIRU may be too low.[8] The upshot is that the level of potential GDP and the NAIRU are highly uncertain. As the nation's unemployment rate recedes toward 6 percent, the Federal Reserve will need to be vigilant to look for signs of labor shortages and other bottlenecks that signal an imminent rise in inflationary pressures.

Politics, Monetization, Money Growth, and Inflation

Most economists agree that severe and persistent inflation is overwhelmingly the result of monetary forces. There has never been an instance of severe and sustained inflation that has not been accompanied by rapid growth of the money supply. Strong support for the monetary explanation of inflation is marshaled when one looks at the relationship between money growth and inflation in a number of countries that have experienced markedly different rates of inflation over the years.

A definite pattern exists in which countries with very high rates of money growth over a long period of years systematically exhibit higher rates of inflation than countries with low money growth rates. For example, Turkey experienced both average money growth and inflation rates in excess of 50 percent annually over the 20-year period ending in 2009. Nigeria and Uganda experienced average money growth rates in excess of 30 percent annually, and inflation above 20 percent per year over this same period. With the exception of China, very few countries exhibiting average annual money growth in excess of 20 per cent escaped double-digit inflation. Japan, which kept money growth to about 3 percent per year, experienced inflation averaging less than 1 percent annually over the 20-year period.[9]

Countries exhibiting very high inflation are typically nations with relatively unstable governments, poorly developed financial markets, ineffective tax systems, and central banks that lack political independence from government officials. In such circumstances, there is a strong tendency for central governments to exhibit very large budget deficits and rely on the central bank to purchase much of the new debt issued each year.

When a government pays for its purchases of goods and services, it essentially writes checks on its account with the central bank. The recipients of the checks deposit them in private banks. Demand deposits, M1, and M2 increase. If the government finances these expenditures through taxes, the public writes checks to the government to pay these taxes, reducing bank demand deposits, M1 and M2. Hence, an increase in government expenditures financed through higher taxes does not increase the money supply. Similarly, when a government issues bonds to the public to finance a budget deficit, bond buyers write checks to the government. The resulting reduction in bank demand deposits cancels out the monetary expansion from the government expenditures, and once again there is no effect on the nation's money supply.

However, when the government finances a deficit by selling bonds to the central bank, this borrowing transaction does not reduce the money supply because no checks are written on private banks to buy the bonds. The check is written by the central bank, and deposits in private banks do not decline. Hence, the net effect of government deficit-spending financed through sales of bonds to the central bank is an increase in the nation's money supply. In this case, the central bank is said to *monetize* the deficit. If conducted on a large scale, the process of monetizing government deficits inevitably leads to rapid money growth and high inflation.[10] Those nations with rudimentary tax systems, primitive financial markets, and subservient central banks typically resort to chronic monetization of deficits.

The U.S. government has been negligent and irresponsible in the new millennium in allowing enormous and potentially long-lasting budget deficits to develop. In fact, the magnitude of the U.S. budget deficit relative to GDP in 2009 and 2010 appeared almost as large as that of Greece, the epicenter of the simmering sovereign debt crisis in Europe. Many households have also been fiscally irresponsible in incurring debt to purchase unaffordable homes, cars, and other items. Because of this public and private debt crisis, and because the political independence of the monetary policy process may be vulnerable to Congressional inroads in the postcrisis environment, some economists fear that this monetization scenario could very well play out in the United States in the next decade. This would bring with it higher inflation.

Inflation has many negative consequences. It arbitrarily and unfairly redistributes the nation's income and wealth, reduces economic efficiency by misallocating resources, and adversely affects investment spending and long-term economic growth. However, inflation does reduce the burden of debt, and extraordinarily high quantities of debt have been taken on by households, firms, and the U.S. government in the twenty-first century. Political forces could dictate that the burden of this debt be reduced through higher inflation.

One example of why higher inflation may be viewed as politically beneficial in current circumstances is that millions of households that took out mortgages during the 2000–2006 period remain underwater on these debts. Their mortgage balance exceeds the value of their home. As the economy gains strength during recovery from the Great Recession and the Federal Reserve boosts interest rates to restore them to normal levels in an effort to keep inflation down, mortgage rates will increase. This means house prices will either fall or rise more slowly than would otherwise be the case, thus exacerbating the hardship for millions of homeowners, mortgage lenders, and the construction industry. In this case, pressure is likely to be brought to bear on the Fed by the congressional and executive branches of government to refrain from boosting interest rates. This suggests the Fed may err in being slow or timid in raising interest rates, thus allowing inflation to increase.

A second example involves the U.S. government's own budget deficit and burgeoning debt. Both of these are on paths that, if sustained, will lead to a U.S. sovereign debt crisis such as experienced by countries like Argentina and Mexico over the years, and by Greece and Ireland more recently. Ideally, our political leaders would attack the problem through cuts in entitlements and other forms of government expenditures, along with tax hikes. Politicians understand, however, that their chances of being elected are severely compromised if they propose serious methods to fix the deficit problem. A more highly stimulated economy with associated higher inflation would bring in more tax revenues and work to reduce the budget deficit.[11] Hence, pressure is likely to be brought to bear by our elected officials on the Federal Reserve to get some inflation going.

The Federal Reserve and the Raw Material for Rapid Money Growth

As indicated in chapter 9, the huge increase in the Federal Reserve balance sheet that took place as the Fed aggressively battled the Great Crisis and its aftermath created the raw material for an extremely rapid expansion in M1 and M2. The expansion of Federal Reserve lending programs, followed by the Fed's huge acquisition of mortgage-backed bonds and other financial instruments, boosted bank reserves from approximately

$42 billion in January 2008 to more than $1,100 billion in fall 2010. The monetary base expanded in the same period from $820 billion to approximately $2,000 billion, an increase of nearly 150 percent. In the event that the money supply multipliers had remained stable, M1 and M2 would have also increased by roughly 150 percent.

Of course, what happened was that the scramble for liquidity resulted in severe declines in the money multipliers (m1 and m2). The willingness of banks to hold excess reserves increased dramatically. In the money multiplier framework, the ratio of excess reserves to demand deposits increased by a factor of more than 500, sharply reducing the m1 and m2 multipliers. In spite of the huge percentage increase in the monetary base, M1 and M2 increased at annual rates of approximately only 10 and 6 percent, respectively, in the period from January 2008 to October 2010.

Eventually, as normal economic conditions reassert themselves, it is expected that banks will reduce their excess reserve holdings toward normal levels. This means money multipliers will revert also to normal levels—they will increase sharply. To prevent a highly inflationary increase in the monetary aggregates, the Fed would need to take actions either to dramatically reduce reserves and the monetary base, or to induce banks to continue to willingly hold an abnormally large quantity of excess reserves. That is, the Fed will have to either sharply reduce the monetary base, implement measures to prevent the natural reversion of the money multipliers to normal levels, or pursue some combination of both actions. The next section will examine the methods and plans which the Federal Reserve has in place to prevent an inflationary surge in the money supply.

V. The Federal Reserve's Exit Strategy

The Federal Reserve has adequate tools to ensure that the abundance of excess reserves in the banking system following the Great Recession does not lead to an inflationary surge in bank lending and the money supply. There are four tools the Fed has at its command to employ at the appropriate time, and the Fed is likely to use several of these in combination. First, the Fed could implement its traditional tool of outright sales of assets, including its holdings of short- and long-term Treasury securities, agency securities, and MBS. Second, the Fed could engage in large-scale reverse repurchase agreements ("reverse repos"). Third, by offering attractive interest rates, the Fed could induce banks to hold term deposits at the Fed as an alternative to lending the funds to private borrowers. Finally, by managing the rate of interest the Fed pays banks on reserves, the Fed can induce banks to voluntarily hold large quantities of excess reserves rather than lending them out. The first three of these alternatives would drain reserves from the banks, thus reducing the monetary base. The fourth option would be used to induce banks to deliberately hold more reserves rather than lending them out, thus preventing an inflationary increase in the money multiplier. All options would boost short-term interest rates. Each of these alternatives will be discussed in turn.[12]

Open Market Sales of Fed Assets

In selling such assets as Treasury bills and bonds, agency securities, and MBS, the Federal Reserve receives payment from the buyers and collects by debiting the reserve accounts of the banks on which the checks are written. Bank reserves and the monetary base fall dollar-for-dollar with such Fed security sales. Selling off part of its enormous holdings of securities would be a straightforward way for the Fed to boost interest rates and reduce the size of its balance sheet, along with bank reserves and the monetary base.

A problem with this approach in the circumstances facing the Fed in the current postcrisis environment is that the predominant portion of the Fed's assets consists of MBS and long-term Treasury and agency securities. In 2010, less than 1 percent of the value of Federal Reserve securities owned outright consisted of Treasury bills. Thus, using this tool to appreciably drain reserves would necessarily involve the Fed selling long-term securities. Heavy sales by the Fed of MBS or other long-term bonds would likely push up mortgage rates and thus hinder the recovery of the severely depressed and fragile housing sector as well as adversely impacting the balance sheets of banks and other lenders that hold mortgages and mortgage-related securities.

Given the apparent success of the Fed in lowering mortgage rates by buying huge quantities of MBS in 2009 and 2010, the Fed is understandably reluctant to reverse this policy as long as the fragile conditions remain in place. In fact, the Fed fears that even an announcement of its intention to commence selling MBS could cause market instability. For this reason, Chairman Bernanke has emphasized that the Fed's exit strategy will lead with the other instruments mentioned above. Reduction of the Fed's enormous MBS portfolio may occur naturally and slowly as individual MBS mature. It is quite possible that elimination of the Fed's holdings of these securities may take a decade or even longer.

Engaging in Reverse Repurchase Agreements

In a reverse repo, the Fed sells U.S. government securities with an agreement to repurchase the securities at a specific future date and price. In the initial sale, the Fed collects payment by debiting the reserve account of the bank on which the buyer of the securities made payment. This reduces reserves and the monetary base on a dollar-for-dollar basis in the same way that an outright sale of securities by the Fed does. In a tri-party reverse-repo transaction, the seller of securities (in this case the Fed) posts collateral—typically Treasury securities—with the dealer involved in the transaction.

Given the enormous magnitude of transactions the Federal Reserve is contemplating in its exit strategy, it is not clear that the government securities dealers can handle the requisite volume. And the Fed may not have sufficient collateral in the form of Treasury securities. Much depends on the speed with which the Fed ultimately finds it desirable to reduce its balance sheet. Given the enormous quantity of MBS owned by the Fed, a very large volume of reserves could be removed through reverse repo transactions that use MBS as collateral. Accordingly, to facilitate an increase in the scale of such operations, the Fed has been examining ways to widen the number of counterparties with whom such transactions can be conducted. The Fed has explored the viability of selling large quantities of securities. One possibility under consideration is conducting reverse repos with money market mutual funds.

Initiating the Term Deposit Facility

In this plan, the Fed will offer attractive interest rates to banks that agree to convert a portion of their excess reserves into term deposits at the Fed. These deposits would not be counted as reserves and would be locked up for the term—perhaps three or six months—and thus unavailable to the banks for short-term liquidity purposes. These term deposits are analogous to certificates of deposits held by customers of commercial banks. The term deposits would be auctioned by the Fed in large magnitudes at regular intervals, permitting the Fed to precisely determine the quantity of term deposits offered and the associated reduction in reserves. Market forces will likely dictate that the yield on term deposits be slightly higher than the rate the Fed pays banks on excess reserves, just as rates paid bank customers on short-term certificates of deposit are slightly higher than those paid on passbook savings accounts. Like reverse repo transactions, each dollar involved in the transaction reduces bank reserves by one dollar. This tool might be superior to reverse repos in that it requires less frequent day-to-day activity by the Fed in the markets, thus being more conducive to market stability.

Paying Banks Interest on Reserves

For decades, the Federal Reserve requested authorization from Congress to pay interest to banks on reserves. Largely because the overwhelming portion of net income earned by the Federal Reserve is routinely turned over to the Treasury, and because payment of interest on bank reserves would reduce the Fed's earnings, the proposal was traditionally rejected. However, in 2008 Congress finally authorized the Fed to pay interest on bank reserves. This is likely to be an important tool for the Fed in the extraordinary conditions the Fed faces as the economy recovers and the Fed unwinds its bloated balance sheet in coming years.

Given the extremely low prevailing federal funds rate (FFR), together with the unprecedented magnitude of excess reserves in the banking system, the Fed is concerned about its ability to boost rates when the appropriate time comes without selling a very large quantity of assets. As indicated, the Fed is unwilling to risk appreciably higher mortgage rates under fragile economic circumstances. It fears that liquidating significant blocks of its assets, which consist overwhelmingly of long-term bonds, would significantly push up mortgage rates. At the prevailing very low FFR, bank demand for excess reserves is likely very elastic with respect to the FFR. This means that to boost the FFR significantly through normal techniques, the Fed would need to sell a large amount of long-term assets. As indicated, the Fed is reluctant to do this.

The payment of interest on bank reserves enables the Fed to place a floor under the federal funds rate and more accurately maintain the FFR at higher target levels without having to sell an inordinate amount of securities. Arbitrage activity by banks likely ensures that the actual FFR would not be significantly lower than the rate paid banks by the Fed on reserves. Suppose the Fed is targeting the FFR at 1.5 percent but the actual FFR is stuck at 1.35 percent because of the enormous quantity of excess reserves. The Fed is reluctant to drain a huge amount of reserves for the reasons just mentioned. If the Fed now agrees to pay 1.5 percent on reserves, banks would enter the federal funds market to borrow billions of dollars (initially at 1.35 percent) and hold the reserves in their accounts at the Fed, earning 1.5 percent. This action would persist until the actual FFR was pushed very close to the 1.5 percent target rate, falling short of that rate only to the extent that transactions costs in the fed funds market exist. The Fed views this tool as allowing it to exert tighter control over the FFR.

Use of this tool would ensure that the Fed could put upward pressure on short-term rates as desired because banks are unlikely to supply funds to the money markets at rates lower than the risk-free rate the Fed is offering on bank reserves. This new Fed tool is likely to be favored in the exit strategy because it has been used with success by the European Central Bank, along with the central banks of Canada, Japan, and a few other nations. When it is time to exercise restraint, the Fed is likely to lead by boosting the rate paid banks on excess reserves, and follow this action with open market security sales, reverse repo transactions, and auctioning of term deposits.

VI. Conclusion

Many analysts fear that the United States and other major nations are on the cusp of an era of appreciably higher inflation in the postcrisis era. In the case of the United States, the Federal Reserve has adequate tools at its disposal to prevent this from happening. But the Fed faces an extremely difficult challenge in choosing the *timing* in which these tools are implemented in unwinding its policy of extraordinary monetary stimulus. Moving to put the policy of restraint in place too early or too forcefully could jeopardize the fragile economic recovery, send the nation back into recession, and cause additional problems in the banking sector. Waiting too long to implement restraint could lead to a costly bout with inflation. The stakes are very high.

The timing issue is particularly challenging because Federal Reserve policy influences economic activity with a significant lag. The Federal Reserve must therefore implement its exit strategy based on its best forecast of economic conditions that will prevail six months or a year in the future. Economic forecasting is fraught with difficulties. Clearly, the Fed is operating in uncharted waters as it contemplates its strategy. It has never been faced with an exit strategy of this order of magnitude. The Fed's judgment and competence will definitely be challenged by an array of uncertainties as it moves to implement measures to reduce bank reserves and the monetary base and boost interest rates. An optimist might note that the intellectual capital in the upper ranks of the Federal Reserve is arguably near an all-time high. Nevertheless, the institution will inevitably be criticized by inflation hawks as having moved too little and too late, or by doves as moving too aggressively and too soon.

Chapter 11

The Taylor Rule and Evaluation of U.S. Monetary Policy

I. Introduction

Among economists, a long-standing debate involves the "rules versus discretion" issue in monetary policy. A monetary policy rule is an arrangement in which the central bank announces in advance a specific objective (or objectives) and commits itself to using its policy instruments rigorously to achieve the explicit objective(s). For example, if a central bank employs an explicit 2 percent inflation targeting rule, it will raise interest rates when actual or expected inflation exceeds 2 percent, and reduce interest rates when inflation or expected inflation falls below 2 percent. This type of monetary policy regime contrasts with a system of discretionary monetary policy, in which the central bank is given maximum latitude to employ its judgment in conducting policy.

Many economists believe that we would be better served if the conduct of monetary policy were governed by a rule rather than by human discretion. This is particularly true of nations with a history of high inflation. This chapter discusses the rules versus discretion issue as it pertains to monetary policy. It gives special emphasis to a specific rule known as the Taylor Rule, in which the central bank moves its short-term interest rate target in response to discrepancies of actual inflation and output from specific desired levels. After discussing limitations and problems in using the Taylor Rule, it is used as a benchmark to evaluate the actual conduct of U.S. monetary policy in the Great Depression and in more recent times.

II. The Case for a Monetary Policy Rule

Proponents of monetary rules offer several arguments in support of their position. First, politicians and policymakers may seek to use monetary policy to further their own political objectives rather than promoting the public interest. To the extent that the central bank is not structured to be independent of the legislative and executive branches of government, the conduct of monetary policy is likely to be influenced by political considerations. Incumbent politicians know that economic conditions at election time are critical in determining the outcome. If unemployment is high, they will pay a price at the polls.

The *political business cycle* involves the manipulation of the economy for political purposes. Incumbent politicians benefit most from a booming economy and the associated low unemployment rate at election time. If a central bank is subject to political influence or is otherwise sympathetic to the incumbents' re-election, monetary policy may be characterized by unwarranted stimulus in the year leading up to the election, followed by severe restraint implemented immediately after the election to combat the inflation and other excesses caused by the earlier monetary stimulus.[1] In this way, discretionary monetary policy may contribute to political business cycles. Such stop-go macroeconomic policies are not good for the nation's economic engine. Rigorous adherence to a monetary policy rule prevents the central bank from contributing to a political business cycle. Given the political forces (discussed in chapter 10) that are likely to be brought to bear on the Fed as the economy recovers from the Great Recession, adoption of a monetary policy rule might save the nation from a costly era of inflation.

Some economists believe that, even if the central bank is totally free from political influence, the inherent difficulties posed by myriad uncertainties, policy lags, forecasting difficulties, and other factors make it unlikely that discretionary monetary policy will consistently contribute to economic stability. Monetarist economists have long argued that the Federal Reserve has historically been a destabilizing force and that adherence to a monetary rule would likely have resulted in greater economic stability. The facts show that over the course of the 16 business cycles since the founding of the Federal Reserve, the monetary base and monetary aggregates have grown more rapidly during periods of economic expansion than in recessions, on average. This has not typically been the case, however, in business cycles after the 1970s.

Finally, even if those in charge of monetary policy are extremely competent at economic forecasting and evaluating the need for policy restraint or stimulus, a strong case for a monetary policy rule can be made on the basis of the *time inconsistency problem*—the tendency of a policymaker to announce a particular policy to influence expectations but then to follow a different policy after the expectations have been formed.

An analogy from international politics is pertinent to the case of the time inconsistency problem facing central banks. Consider government policy toward terrorists who contemplate taking hostages. To reduce incentive of terrorists to take hostages, governments often have a stated policy that there will be no negotiation with the terrorists. Governments believe that their stated policy reduces the incidence of hostage-taking. However, if hostages are taken, a government faces tremendous pressure to negotiate their release, in spite of its stated position to the contrary. Rational terrorists, aware of the time inconsistency dilemma, often take hostages. If officials' authority to negotiate with terrorists were removed by explicit law, the incentive for rational terrorists to take hostages would be eliminated. Hostage-taking would almost certainly decline because terrorists would have nothing to gain by taking hostages. Ironically, elimination of policy discretion likely yields a better outcome in this case.

This analogy is clearly pertinent to monetary policy. Consider a central bank that wishes to achieve both low inflation and low unemployment. The Phillips curve depicts the existence of a short-run trade-off between unemployment and inflation, ceteris paribus. Holding other factors constant, lower unemployment is accompanied by higher inflation. The *position* of the Phillips curve depends on the inflation outlook—if expected inflation is higher, the short-run Phillips curve lies farther to the right. In other words, the inflation rate associated with any given unemployment rate will be higher if expected inflation is higher. For this reason, central bankers have a powerful incentive to foster low inflation expectations through speeches of Fed officials, public statements, and so forth.

However, once inflation expectations are set, political considerations may cause the central bank to exploit the short-run Phillips curve—it may be tempted to buy a near-term reduction in unemployment at the cost of higher inflation a bit later. Because informed economic agents are aware of the time inconsistency problem, the central bank does not have full credibility when it makes reassuring statements about the inflation outlook. The surprising result is that implementation of a strict rule governing central bank policy improves the outcome by eliminating the time inconsistency problem. Implementation of the rule increases the central bank's credibility in dealing with inflation. It reduces inflation expectations, shifting the short-run Phillips curve downward toward the origin, thus permitting any given unemployment rate to be accompanied by a lower rate of inflation.

III. Passive and Active (Feedback) Rules

A monetary rule can be either passive or active. In a passive rule, the central bank does not respond to ongoing or expected economic developments. A prime example is the constant money growth rule, in which the central bank commits itself to simply increasing the money supply at some relatively low and constant rate, irrespective of contemporary or prospective economic conditions. It does not change its policy, for example, if inflation or unemployment increases sharply. In an active or feedback rule, the central bank changes its instruments aggressively, if necessary, to achieve the specific goal specified in the rule. In the Taylor rule, to be discussed in depth in this chapter, the central bank moves short-term interest rates in response to deviations of both inflation and unemployment from specified target levels.

The Constant Money Growth Rule

From the late 1940s through the 1970s, the velocity of money—the multiplier that links the money supply to aggregate GDP expenditures, was relatively stable. It trended upward over time at an annual rate of about 3 percent per year, and year-to-year deviations from this growth rate were relatively modest. This suggests to advocates of the constant money growth rule that low and stable growth of the money supply would likely have been accompanied by relatively stable growth in GDP expenditures and modest inflation, on average. Had a constant money growth rule been in place, business cycles would certainly not have been eliminated but it is unlikely that we would have experienced the double-digit inflation that occurred in the late 1970s. Nor would we have experienced the Great Depression of the 1930s had the Fed maintained positive money growth as prescribed by the constant money growth rule.

Monetarist economists take the position that not only would these extreme episodes have been avoided, but also that output and inflation would generally have been more stable over the years had the Fed been constrained by a constant money growth rule. This is a highly controversial issue. There is a consensus among economists that the conduct of Federal Reserve policy over the past 30 years has generally been far superior to that of earlier times. Most economists today believe that, in this period, the Fed delivered an outcome superior to that which would have occurred had it employed a constant money growth rule. After 1980, when major deregulation of the financial system was implemented, and when the pace of financial innovation accelerated, velocity of M1 and M2 became appreciably more volatile. Sentiment for adopting the constant money growth rule probably reached its apogee near the end of the 1970s. It has seldom been proposed in recent times.

Inflation Targeting Rule

Beginning with New Zealand in 1989, central banks in more than 20 nations have initiated inflation targeting (IT) regimes. When a nation implements an IT regime, it announces a specific numerical inflation target level (say 2 percent) or range (perhaps 1–3 percent) at or within which the central bank commits to maintain inflation. The central bank backs up the announcement with a systematic, credible plan for achieving the target. Many countries have an escape clause permitting temporary deviation from the target in the event of a major supply shock. In an IT regime, the monetary authorities must develop a methodology for forecasting inflation that involves a macroeconomic model or a set of indicators containing information about future inflation. The central bank implements a set of forward-looking operating procedures in which short-term interest rates are adjusted in response to deviations between the central bank's inflation forecast and the specific inflation target.

Inflation targeting is believed to provide an anchor that ties down inflation expectations and strongly assures the public that development of serious inflation will not be allowed to occur. In the absence of such an anchor, monetary policy actions may drift in response to near-term economic and political forces and become inconsistent with long-term policy goals. Adoption of an IT regime increases a central bank's transparency and accountability. If a central bank announces a 2 percent inflation target, its intentions are more transparent than if it simply states that its goal is to "maintain relatively stable prices over the long run." With increased transparency comes increased accountability. When an IT central bank significantly misses its inflation target, policymakers must typically provide an explanation. In some instances, failure to hit the target may be justified. An example might be a major increase in oil prices, which makes a near-term increase in inflation almost inevitable. In other instances, the government may hold officials of the central bank accountable—in an extreme case even removing them from office.

Inflation targeting largely circumvents the time inconsistency problem of monetary policy. By providing the central bank with maximum credibility regarding its commitment to low inflation, an IT regime presents policymakers with a favorable short-run Phillips curve. Advocates of IT argue that its implementation facilitates the battle against inflation in nations that suffer from chronically high inflation. The *sacrifice ratio*— the percentage of one year's output a nation must forgo or "sacrifice" to reduce inflation by one percentage point—may be reduced if a country adopts IT.

The Federal Reserve has never adopted an explicit IT regime. However, given the enormous increases in public and private debt incurred in recent years, along with the unprecedented quantity of excess reserves pumped into the banks by the Fed during the Great Crisis and its aftermath, many observers have been nervous about the prospects for higher inflation in the not-too-distant future, as discussed in chapter 10. The time may be at hand for the Fed to implement an explicit IT regime.

IV. The Taylor Rule and U.S. Monetary Policy

The conduct of Federal Reserve policy is ultimately driven by the Fed's dual mandate: maintaining reasonable price level stability and fostering stability of the nation's output at levels consistent with high employment. Over the years, the Federal Reserve has employed various approaches in an effort to achieve these goals. In the 1970s, for example, the Fed (and many other central banks) set targets for growth rates of monetary aggregates such as M1 and M2 that were thought to be consistent with fostering the goals of price stability and high and stable levels of output and employment.

Beginning in the 1980s, the Fed has employed the federal funds rate (FFR)—the interest rate at which banks lend their reserve deposits at the Federal Reserve to each other—as its instrument in seeking to achieve these objectives. The FFR strongly influences a multitude of other short-term interest rates, including the commercial paper rate and the Treasury bill rate. It determines the prime loan rate that major banks use as a standard in setting various loan rates because the prime loan rate is set at a fixed margin (3 percentage points in recent years) above the FFR target. When the Fed changes the FFR target, an array of bank loan rates change in lockstep. The Fed buys and sells Treasury securities in the open market in order to keep the actual federal funds rate as close to its target level as possible. If market forces drive the FFR above the Fed's target, the Fed purchases securities, thereby increasing bank reserves and lowering the actual FFR. If market forces cause the FFR to drop below the Fed's target, the Fed sells securities, draining reserves from the banking system and thereby working to boost the FFR.

Two principles are paramount. First, when inflation rises above acceptable rates, the Fed must raise its FFR target, thereby pushing up interest rates across a broad spectrum of financial instruments and maturities. This slows the growth of aggregate spending, which, in turn, reduces inflationary pressures. Second, when output slows sharply or declines and unemployment rises above acceptable levels, the Fed must reduce the FFR to bring down interest rates more broadly, thereby stimulating aggregate demand, output, and employment.

Formulation of the Taylor Rule

In 1993, Professor John Taylor of Stanford University proposed a monetary policy rule in which the central bank moves its federal funds rate target in response to changes in both inflation and the nation's output gap—the gap between potential real GDP and actual real GDP. The general form of the Taylor Rule for setting the federal funds target rate is expressed as follows:

$$\mathbf{FFR} = r^* + \pi + w_1 \, (\pi - 2\%) + w_2 \, [(Y - Y^*)/Y^*] \times 100 \qquad (11\text{-}1)$$

In this expression, FFR represents the federal funds rate target to be set by the central bank. On the right-hand side, r^* is the neutral real interest rate—the real rate consistent with long-run equilibrium in the economy. This neutral real rate fluctuates over time and is typically taken to be 2 percent, on average, which is very close to the average real federal funds rate of 1.8 percent over the past 50 years. The Greek letter π is the ongoing inflation rate. The term $(\pi - 2\%)$ in the equation is the inflation gap—the amount by which inflation differs from the implicitly desired inflation rate of 2 percent per year.[2] Real GDP is designated by Y, and Y^* is potential real GDP.

The last term in the equation includes $Y - Y^*$, that is, the magnitude of the output gap, expressed in dollars. This gap is divided by Y^* and taken times 100 so that the gap is expressed as a percentage of potential output. A positive output gap indicates an economic boom is in place, with real output (Y) above potential real output (Y^*) and the unemployment rate below the NAIRU. A negative output gap indicates the presence of slack in the economy with actual real GDP below potential real GDP and with the unemployment rate above the NAIRU.

The parameters w_1 and w_2 are the weights applied in the reaction of the central bank to the inflation gap and the output gap, respectively. Economists disagree about the appropriate weights to employ in the Taylor rule. There are disagreements about the appropriate relative magnitude of w_1 and w_2, as well as whether the both weights should be small or large. Inflation hawks, concerned with the economic consequences of high inflation, would favor placing a higher weight on the inflation gap than on the output gap ($w_1 > w_2$). Those more concerned about the costs of high unemployment tend to advocate a higher weight placed on the output gap ($w_2 > w_1$). For example, when President Obama contemplated filling three vacant positions on the 7-member Board of Governors in 2010, the unemployment rate hovered near 10 percent. With inflation pressures expected to be very low in the near term, news commentators suggested that he would be inclined to favor candidates with sympathies aligned with the unemployed, that is, those candidates who prefer $w_2 > w_1$.[3]

Also, note that larger weights on both w_1 and w_2 imply a more aggressive response by the central bank to changes in both inflation and in output than do smaller weights, as is illustrated in Table 11-1.

Professor Taylor, in his 1993 original exposition of the Taylor rule, chose equal weights of 0.5 for w_1 and w_2. If we adopt those weights, assume r^* is 2 percent, and move inflation (π) to the left-hand side of the equation, equation 11-2 indicates the formulation of the prescribed real federal funds rate in the Taylor rule. Note that the rule calls for the central bank to move the *real* federal funds rate in response to changes in the inflation gap and the output gap, with weights of 0.5 for both w_1 and w_2.

$$\text{FFR} - \pi = 2\% + 0.5\,(\pi - 2\%) + 0.5\,[(Y - Y^*)/Y^*] \times 100 \qquad (11\text{-}2)$$

Consider the second term on the right-hand side of the equation. It indicates that, given the size of the output gap, the rule requires the Fed to boost the *real* FFR if the inflation rate moves above 2 percent per year and reduce the real FFR if the inflation rate declines below 2 percent per year. If the actual rate of inflation is 2 percent and there is no output gap, i.e., if actual GDP is on potential, the real FFR called for by the rule is 2 percent, with the nominal rate at 4 percent. If inflation increases to 4 percent and the output gap remains zero, the Taylor rule calls for the Fed to set the real FFR at 3 percent, and the nominal rate at 7 percent.

It is important to note that a central bank that adheres to the Taylor rule will boost real interest rates when inflation rises and reduce real interest rates when inflation declines. This important policy prescription has become known as the *Taylor principle*. Such a countercyclical policy tends to help stabilize the inflation rate. Serious policy errors have been made in the past by central banks that have not followed the Taylor principle, as we note later in this chapter.

Table 11-1 illustrates the nominal and real FFR rate prescribed by the Taylor rule for various inflation and output gap scenarios, under the assumptions of equal weights for w_1 and w_2 of 0.5, and for equal weights of 1.0.

Table 11-1   Federal Funds Rate Prescribed by Taylor Rule

Scenario	π (%)	$\pi - 2\%$ (%)	W_1	% Output Gap	W_2	Taylor Rule FFR (%)	Taylor Rule Real FFR (%)
A	2	0	0.5	0	0.5	4	2
B	4	2	0.5	+2	0.5	8	4
C	0	-2	0.5	-4	0.5	-1	-1
D	2	0	1	0	1	4	2
E	4	2	1	+2	1	10	6
F	0	-2	1	-4	1	-4	-4
...	...	...	...	...	...	...	...
G	-10	-12	0.5	-30	0.5	-29	-19

Source: Calculated using equation 11-1.

In Scenario A, as noted, with inflation of 2 percent, a zero output gap, and weights of 0.5 for w_1 and w_2, the Taylor rule calls for a real FFR of 2 percent and a nominal FFR of 4 percent. In scenario B, an economic boom situation with inflation of 4 percent and a positive output gap of 2 percent, the rule calls for a real FFR of 4 percent (nominal FFR of 8 percent). Note that relative to case A, case B involves a significantly higher real FFR. As the economy moves from Scenario A to Scenario B, the Fed is "leaning against the wind," raising real interest rates to combat higher inflation.

Scenario C is representative of depressed economic conditions. Inflation is zero and a negative output gap of 4 percent exists. In this case, the Taylor rule calls for a nominal (and real) FFR of negative 1 percent. Given the lower bound on nominal interest rates of zero, this means the Fed is incapable of adhering to the rule. An extreme instance of this problem is illustrated in Scenario G, representative of the trough of the Great Depression of the early 1930s. In this scenario, with inflation running at negative 10 percent and with an output gap of negative 30 percent, and with weights on both the inflation and output gaps at 0.5, the Taylor rule calls for a real FFR of negative 19 percent and a nominal FFR of negative 29 percent! Given the zero lower bound problem, one can understand why Keynes argued that monetary policy was inherently incapable of extricating the economy from depression in 1932 or 1933.

Scenarios D, E, and F in the table illustrate the Taylor rule response to changes in inflation and the output gap in the case in which the weights are both increased to 1.0. In comparing the results as we move from Scenario A to B with those in moving from D to E (a move to boom conditions in both instances), note that the Taylor rule mandates a more aggressive response in the latter case of larger weights. Rather than moving the nominal FFR from 4 percent to 8 percent, as when the weights are 0.5, the Fed jumps this FFR from 4 to 10 percent when the weights are 1.0. Rather than boosting the real rate from 2 to 4 percent as in the former case, the Fed has boosted it from 2 to 6 percent in the latter. Those who advocate a generally more aggressive stance on the part of the Fed would prefer larger weights for both w_1 and w_2, as in scenarios D, E, and F.

The Taylor Rule and Inflation Targeting

A larger positive output gap or smaller negative gap, as defined in equations 11-1 and 11-2, implies a more robust economy. Because a nation's unemployment rate is strongly (and inversely) related to the size of the output gap, an obvious way to view equations 11-1 and 11-2 is as a rule that requires the central bank to respond with equal vigor to developments on the inflation front and on the unemployment front. Those who support a policy of strict inflation targeting might advocate leaving off the last term of the Taylor rule, instead focusing attention entirely on inflation. That is, they would ignore the output gap and the associated unemployment rate, setting a weight for w_2 of zero.

However, one can interpret the Taylor rule as stated in equations 11-1 and 11-2 as being consistent with the objective of those who favor a policy of inflation targeting. In the absence of major supply shocks, the size of the output gap is typically an important indicator of the likely change in *forthcoming* inflation. A positive output gap, with the current unemployment rate being below the NAIRU, indicates that inflation will be rising. The forthcoming rate of change of inflation is positively related to the size of the output gap. A negative output gap, with the unemployment rate above the NAIRU, suggests that inflation will be declining. Hence, one can view the Taylor rule as providing an operating procedure that generally facilitates the Fed's ability to hit an inflation target.

In the event of supply shocks, the central bank is confronted with a trade-off between output stability and inflation stability. A sharp increase in energy prices, for example, exerts upward pressure on inflation and downward pressure on output. If the Fed aims to maintain price stability, it must raise interest rates to reduce aggregate demand. This, however, reduces output and increases unemployment. In this instance, price stability is maintained only at the cost of increased instability of output and employment. There is disagreement among economists in this case about the optimal response of the central bank.

Problems in Implementing the Taylor Rule

In practice, there are several problems associated with using the Taylor rule. For one thing, there are difficulties in measuring both the inflation gap and the output gap in equations 11-1 and 11-2. There are several different prices indexes, and the inflation rate (and Taylor rule FFR) one calculates differs depending on the index employed. And there is disagreement about whether core measures of inflation that strip out volatile food and energy prices or "headline" inflation that includes those items should be used in calculating inflation. More fundamentally, while we have reliable measures of real GDP, we cannot measure potential real GDP and the NAIRU. We must rely on estimates, and economists differ in their estimates of these variables. For these reasons, there is uncertainty about the magnitude of the output gap—and therefore in the interest rate prescribed by the Taylor rule.

In addition, there are fairly long and variable time lags between the point in time at which monetary and/or fiscal policy would ideally be put in place and the time at which the policy ends up influencing economic activity. These lags might be termed the recognition lag, the implementation lag, and the impact lag, and their existence complicates the effective use of both the Taylor rule and discretionary monetary policy.

The recognition lag encompasses the time that elapses between the point at which policy actions would ideally have been implemented (known only with hindsight) and the point at which policymakers become aware of the need for action. Data for such key variables as GDP, industrial production, and various price indices become available only periodically rather than continuously. And they are sometimes later revised significantly. This means a recognition lag is inevitable.

The implementation lag is the time that elapses between the point at which the need for a change in policy is recognized and the point at which the policy is implemented. Because the Federal Open Market Committee meets eight times each year in Washington, and because the Fed chairman can call additional meetings as needed, the recognition lag for monetary policy is normally brief. When Lehman Brothers failed in September 2008, the Fed acted within hours to implement appropriate policy measures. Fiscal policy actions encounter much longer implementation lags because such actions require congressional approval, and serious political obstacles are frequently involved.

The impact lag is the time that elapses between the point at which policy is implemented and the point at which it begins to influence economic activity. Monetary policy influences GDP with a significant lag because it must first influence such variables as bank lending, interest rates, exchange rates, asset prices, and wealth. Business investment and housing construction do not respond immediately to changes in interest rates and credit availability. Plans must be drawn up, bids taken, contractors hired, and financing arranged. And consumption spending responds to changes in interest rates and wealth with a lag. Monetarist economists have long pointed out that monetary policy impinges on GDP and the price level with a rather *long* and *variable* lag.

Existence of these lags imply that to be highly effective, it is essential that *expected future* inflation and output gaps be employed in the Taylor rule, rather than *contemporaneous* gaps. This means that effective use of the Taylor rule requires reasonably accurate economic forecasting. This is a major challenge, in part because it is extremely difficult to forecast GDP, potential GDP, and inflation, especially for horizons a year or more in the future.

A third problem confronting the use of the Taylor rule is that the structure of the economy changes over time due to changes in technology, regulations, market structures, and many other forces. This suggests that the optimal weights used in the Taylor rule (w_1 and w_2) might need to change over time.

Finally, the Taylor rule does not take financial crises into consideration. One problem is that yield spreads on various debt instruments are strongly influenced in times of crises. For example, the spreads between corporate bond yields and Treasury bond yields, and between commercial paper yields and Treasury bill yields widened sharply in 2008 during the crisis. Because the corporate bond and commercial paper yields are important in influencing investment decisions by firms, and because in crises these yields increase relative to the level of the FFR, the FFR appropriate in a financial crisis is likely to differ from that in normal times, given the size of the inflation and the output gaps.

Before the recent financial crisis, opposition to the idea of the Federal Reserve taking action to combat incipient bubbles was predominant among U.S. central bankers. Alan Greenspan, Fed chairman from 1987 to 2006, strongly opposed the idea of the Fed attempting to deflate bubbles before they become dangerously large. And Chairman Bernanke, who replaced Greenspan in 2006, never distanced himself from Greenspan on this issue. However, given the enormous costs to countries throughout the world created by the 2007–2009 collapse of the housing and credit bubbles, many economists have changed their view on this issue. And the Federal Reserve is now apparently undertaking studies to examine the feasibility of using its tools to combat the development of dangerous bubbles.

The proposal to combat bubbles through monetary policy implies that an additional term should be added to the right-hand side of equations 11-1 and 11-2. This variable would be some measure intended to pick up the development of bubble conditions. This issue is highly contentious because identifying a bubble is inherently very difficult. Only a small minority of economists expressed the view that a bubble in house prices was in effect during the period preceding the collapse of house prices in 2007 and 2008.

All of these problems indicate that a strong dose of judgment needs to be added before a central bank decides to mechanically adhere to the Taylor rule. Nevertheless, if the central bank sets short-term interest rates at large variance from the rate prescribed by the Taylor rule, the central bank ought to have cogent reasons to justify the discrepancy.

V. Using the Taylor Rule as a Standard to Evaluate Monetary Policy

Because of numerous uncertainties, it is inevitable that policy mistakes will sometimes be made by those responsible for the conduct of monetary policy. It is interesting and useful to employ the Taylor rule as a benchmark for the purpose of evaluating the conduct of monetary policy after the fact. With the aid of hindsight and the Taylor rule, it is possible to pinpoint occasional episodes in which the Federal Reserve appears to have erred in being either too restrictive or too expansionary in its conduct of monetary policy. In the past 80 years, five such episodes seem particularly apparent. These episodes include 1930–1933, 1965–1969, 1974–1979, 1982–1986, and the recent period 2002 through 2005, when the U.S. housing and credit bubbles were rapidly inflating.

The Taylor Rule and the Great Depression

Establishment of formal national income accounting did not commence until after World War II. Also, the federal funds market did not exist until the 1950s. These facts complicate the calculation of the Taylor rule for the Great Depression of the early 1930s. However, data for short-term Treasury bill yields, a good proxy for the federal funds rate, are available for the 1920s and 1930s. And Nathan Balke and Robert Gordon have compiled a quarterly series for real GDP and trend real GDP that makes possible the calculation of output gaps for the period encompassing the Great Depression. Using the Taylor rule specification with weights of 0.5 for both the inflation and output gaps, the Taylor rule prescription for the Treasury bill yield for the 1928–1938 period along with the actual Treasury bill yield, are shown in Figure 11-1.

Note that in mid-1929, the Treasury bill yield was pretty much the same as would have been prescribed by a Taylor rule. In August 1929, a recession started (later degenerating into the Great Depression) and a negative output gap began to develop, causing a decline in the short-term interest rate prescribed by the Taylor rule. This prescribed rate became negative in the first quarter of 1930. By mid-1930, mild deflation had set in and the negative output gap had become more severe. This meant the Taylor rule called for even lower interest rates. Actual Treasury bill yields were extremely low after the end of 1930, averaging about 1.20 percent in 1931 and less than 0.25 percent from mid-1932 to mid-1934.

By the middle of 1930, the Taylor rule was calling for double-digit negative Treasury bill yields. The Fed, of course, was constrained by the zero bound on nominal interest rates. There was virtually no scope for further reductions in interest rates. The negative output gap continued to widen as the economy cascaded downward. This negative gap surged to more than 25 percent in fall 1931 and reached a peak of 35 percent

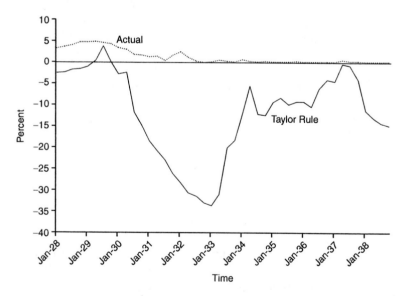

Figure 11-1   Actual vs. Taylor Rule Treasury bill rate, 1928–1938.

Source: Treasury bill yields are from Board of Governors of Federal Reserve System, *Banking and Monetary Statistics* (Washington, DC: National Capital Press, 1943), p. 460. Taylor rule rates are calculated from data in FRED database and Nathan Balke and Robert Gordon, "Data Appendix," in Robert J. Gordon (ed.), *The Business Cycle: Continuity and Change* (Chicago, IL: University of Chicago Press for NBER, 1986), pp. 781–850.

in the first quarter of 1933. The rate of deflation increased to around 10 percent during the period extending from the middle of 1931 to the fourth quarter of 1933. With a negative output gap of more than 30 percent and double-digit deflation, the Taylor rule called for short-term interest rates lower than negative 30 percent in most of 1932 and early 1933. The hugely negative rate indicated by the Taylor rule is consistent with Keynes' view that "you can't push on a string"—the idea that once an economy is mired in depression, monetary policy becomes impotent.

This is not to say that the Fed is not culpable in the economic disaster of the Great Depression. The blunders committed by the Fed in tightening its discount policy, failing to respond appropriately to the waves of banking panics, and allowing bank reserves to decline in the face of large declines in the money supply multiplier and the velocity of money must be counted as major sources of the severity of the depression. Once the Fed's early mistakes had permitted severe deflation to set it, however, the power of monetary policy was severely compromised.

The Taylor Rule and Actual Federal Funds Rate, 1960–2010

Figure 11-2 indicates the actual federal funds rate (heavy line) over the period extending from 1960 through the early portion of 2010, along with the rates prescribed by the Taylor rule using two different measures of inflation. Rule 1 uses the GDP deflator as the measure of the price level. Rule 2 uses the core GDP deflator—the GDP deflator with food and energy prices stripped out. Both rules employ the average inflation rate over the previous 12 months, along with the contemporaneous size of the output gap. The output gap is calculated using actual real GDP along with the Congressional Budget Office measure of potential real GDP. This figure will be used to discuss several policy errors committed by the Federal Reserve over the past 50 years.

The Vietnam War Episode of Rising Inflation (1965–1969)

By mid-1965, the U.S. economy was in the fifth year of an economic expansion that followed the 1960–1961 recession. The unemployment rate was around 4.5 percent, likely not far from the contemporary NAIRU, when the United States made a decision to escalate its military commitment in Vietnam. The increase in military expenditures boosted aggregate demand, and the inflation rate escalated from less than 2 percent in 1965 to more than 5 percent by 1969. The Fed was slow to boost the federal funds rate as inflationary pressures were building.[4] It failed to follow the Taylor principle. In contrast to what the Taylor rule would have prescribed, the Fed allowed the *real* FFR to decline significantly. In

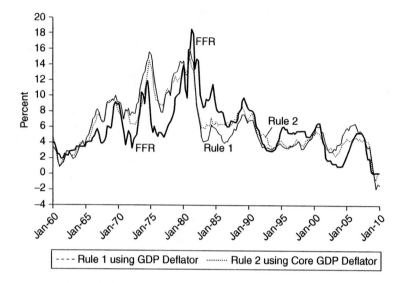

Figure 11-2   Actual Federal Funds rate and Taylor Rule rate, 1960:1–2010:1.
Source: Federal Reserve Bank of St. Louis, FRED Database.

the 14 quarters extending from 1965:4 through 1969:1 the actual FFR was lower than the rate prescribed by Taylor rule 1 by an average of 280 basis points (2.80 percentage points). Together with the falling real FFR and the increase in money growth rates during this period, the Taylor rule implicates the Federal Reserve in the rising rate of inflation.[5] This episode is an unambiguous example of a policy mistake by the Federal Reserve.

The Inflationary 1970s

The U.S. economy entered a one-year recession in November 1969. This, coupled with an experiment with wage-price controls initiated in August 1971, brought the inflation rate down to approximately 3.5 percent by the end of 1972. A severe supply shock in the form of a major increase in crude oil prices triggered an episode of stagflation beginning in 1973. Both inflation and unemployment increased sharply. In mid-1974, one-third of the way through a severe recession, the Fed began aggressively reducing the FFR.

As indicated in Figure 11-2, the Fed maintained the FFR at levels far below the rate prescribed by the Taylor rule for several years. The U.S. inflation rate ratcheted higher and higher, peaking at about 13 percent per year in early 1980. As the figure indicates, Federal Reserve policy was consistently too expansionary relative to the Taylor rule benchmark throughout the decade of the 1970s, helping account for the fact that the inflation rate averaged approximately 8 percent per year in this decade.[6] Over a period of five and a half years (1974:1 to 1979:3), the federal funds rate was maintained some 440 basis points lower than the rate prescribed by Taylor Rule 1, on average. The predominant consensus among economists is that the Fed committed an important policy error in the second half of the 1970s. Policy was too stimulative.

It is not likely that the Fed deliberately conducted an inflationary policy. What explains the Fed's error? There is some disagreement about this. Professor Taylor argues that the Fed was relatively unsophisticated and failed to take account of the difference between nominal and real interest rates before the installation of Paul Volcker as chairman in August, 1979. In terms of the left-hand side of equation 11-2, the Fed essentially omitted the π term. It raised nominal interest rates as inflation increased, but it failed to raise them as fast as inflation was rising. Hence, real interest rates declined while inflation expectations were increasing, leading to even higher inflation. In this view, because of its failure to focus on real interest rates, the Fed was inadvertently pursuing a procyclical policy rather than a countercyclical one.

The other view of what happened argues that the Fed failed to take account of changes that had occurred in the NAIRU and potential GDP in the 1970s. As the baby-boomers entered the labor market in rapidly increasing numbers in the 1970s, both frictional and structural unemployment increased, thus boosting the NAIRU. Failure to account for this phenomenon means the Fed underestimated the NAIRU and overestimated the size of potential GDP. In terms of equation 11-2, the Fed thought the United States had a larger negative output gap than actually was the case. The Fed mistakenly believed that there was a lot of slack in the economy and therefore pursued a policy that turned out to be excessively stimulative.[7] This episode illustrates a major challenge confronting the use of the Taylor rule—the uncertainty about the level of the NAIRU, potential GDP, and the output gap.

The Volcker Disinflation (1981–1986)

In August 1979, President Jimmy Carter appointed Paul Volcker to the position of chairman of the Board of Governors of the Federal Reserve. Volcker viewed his appointment as a mandate to bring down inflation. Inflation had been ratcheting upward since the mid-1960s and was running at an annual rate above 12 percent at the time of Volcker's appointment. In a series of moves, the Fed boosted the FFR target from 11 percent in August 1979 to 20 percent by July 1981.[8]

Because inflation had been building momentum for 15 years, and with inflation expectations now solidly entrenched in the public's psyche, the Fed resolved not to take its foot off the brakes until inflationary psychology had been soundly defeated. Even though actual inflation came down sharply from 12 percent in 1980 to around 4 percent in 1983, the Fed maintained the FFR above 8 percent until early 1986. In the period from the first quarter of 1982 through the second quarter of 1986, the Fed maintained its fed funds target some 430 basis points above that prescribed by Taylor rule 1, on average (review Figure 11-2).

Interest-sensitive industries such as construction and automobiles were hammered by the sky-high interest rates. In July 1981, the United States entered into an extremely severe recession. The nation's unemployment rate rose to 10.8 percent in November 1982, the highest rate since the Great Depression. It stood at 7.2 percent as late as the middle of 1986. With hindsight, this highly restrictive policy was probably maintained for an excessive period of time, and some observers charged Volcker's Fed with overkill. Others regard Volcker as a hero, and perhaps the greatest Federal Reserve chairman of all time. They credit him with having the courage to stick with his restrictive monetary medicine until inflation was vanquished, thus paving the way for Greenspan's Fed to preside over 20 years of prosperity combined with unusually low inflation.

Chairman Greenspan, Easy Money, and the Housing Bubble (2002–2005)

Alan Greenspan was appointed to succeed Volcker in August 1987, and remained as chairman until 2006, when he stepped down to be replaced by Ben Bernanke. During this period, the Greenspan-led Fed was widely praised for its role in fostering the "Great Moderation," a period in which both output and inflation were unusually stable.[9]

The Greenspan-led Fed followed the Taylor rule more closely than did his predecessors, as the FFR tracks the Taylor rule fairly closely after 1987. However, note in Figure 11-2 that following the 2001 recession, the terrorist attacks of September 11, 2001 and the stock market meltdown (the "tech wreck") of 2000–2002, the Federal Reserve set the FFR far below the rate prescribed by the Taylor rule. For more than three years extending from the fall of 2002 through the end of 2005, the FFR was maintained, on average, more than 270 basis points below the rate prescribed by Taylor rule 1. This gap is particularly large relative to the low contemporary levels of interest rates in general. Many commentators have remarked that this episode was an important source of the bubbles in house prices and credit that eventually burst and touched off the Great Crisis.

The conventional interpretation of this episode is that the Greenspan Fed was very concerned at the time that the U.S. economy might be on the cusp of an episode of deflation. Japan was experiencing a prolonged period of modest price-level deflation in which economic activity remained stagnant and unemployment was much higher than traditional levels. The Fed likely perceived its low interest-rate policy as insurance protection against Japanese-style deflation and stagnation.

As it turned out, the policy contributed to the granting of a huge number of variable-rate mortgages with extraordinarily low initial rates. As these rates reset at significantly higher levels beginning in late 2005, increasing numbers of households found themselves unable to make their payments. This set in motion the wave of mortgage defaults, foreclosures, and forced sales of houses that contributed strongly to the enormous decline in house prices that touched off the Great Crisis.

VI. Conclusion

Existence of numerous uncertainties makes it challenging to conduct monetary policy in a way that contributes significantly to economic stability. If one thinks in terms of the simple aggregate demand/aggregate supply framework of elementary macroeconomic analysis, the positions of the AD and AS curves are uncertain. While professors may confidently draw these curves on the board, policymakers do not know their positions. They are also uncertain about the strength of the nonpolicy forces currently working to shift these curves. They are uncertain about the dynamics—how rapidly these curves are shifting over time and how quickly output and the price level adjust to a new equilibrium. There is also uncertainty about the level of full-employment output and the corresponding level of the NAIRU. In addition, policymakers face uncertainty about the structure of the economy and the transmission mechanism of monetary policy—the strength of the various channels through which monetary policy influences economic activity. These forces are changing over time.

This means that errors in the conduct of monetary policy are inevitable. This is true whether monetary policy is guided by a rule or is conducted on the basis of discretion. One can conduct an ex post evaluation of monetary policy by examining, during and immediately preceding periods of instability, short-term interest rates set by the central bank relative to rates prescribed by the Taylor rule. In so doing, one can pinpoint several important errors made by the Fed during its 100-year history. However, such a study would also reveal numerous instances in which the Federal

Reserve delivered a performance superior to that had the Fed surrendered its policy to mechanical application of the Taylor rule.

It is likely that, in the case of a country with a weak government and a history of severe inflation, the nation would be well served by replacing monetary discretion with a rigorous monetary rule. In the case of developed nations with strong and stable governments, the jury is out. Economists disagree about whether the Federal Reserve would better serve the nation by adopting some form of a monetary policy rule. Abandoning discretion in favor of a constant money growth rule or Taylor rule before the Great Depression may have allowed the nation to avoid the severe deflation that was instrumental in fostering the catastrophe. However, given advances in the art and science of conducting monetary policy, it seems likely that a highly competent team of central bankers might be capable of delivering a superior performance by continuing to employ discretion in the conduct of monetary policy.

Chapter 12

Regulatory Reform Proposals

I. Introduction

It would be difficult to find a professional economist who believes that a set of regulatory reforms can be drawn up that would put an end to U.S. financial crises. Crises appear to be endemic to capitalistic systems in which innovation is strongly rewarded and calculated risk-taking is an essential ingredient. Most believe, however, that a carefully designed set of reforms focused on correcting numerous socially perverse incentives would reduce the frequency and severity of future crises.

In response to the massive crisis known as the Great Depression of the early 1930s, Congress acted decisively and enacted dramatic legislation. It implemented federal deposit insurance, strengthened the Federal Reserve System, and created the Securities and Exchange Commission to reduce the incidence of fraud and other egregious behavior on Wall Street. It passed the Glass-Steagall Act, which separated commercial banking from investment banking. As a result of these important legislative actions, crises in the ensuing 70 years were relatively mild and infrequent. Ironically, the ingenious and aggressive measures instituted during the Great Crisis by the Federal Reserve and other central banks that saved the world from Great Depression II may have had the unfortunate side effect of blunting essential financial reforms this time around. The Wall Street Reform and Consumer Protection Act, signed into law by President Obama in July 2010, contained several important provisions. However, it fell short of what might be considered an appropriate and warranted bill.

The U.S. financial industry wields enormous political clout, and it sometimes appears that the industry owns not only the regulators but also the U.S. government. In 2009 the industry reportedly invested nearly $500 million in lobbying activities in a determined effort to minimize the effects of proposed financial reforms on the bottom line of firms in the industry. The lobbying expenses appear likely to yield a high rate of return for the financial industry, as several key provisions aimed at reducing the vulnerability of the system to crises in the proposed legislation were deleted or watered down in the final bill that was enacted.

To think about appropriate reforms in response to the Great Crisis, one must objectively assess its origins. Contributing causes are numerous, complex, and interconnected. Economists disagree about the relative weight of the roles played by the various contributing elements. Some place the heaviest blame on the government, defined loosely to include the Federal Reserve. For example, some fault the Fed for keeping its target federal funds rate (FFR) extremely low while the twin credit and housing price bubbles were inflating most rapidly. Others focus their ire on the Community Reinvestment Act (CRA), which encouraged certain mortgage lenders to increase loans to households with low incomes and other characteristics that had previously constrained their ability to purchase homes. Still others blame our housing GSEs (government-sponsored enterprises)—Fannie Mae and Freddie Mac—for purchasing enormous quantities of subprime mortgage-backed bonds, thereby helping stimulate excessive production of these instruments that boosted the flow of credit to the housing sector.

The thesis of this book, while acknowledging a contributing role for the three above-mentioned factors, is that the twin bubbles stemmed predominantly from actions taken in the private sector of the economy. Beginning in the late 1990s, large and enormously interconnected firms in the financial services industry took on larger and larger risks in an increasingly aggressive and reckless quest for quick financial gain. These risks, taken in pursuit of self interest, were incompatible with the best interests of society as a whole. A pervasive misalignment of private incentives in a variety of areas goes a long way in explaining the chain of events that created the financial catastrophe. Financial reforms must effectively realign these private incentives so that they are consistent with social goals if an even more devastating crisis in the next few years is to be averted. Because of powerful financial incentives, however, any set of new regulations will inevitably induce compensatory actions by the regulated firms that partially or entirely circumvent the regulations. Such is the history of financial regulations. New reforms will need to be implemented periodically.

II. Who Are the Villains: The Government or Private-Sector Entities?

Professional economists are trained to strongly appreciate the beneficial forces of unfettered free markets in instances in which a high degree of competition is prevalent. Adam Smith's concept of the Invisible Hand—the view that each individual pursuing his/her own self interest also inadvertently contributes to the best interests of society at large—has long held sway among professional economists. Many economists instinctively look for other explanations when it is proposed that market failure lies at the heart of a financial crisis. Since unregulated competitive markets typically foster economic efficiency and generally yield optimal results, there is a natural tendency to blame government instead. Thus, conservative economists typically assert that the Great Crisis resulted from government failure, not market failure.

Those who blame the Federal Reserve point out that the Fed held interest rates at abnormally low levels during the 2002–2005 period in which the bubbles were rapidly inflating. As indicated in chapters 4 and 11, the Fed did keep its FFR at extraordinarily low levels during 2002–2005. This rate was maintained several hundred basis points below the Taylor rule prescription during this period. With perfect foresight, the Fed would undoubtedly have kept rates higher and started raising its interest-rate target 12–24 months sooner than it did. But neither the Fed nor 99 percent of professional economists saw the crisis coming.

It is important to remember the central responsibility of the Federal Reserve, as mandated in the Employment Act of 1946: maintaining high levels of employment and fostering reasonable price level stability. The Fed's principal focus should not be aimed at stabilizing any particular sector of the economy—for example, the stock market or housing market. The Fed's low interest-rate policy was implemented out of a legitimate concern that the nation was on the cusp of deflation. Were deflation to materialize and become persistent, the central bank potentially could lose traction and become unable to extricate the country from a lengthy period of stagnation. Such an outcome would carry a very high price, as attested by Japan's "lost decade."

The "blame the Fed" camp fails to acknowledge that the housing bubble began to form in the late 1990s, a period in which the FFR was appreciably higher and in accord with the Taylor rule. Also, the easy money policy implemented by the Fed in 2002–2005 did not appreciably reduce rates on 30-year fixed-rate mortgages, traditionally the predominant mortgage instrument. The argument that low short-term interest rates were the principal cause of the twin credit and house price bubbles is belied by the fact that both Germany and Canada also maintained extremely low short-term rates during this period but were able to avoid serious housing price bubbles.

It cannot be denied that extremely low short-term rates fostered by the Fed made it possible for predatory lenders to induce gullible buyers to take out variable-rate mortgages with exceptionally low initial rates that made unaffordable homes appear affordable. And low rates enabled reckless buyers to upgrade to extravagant homes that would knowingly be affordable only through Ponzi finance—that is, only if future payments were to be made through refinancing made possible by continued rapid appreciation of the price of the house. The real villain here is not Federal Reserve monetary policy, but the laissez-faire attitude of the regulatory and supervisory authorities (including the Fed) who looked the other way while hundreds of thousands of mortgage loans that obviously had a very high probability of going bad were granted.

The Community Reinvestment Act (CRA) also had an influence on the development of the twin bubbles in that it required banks to increase mortgage loans to low-income households. However, the CRA was passed in 1977. If it was the principal cause, why didn't the Great Crisis occur sooner? Most of the subprime loans that failed were made by mortgage brokers and mortgage bankers that were outside of the purview of the CRA. Large bank holding companies with mortgage-lending subsidiaries were not required to include their subsidiaries when calculating their CRA requirements. Clearly, the CRA cannot be regarded as the fundamental cause of the crisis.

Fannie and Freddie are also culpable in contributing to the crisis. While these firms were not involved in securitizing subprime mortgages, they purchased large quantities of bonds backed by subprime mortgages, thus helping generate the excessive pipeline of credit to the housing sector. Their performance during 2002–2006 was reprehensible as they loaded up on risky mortgage-backed bonds and ramped up leverage. They were private firms, however, whose top officers were motivated to take unreasonable risks by prospects of earning multimillion dollar annual bonuses. Also, it is important to note that the extreme problems encountered by such firms as Lehman Brothers, Merrill Lynch, Bear Stearns, and Citigroup resulted from their holdings of "private label" securities that were made up of subprime mortgage loans put together by firms like Morgan Stanley, Goldman Sachs, and Lehman Brothers, not by Fannie and Freddie.

The most valid sense in which government is responsible for the Great Crisis was the failure of the regulatory and supervisory apparatus to maintain pace with the rapidly evolving financial technology. This is in large part the result of powerful incentives of private entities to circumvent regulations in the interest of pursuing enormous profits. The behemoth investment banks and bank holding companies maintain a large cadre of very smart lawyers and creative financial engineers whose job is to find new ways to evade the intent of regulations that are intended to limit risk and prevent crises. Government regulators are likely to always be understaffed and underpaid relative to those working for such firms as Goldman Sachs and Morgan Stanley. For this reason, financial crises are unlikely to one day disappear.

III. Proposed Reforms: Fundamental Considerations

In thinking about essential reforms, we should first consider changing the way we think about the financial industry. The share of the nation's GDP emanating from the financial services industry has tripled since World War II. In a recent year, more than one-third of aggregate profits of firms counted in the Standard & Poor's 500 accrued to this industry. In a good year, income earned by the 25 most highly paid hedge fund managers typically exceeds that of all the S&P 500 CEOs combined. Therefore, especially in the past couple of decades, finance has become an increasingly glamorous prospective vocation, enticing to ambitious young individuals as they contemplate their careers. The venerable investment bank Goldman Sachs reported that in 2009, a very bad year, its 30,000 top employees earned salaries and bonuses that averaged $600,000. Thousands of Goldman traders, managers, and officers were paid in excess of $1 million. Largely because of the fabulous lifestyles potentially within reach of intelligent and ambitious individuals, many of the nation's brightest college graduates have been pursuing careers related to Wall Street finance. For example, in a recent year, more than 40 percent of male graduates of such prestigious institutions as Harvard and Cal Tech reportedly traveled this route. Fewer talented students are majoring in lower-paying but arguably more important fields such as engineering, science, and education.

It seems likely that the enormous growth of the financial industry in the past quarter century is indicative of a socially undesirable misallocation of national resources. Market forces induce resources to flow to areas where rates of return are highest—often a socially desirable phenomenon. However, false signals likely have attracted excessive resources to the financial sector. Economists believe that, in the presence of "black swan" events—those in which a very low probability exists that an ultimately inevitable disaster will occur in any given year—markets fail to allocate resources efficiently. Markets tend to ignore the possibility that such disastrous events might occur. An example of such misallocation is 100-year floods and construction of homes on flood plains. If one thinks of the Great Crisis as a "black swan" event and also considers that the gradual dismantling of financial regulations since 1980, globalization, and financial engineering have induced firms to take on increased leverage and ramp up risk while ignoring the risk of the inevitable occasional disaster, it is not unreasonable to argue that the market allocated excessive resources to the financial sector in the years leading up to the crisis. Government intervention in the market may be warranted, as is the case when construction of homes on flood plains is proposed.

What has been the payoff to society of the extraordinary financial-sector growth? Undeniably there have been numerous important benefits. Many financial markets have become more competitive, with lower transactions costs accruing to participants. Emergence of discount brokerages, on-line trading, and exchange-traded funds has made purchase of a diversified portfolio of stocks—formerly an option only for the well heeled—a realistic possibility for thrifty middle-class Americans. Emergence of money market funds has given millions of households a superior alternative to low-yielding passbook savings accounts. Development of efficient futures markets has enabled farmers, public utilities, and many others to hedge against adverse changes in prices. Financial innovation can be, and typically has been, socially beneficial.

On the other hand, as viewed from the perspective of 2010, a revolution in esoteric financial engineering by Wall Street firms was instrumental in developments that ended up separating 8 million Americans from their jobs, initiating fiscal crises in all levels of government in the United States and many other nations, and potentially compromising the political independence of the Federal Reserve. In Europe, sovereign debt problems caused by the Great Crisis and efforts to deal with its aftermath have resulted in implementation of austerity programs that threaten to send North America and Europe into an extended period of economic stagnation. The existence of the 16-nation euro zone has been placed in jeopardy. With the exception of the Great Depression, the mindboggling costs of the Great Crisis are without precedent in U.S. history.

From a public policy perspective, perhaps the time has come to think about the financial industry the way we view a public utility—as an industry that is critically important to our well-being, but which must be monitored and carefully regulated so that it operates in the interest of the public. Given the tradeoff between financial firms' quest for profits and safety, the experience of the Great Crisis indicates that public policy needs to nudge decision-making in the direction of safety. This may be in society's interest even if it means slowing the growth of financial technology and making the industry less glamorous. The Great Crisis has made clear that the financial industry should be viewed in the same light as the nuclear energy and tobacco industries—industries whose production involves toxic products that potentially impose large negative externalities on society at large. Negative externalities occur when the production or consumption of a good imposes costs on third parties—those that neither produce nor consume the good. Think of lung disorders due to second-hand smoke, cancer related to nitrates in water systems attributable to farming processes, and highway deaths due to drunken drivers.

A useful way to think about modern financial crises is to view them as negative externalities imposed on society by enormous financial firms motivated to take on socially excessive risk in an environment in which gains accrue to those who bet correctly and losses are socialized through bailouts funded by taxpayers. In the presence of negative externalities, even the most ardent free-market economists agree that market failure occurs because not all of the costs associated with production of a good are charged to the firm that produces the good. If firms are free to ignore these external costs, the free market sets the price of the good or service too low. This means the quantity produced and exchanged will be too high from society's perspective. Examples include production of cigarettes, alcohol, and gasoline. Economists agree that an efficient way to correct this problem of market failure is to force the firm to internalize the external costs. One way to do this is by levying a tax on the product. This justifies our taxes on cigarettes, alcohol, and gasoline.

A tax imposed on financial institutions in proportion to their likely contribution to future systemic crises could reduce their propensity to engage in socially excessive risk. This tax, if designed efficiently so that the tax rate rises in step with the size, interconnectedness, and risk taken by the firm, would provide incentives for firms in the financial industry to reduce risky behavior. It would also provide a fund so that taxpayers do not incur the cost of bailing out failing banks and other financial firms. Britain implemented a tax of this nature. In last-minute negotiations, however, a proposed tax of this nature was stripped out of the final 2010 U.S. reform bill in order to obtain the necessary votes for passage of the legislation.

Too Big to Fail

Conservatives often argue that to prevent excessive risk-taking by large financial firms, we must simply allow them to fail. "Creative destruction"—the ultimately beneficial effects of letting weak and inefficient firms die—is one of the facets of capitalism that have enabled this form of economic organization to consistently yield higher and more rapid growth of living standards than planned economies. But the folly of the viewpoint that government should not intervene to prevent bankruptcy of huge and massively interconnected financial firms is indicated by the immediate aftermath of the 2008 decision to let Lehman Brothers fail. Were it not for the extraordinarily prompt, creative, and aggressive actions taken by central banks and governments in the United States and Europe, this decision very likely would have plunged the world into Great Depression II.[1] Any administration, liberal or conservative, Democratic or Republican, must and will act in the future to prevent such systemically important firms from failing. To believe otherwise is to engage in delusion.

Simon Johnson has argued that the moral hazard problem arising from the fact that big banks, hedge funds, and insurance companies are keenly aware that government views them as too big or too interconnected to be allowed to fail means that periodic crises are inevitable.[2] The behavior of such firms is inevitably tilted in the direction of taking more risk. Johnson argues that firms will inevitably find ways to circumvent regulations and take on excessive risk in the pursuit of profit, as they have in the past. In this view, the only way to resolve the moral hazard problem is to make sure that no firm is too big or too interconnected to fail.

This can only be accomplished by seeing to it that large, interconnected financial firms are broken up into units sufficiently small so that their failure would not jeopardize the financial system. Citigroup, for example, has total assets in the neighborhood of $2 trillion. Johnson, supported by myriad economic studies, argues that economies of scale and scope in banking are exhausted well before a bank reaches total assets of $100 billion. Most empirical studies indicate the scale threshold of maximum bank efficiency is considerably lower than this figure. The implication: If there are no efficiencies or other benefits associated with behemoth organizations like Citigroup and Goldman, whose propensity to take risks endangers the financial system, we should break them up into smaller institutions that can safely be permitted to fail. For example, break Citigroup up into at least 20 separate firms, none of which has total assets in excess of $100 billion. In the interest of survival, these new small-enough-to-fail firms would have powerful incentives to reduce the level of risk they engage in.

An efficient way to accomplish this goal would be to provide incentives for firms like Citigroup to voluntarily spin off portions of the firm. The most obvious way to accomplish this would be to impose a progressive system of capital requirements—one in which required capital ratios (capital/total assets) become progressively higher as bank size increases. A 12 percent capital requirement on bank assets between $25 billion and $100 billion and a 20 percent requirement on assets above $100 billion, coupled with rigorous measures that make it impossible for banks to evade capital requirements through financial engineering, moving assets off balance sheet, and other tactics, would induce Citigroup to become dramatically smaller. Provision of tax incentives is an alternative method of effecting voluntary downsizing of huge, interconnected financial firms.

Unfortunately, the U.S. financial industry is moving in the other direction—it is becoming increasingly concentrated. Investment banking is essentially an oligopoly featuring very few extremely powerful firms like Goldman Sachs and Morgan Stanley. Lehman Brothers is gone, so the industry has become even more concentrated. Commercial banking has become more concentrated as larger banks have taken over the more than 250 smaller banks that failed in 2009 and 2010. European and Canadian banking systems have always been highly concentrated. Neither the Obama administration nor the Federal Reserve has supported the proposal to downsize the systemically important firms. The top regulatory authority on the Federal Reserve's Board of Governors, Daniel Tarullo, while not intellectually opposed to the proposal, views it only as a last resort. So it turns out that the proposal to break up the huge, interconnected banks has never really been on the table.

While the financial reform legislation enacted in 2010 did nothing to break up large financial firms, it did provide federal authorities both the responsibility and authority to dismantle and liquidate large, systemically important financial firms that are failing without going through lengthy and costly bankruptcy proceedings. This includes new authority to seize and dismantle such noncommercial bank companies as insurance companies and investment banks. However, the legislation does not rule out the possibility of taxpayer bailouts of failing firms, and skeptics question the likelihood that the resolution authority will actually be exercised, even when warranted.

IV. Specific Problems Needing to be Fixed

As indicated, the formation of the twin bubbles that gave us the financial crisis and the costly aftermath can be attributed to a series of misaligned or socially perverse incentives. Incentives facing various private parties are at odds with those that would serve the public interest by reducing the frequency and severity of financial crises. Several of these misalignments and proposed remedies will be discussed in this section.

The Compensation System

At the heart of the problem are the financial incentives facing Wall Street traders and officers of large investment banks, bank holding companies, hedge funds, insurance companies, and other companies in the financial services industry. While the overwhelming majority of the owners of these firms—the stockholders—are interested in maximizing long-run returns on their investment, managers, traders, and CEOs have powerful incentives to maximize near-term payments and bonuses. Given asymmetric information—the fact that managers and traders inevitably have better information about activities and risk taking place in the firm than do the stockholders—the stockholders (the principals) are unable to induce traders and managers (their agents) to take a viewpoint that fosters the long-run well-being of the firm and its stockholders. This is an example of the well-known principal–agent problem.

Examples of risk-taking activities include purchasing risky securities like collateralized debt obligations (CDOs) and other complex instruments, operating with very high leverage, and issuing short-term debt to fund purchase of long-term securities. Enormous incomes that can be reaped in very short periods—many managers and traders can earn considerably more in a year than typical workers earn in a lifetime—give rise to the "I'll be gone, you'll be gone" attitude. That is, if the risks come home to roost and the firm is closed down three years later, so what? Sufficient income will have been earned by key operatives in the firm in a short time period to fund a comfortable early retirement.

To promote incentives of traders, managers, and top officials to take a long-run view that would promote financial stability, the compensation system needs to be revamped. One proposal would have firms provide compensation through payment in restricted shares—shares of stock in the firm that vest with the recipient only after several years have elapsed. Some have suggested a decade would be appropriate. Even better, a major portion of the payment could be held until retirement. In the current culture of Wall Street, traders and officers are heavily rewarded when the firm has good years, but not penalized in bad years. They receive large bonuses in years in which their activities earn their firms tens of millions of dollars of profits, but pay no penalties in years in which their bets go south and cost their firms dearly. This arrangement strongly tilts incentives toward taking more risk. A change in compensation policy in which firms pool bonus funds and average the performance over a ten-year period in determining payouts would moderate the incentive to take risk.

An even more powerful incentive for firms to monitor and reduce risk would be to mandate that the pool of funds to be paid out later in bonuses be constituted by slices of the same CDOs and other esoteric securities the financial engineers of the firm have been cooking up. This would put a large dose of "skin in the game." Credit Suisse implemented such a plan in 2009 when it moved $5 billion of toxic CDOs from its balance sheet to a fund out of which future bonuses were to be paid. Such a plan, if announced in advance and accompanied by measures prohibiting prospective bonus recipients from taking actions that hedge against a decline in the value of the securities, would strongly align incentives of traders and managers in the public interest and reduce the likelihood of a future systemic collapse of the financial system.

If these changes in compensation systems were adopted unilaterally by one firm, it would lose many of its top employees to other firms in the industry. Hence, in the event corporate boards of directors refuse to act, the U.S. government may need to implement and enforce any major change in the system of compensation. One might argue that government authority to do this may be warranted by the hundreds of billions it has paid out to save private firms and prevent Armageddon, together with the prospect that a repeat performance is likely if essential reforms that happen to be painful to the financial industry are not implemented. Ideally, reforms of this nature would be put in place simultaneously by many of the world's leading nations—a difficult goal to achieve. The financial reform legislation of 2010 did not come to grips with the issue of compensation.

Capital and Liquidity Requirements

The capital of a financial firm is its equity or net worth—the amount by which the value of its total assets exceeds the value of its total liabilities. This equity accrues to the owners of the firm. Regulatory authorities set capital requirements to be maintained by commercial and investment banks—that is, the authorities set minimum standards for capital/total assets. As indicated in chapter 4, such investment banks as Lehman Brothers, Goldman Sachs, and Merrill Lynch were legally operating with capital/total asset ratios as low as 3 or 4 percent at the time the crisis struck in 2007. Such capital requirements are far too low.

Leverage of a financial firm may be defined as the ratio of total assets to capital—the reciprocal of the capital/total assets ratio. These huge investment banks were leveraged to the tune of 25:1 and 33:1, each dollar of capital or equity supporting loans and other assets of $25 to $33. In good times, high leverage provides tremendous rates of return on equity for the owners. In bad times, it results in large negative returns that can render firms insolvent. In 2004, the investment banks successfully lobbied the Securities and Exchange Commission (SEC) to permit a large increase in leverage (decline in capital requirements).[3] Unfortunately, because Lehman was leveraged 25:1, a 4 percent decline in the value of its assets would render the firm insolvent. That is exactly what happened as many of the risky mortgage-related assets on Lehman's books declined in value.

If a bank or other firm is required to abide by higher capital requirements, its owners have more at stake in the event of failure and the firm is therefore likely to pursue less risky activities. Higher capital requirements would therefore reduce the moral hazard problem. In addition, of course, a bank is less likely to fail if it has a higher capital cushion because it would take a larger shock to knock out the bank's capital and render it insolvent. For these reasons, almost all economists favor higher capital requirements as an essential part of a viable reform program. Importantly, capital requirements also need to be extended to insurance companies and other nonbank financial firms that constitute the shadow banking system.

An interesting proposal that has gained increasing support of economists from diverse philosophical camps is to require systemically important financial firms to maintain a stock of contingent capital on their balance sheets in the form of hybrid debt-equity securities. These bonds issued and held on the books by the financial firm would automatically be converted into equity or capital in the event the actual capital ratio of the firm declined to some triggering threshold. Suppose, for example, financial firms were required to maintain such contingent capital in the amount of 10 percent of their total assets in addition to abiding by an 8 percent minimum capital ratio requirement. In the event financial losses drove the existing capital ratio from the required 8 percent to the trigger level—say 2 percent—a sufficient amount of the hybrid debt would automatically be converted to capital to push the capital ratio back to 8 percent. The firm's creditors (bondholders) would be forced to exchange some of their holdings of bonds for shares of bank stock.

This proposed contingent capital requirement would provide a cushion that increases the safety of the institution and reduces the likelihood that government would need to become involved in costly bailouts of impaired firms. And because the market would dictate that higher yields be paid on the contingent bonds issued by riskier institutions, financial firms would have a strong incentive to hold down risk. Bankers strongly oppose this proposal (and most others) because it would raise the cost of doing business, but isn't it time we stop the banks from dictating public policy to Congress?

The financial reform bill enacted in 2010 includes provisions mandating that regulators enforce higher capital standards. However, as in numerous other aspects of the legislation, wide latitude over the details of this provision is left to the discretion of the regulatory authorities.

The Basel Committee on Banking Supervision, under the auspices of the Bank for International Settlements in Basel, Switzerland, establishes a common set of capital requirements that have been adopted by more than 80 countries, including the United States. These complicated standards, known as the Basel Accords, are being renegotiated with a view toward generally implementing higher capital standards. A new "Basel 3" set of accords, under consideration in 2010, will phase in somewhat more rigorous capital requirements over a period of many years.

Liquidity refers to the ease with which assets can be converted to cash to pay depositors or provide funds for other uses. The Great Crisis began as a liquidity crisis resulting from the fact that many financial institutions—especially shadow banks—had funded purchase of relatively illiquid and risky longer-term assets like CDOs through such short-term liabilities (sources of funds) as commercial paper and repos. This practice necessitated frequent refinancing—often almost daily. As the value of mortgage-related securities fell with the decline in house prices, these investment banks and other shadow-market institutions found themselves unable to roll over their short-term debt. Lenders to the institutions balked because they feared that they would not be repaid. This, in turn, forced financial firms to sell illiquid longer-term securities under conditions of stress, contributing to the contraction of asset values that helps explain how a liquidity crisis evolved into a solvency crisis. If a larger portion of financial firms' liabilities had been of longer-term maturity, or if the financial firms had been holding a larger stock of highly liquid assets, their exposure to this sort of problem would have been less severe. Thus, higher liquidity standards for financial firms should be part of a viable reform package.

Credit Rating Agencies

Agencies that rate the quality of bonds and other debt instruments have been around for the better part of 100 years. In the early years, the major function of these agencies was to rate the quality of bonds held by banks. Following a period of relative economic stability from the 1940s through the 1960s, the rating agencies took on increasing prominence in the 1970s when deteriorating conditions resulted in a spate of bond defaults. In 1975 the Securities and Exchange Commission mandated that any entity issuing new debt was required to first obtain a rating from a Nationally Recognized Statistical Rating Organization (NRSRO). Prominent among the handful of ratings firms granted this coveted status by the SEC were Fitch, Moody's and Standard & Poor's. These three firms continue to dominate the ratings industry today, although a few additional firms have been granted NRSRO status by the SEC in recent years.

In the beginning, the rating agencies collected fees for their services from a large variety of investors. But the free-rider problem made this business model obsolete as individuals and firms learned they could obtain the information they wanted free of charge from the diminishing pool of those who paid for this service. With assistance of the SEC requirement that issuers of new debt were responsible for obtaining ratings, the agencies began charging security issuers for the ratings.

An obvious conflict of interest is inherent in this arrangement. The decision of large investors to purchase CDOs and other securities is critically dependent on their rating. For example, pension funds and many other buyers are required to limit themselves strictly to AAA-rated securities. The hefty fees received from security issuers by the oligopoly of rating agencies, together with regulatory arbitrage—the search by the issuers of the instruments for the highest ratings among the agencies— have corrupted the ratings process. In fact, a "race to the bottom" occurred because a rating agency failing to provide an AAA rating on a CDO security built from subprime mortgages stood to forfeit millions of dollars in fees. Unfortunately, many buyers of CDOs and other exotic securities took the ratings at face value and were badly burned as a result, as attested by numerous lawsuits pending against the credit rating agencies. The relationship between the investment banks and other firms that create the securities and the rating agencies has become so cozy that the rating agencies now collect large "consulting" fees for providing advice to security issuers on combining tranches of underlying asset-backed securities of various degrees of risk into CDOs in a way that minimally qualifies for AAA-rating status.

Several reforms aimed at fixing this corrupt and socially costly system have been suggested. First, consulting activities conducted by rating agencies should be prohibited. Second, the agencies should not be funded through fees charged to originators of securities. One proposal would have them funded by the federal government which, in turn, could cover this expense through taxes levied on institutions issuing the securities to be rated. Alternatively, institutional investors could be required to pay into a common pool that could be used by regulators to purchase ratings from the agencies. Also, reducing the considerable barriers to entry into the ratings industry might promote more competition and improve quality of the ratings, although this is uncertain. More radically, the requirement that securities be rated by the agencies could be abandoned entirely. The various regulatory agencies could then implement their own measures for assessing and monitoring risk. This approach, however, may lead to costly duplication of expenses. The financial reform bill enacted in 2010 does not address the issue of incompetent or corrupt credit ratings.

Derivatives Markets

Relatively new derivatives such as CDOs and credit default swaps (CDS) played a major role in promoting the elevated risk-taking that led to the Great Crisis. CDS were especially instrumental in this regard. The CDS market, which exploded from virtually nil in the early 1990s to a peak notional value of more than $60,000 billion in 2008, has gone largely unregulated. This stems from actions of former chair of the Senate Banking Committee, Phil Gramm, who in 2000 slipped into the Commodity Futures Modernization Act a clause that exempted complex over-the-counter derivatives like CDS from regulation by the pertinent agency, the Commodity Futures Trading Commission. (Gramm later left the Senate to become a lobbyist for the financial industry, an example of the "revolving-door" syndrome that needs to be constrained.) These markets are not only largely unregulated, but information about transactions conducted in them is notoriously inadequate. The financial disaster incurred by AIG, which directly cost U.S. taxpayers some $180 billion, resulted from CDS issued by AIG to insure holders of AAA-rated securities built from subprime mortgages against losses on the securities.

As the prices of the CDOs and other securities tanked in 2008, AIG was required to post collateral to make good on losses on securities it had insured through the CDS. But its exemption from capital requirements meant it had nowhere near enough capital to cover the losses incurred by its counterparties on more than $400 billion of risky CDOs it had insured through CDS transactions. Were it not for timely government intervention, AIG would have quickly become insolvent, likely triggering a meltdown of the financial system. In the wake of the pandemonium created by the failure of Lehman the previous day, the Fed and Treasury felt that there was no alternative to preventing the bankruptcy of AIG. The company was far too interconnected, having written CDS contracts with thousands of firms, hundreds of which would likely have gone bankrupt if AIG been allowed to fail.

Banks and dealers have opposed proposals that would make derivatives markets more transparent. Absence of information in these markets allows banks to extract huge fees in derivatives transactions and enables dealers to maintain artificially large bid-ask spreads that produce very large trading profits. Once again, we have a misalignment of incentives. Originators of CDOs, CDS, and other derivatives are motivated to keep markets as opaque as possible to minimize the flow of information and extract outsized profits. The public interest dictates maximizing the flow of relevant information to the public so that transactions costs are minimized and so that regulators have access to information that would enable them to monitor risk in the financial system.

The AIG fiasco reveals a clear need for increased transparency in the markets for derivatives, including the extremely opaque over-the-counter market. Where feasible, credit derivatives should be standardized and traded on a central exchange, which could provide timely information to the public and enforce the posting of adequate collateral by firms issuing the derivatives. The more specialized and esoteric derivatives that cannot be standardized and traded on an exchange are traded over the counter. These bilateral contracts between two parties should be registered in a centralized clearinghouse that would be responsible for the contract and would be required to post substantial collateral. More rigorous capital standards should be applied to such over-the-counter transactions than to those standardized transactions conducted on an exchange, providing incentives to standardize these transactions whenever possible. Data pertaining to both types of derivatives should be collected and made publicly available so that transaction costs are reduced and regulators can identify risks as they develop.

The 2010 financial reform legislation represents a substantial improvement in this regard. The new law requires that most derivatives be traded openly on exchanges. The more complicated derivatives transactions will trade through clearinghouses for the first time. Also, the legislation prohibits banks from trading certain derivatives deemed to be highly risky.

Regulatory Arbitrage

Regulatory arbitrage involves deliberate measures taken by firms for the purpose of evading regulatory oversight. This is a serious problem that needs to be addressed in the interest of reducing the susceptibility of the financial system to crises. Financial firms have practiced regulatory arbitrage in a number of ways. Two of the most important involve exploitation of the maze of regulatory agencies that exist through "regulatory shopping," and purposeful movement of activities previously subject to restraints into the relatively unregulated shadow-banking system. Both of these actions have served to exacerbate systemic risk.

U.S. history has produced a complicated, overlapping financial regulatory structure. For example, each of the 50 states has established its own separate commissions responsible for overseeing banks and insurance companies in the state. Many states also have their own regulatory authorities that oversee credit unions and issuers of securities. On top of this decentralized system, the federal government has an abundance of regulatory bodies responsible for overseeing financial firms. These include the FDIC, the Federal Reserve, the Comptroller of the Currency, the SEC, and the Commodity Futures Trading Commission, among others. There is often overlapping authority, with more than one agency responsible for supervising a particular type of financial institution. In large part, this system is the product of our federal system of government, along with piecemeal legislation implemented in the 1930s in response to the Great Depression.

Some have defended the existing system, claiming that it promotes beneficial competition and efficiency as well as providing checks and balances that foster safety in the financial system. This seems unlikely, largely because this system promotes regulatory arbitrage as financial firms arrange matters so that they fall under the purview of the least rigorous regulator. For example, a commercial bank has the option of receiving its operating charter from the state in which it originates or from the federal government. If it elects to be chartered as a state bank, it then has the option of becoming a member of the Federal Reserve System. These choices determine whether the bank falls under the regulatory authority of the Federal Reserve, the FDIC, or the Comptroller of the Currency, as well as state regulatory authorities. Evidence indicates that not only do banks tend to gravitate to the least rigorous regulatory authorities, but the existence of this regulatory shopping creates incentives for the various regulators to ease restraints on banks in order to protect their domain and preserve their reason for existence. In these ways the current system has worked to weaken banking regulation and supervision.

The complicated, overlapping system of regulation and supervision needs to be consolidated and simplified in the interest of efficiency and financial stability. Turf battles have made this difficult in the past, as was discovered when the Clinton administration proposal to collapse the complicated overlapping structure into a single new regulatory agency met with strong resistance from the Federal Reserve and other agencies whose domain of authority stood to be reduced. The Federal Reserve is probably the logical place where centralized regulatory authority should reside. This follows from the importance of coordinating regulatory policy with monetary policy, together with the existing expertise and relative political independence of the Federal Reserve. Unfortunately, the financial reform legislation enacted in 2010 leaves the patchwork regulatory framework largely intact.

Regulatory arbitrage has also occurred through bank exploitation of the shadow banking system. This has become a serious problem in recent years. Until the past decade or two, commercial banks seemed content to submit to regulations in return for a quid pro quo in the form of the government "safety net." The safety net includes provision of federal deposit insurance and access to the Federal Reserve discount window, both of which reduce the susceptibility of the system to crises. In the quest for larger profits made possible by taking greater risks, banks began shifting more activities to the shadow banking system—firms that perform banking functions but are not regulated like banks. These actions, coupled with financial engineering, enabled banks to evade capital requirements and ramp up leverage. Given that many of these shadow banks are systemically important, as indicated by the AIG and Lehman fiascos, they should be regulated like regular banks. They should be subjected to capital requirements and other restraints as regular banks are. And the regulations must be applied to smaller as well as larger entities in the shadow banking system. Otherwise, a new form of regulatory arbitrage will emerge in the form of massive shifting of activities from larger firms to smaller ones. Collectively, small firms can behave in ways that have major systemic consequences.

Incentives of Regulators

Even if appropriate regulations are in place, they are likely to be ineffective if regulators and supervisors lack the competence, will, or incentives to enforce them. Many commentators have argued that the problems that produced the Great Crisis stemmed not from absence of appropriate regulations but from lack of competence and motivation of those charged with enforcing the regulations. Regulators have been slow or reluctant to intervene with appropriate actions. For example, regulators are often reluctant to close down a failing large financial firm, perhaps in part because of uncertainty and anxiety about the prospective fallout. Under intense pressure from lobbyists, the tempting path for regulators is to opt for "forbearance." They may fail to close down firms that are insolvent, a pervasive problem in the Savings and Loan fiasco of the 1980s. And a revolving door of employment between the regulators and the regulated firms has created an egregious conflict of interest that complicates such decisions.

Regulators receive only a fraction of the remuneration paid to those holding positions of comparable training and importance in the regulated firms. In the conventional wisdom, regulators are deemed inferior in intellect and motivation to those they are charged with regulating. Given the enormous consequences of the regulatory failures of the past decade, the regulatory positions need to be upgraded in the public's psyche so that they are regarded as critically important and prestigious. The public must be informed about the social value of such positions, and compensation of regulatory authorities needs to be boosted sharply. We need to attract idealistic individuals with a mission and sense of public purpose—people of the ilk of a Ralph Nader or Elizabeth Warren—into key positions in the regulatory system.

An interesting proposal with a market-based slant has recently been proposed by professors at Harvard and the University of Chicago. Oliver Hart and Luigi Zingales have suggested using market signals to force lethargic regulatory authorities to swing into action.[4] Here is how the proposal would work: As in the contingent capital plan, financial firms would be required to have two layers of capital on their books. In addition to the capital requirement they are normally required to meet, the firm would be required to issue junior long-term debt—debt that would be repaid only after all other debt had been paid. These bonds would be tradable in the market. If the bank experienced problems and its capital became impaired, the price of the bonds would decline, signaling problems to the public. But the corporate bond market is relatively thin and illiquid, so prices and yields may at times provide unreliable signals. Hart and Zingales argue that a more liquid security that accurately reflects the financial condition of the firm is the much maligned credit default swap. The price of the CDS that insures each bank's bonds reflects the likelihood that the bank's debt will not be paid in full.

If the price of the credit default swap were to rise to a certain specified threshold level suggesting that markets perceive significantly elevated risk in the bank, regulators would be required to step in and conduct "stress tests." The regulators would examine how various hypothetical shocks would affect the bank's financial viability. If the bank passed the stress test, it would be deemed adequately capitalized. If it failed, the test it would be required to raise additional capital. If that effort failed, the firm would be placed in receivership and sold, stockholders being wiped out. This proposal, assuming the CDS market provides reliable advance signals of impending problems, would induce critical regulatory actions that may otherwise be absent. By removing discretion from regulators reluctant to act, the proposal addresses the problem of regulatory forbearance and provides a mechanism that ensures timely intervention.

The Mortgage GSEs

The rationale for the creation of Fannie and Freddie was to promote homeownership by improving the functioning of mortgage markets and lowering the cost of mortgages—one of many subsidies accorded to U.S.

homeowners. Some have questioned the fairness of this favorable treatment of homeowners vis-à-vis renters. Others dispute the merits of the goal of fostering homeownership. These individuals advocate abolition of the GSEs.

Others believe that homeownership is a worthy social goal and advocate continued subsidies that promote this goal, including continuation of the GSEs. If this is to be done, it is imperative that the inherent conflict in the dual GSE goals of promoting the public interest on the one hand and maximizing private profits and bonuses for top officers on the other be eliminated. One way to do this would be to return Fannie and Freddie to their original purely public status, with officers paid salaries commensurate with their skill and experience, but with elimination of bonuses based on short-term profits. The re-oriented firms would resume their original function of securitizing and guaranteeing mortgages that meet rigorous standards that ensure a very low level of risk to taxpayers. The Wall Street Reform and Consumer Protection Act (Dodd-Frank Act), enacted in 2010, failed to address the status of Fannie and Freddie. This contentious issue is likely to occupy the attention of Congress in 2011 and 2012.

V. Conclusion

In testifying before Congress, Goldman Sachs CEO Lloyd Blankfein spoke of the Great Crisis as if it was a random, unpreventable event—almost an Act of God. This inference is incorrect and even dangerous because it deemphasizes the urgency of implementing appropriate regulatory reforms. In reality, the severe crisis was a predictable consequence of the pattern of incentives that was allowed to develop over a period of many years. Only the *timing* of the disaster was unpredictable.

There are two broad avenues of reform that would diminish the susceptibility of modern economies to enormously costly financial crises. The more radical approach would reform the structure of the financial institutions to eliminate the possibility that failure of any one or two players could compromise the safety of the financial system. This would necessitate a major restructuring of the financial industry to make individual units sufficiently small so that any firm could responsibly be allowed to fail. This radical approach was eschewed in the financial reform legislation enacted in 2010. The more practical approach is to institute a series of reforms largely intended to align incentives of individual players in the financial system so that they are compatible with longer-term financial and economic stability. This was the approach taken in the financial reform legislation enacted in 2010. However, several constructive features of proposed legislation were deleted in the final compromise bill that was passed by Congress and signed by President Obama. If this legislation fails to prevent a repeat of the Great Crisis in the next decade or two, the public's anger directed at huge financial organizations may suffice to induce more radical reform of our financial institutions.

I Financial Crises: An Overview

1. If a nation's deficit/GDP ratio exceeds the trend growth rate of its GDP, the nation's debt grows faster than GDP and its debt/GDP ratio increases over time. When this ratio reaches a critical threshold of uncertain magnitude, investors begin to anticipate possible default and therefore demand a premium in the form of higher yield to induce them to buy the bonds (lend to the country). As indicated in Table 1-1, Greece appears more vulnerable to this development than other countries and, in fact, crossed the critical threshold in 2010. With the notable exception of Germany, all other countries represented in the table, including the United States, are also vulnerable to a potential rapid shift in investor sentiment that could force them to pay appreciably higher yields on their bonds, thus exacerbating their fiscal problems. For this reason, additional fiscal stimulus, while needed for purposes of economic stabilization, appears to be ruled out for the medium term. Indeed, numerous countries introduced severe austerity programs in the second half of 2010 that are likely to impede the world-wide economic recovery from the Great Recession.

2. In April 2010, risk premiums in Greek bonds soared as investors dumped these bonds in favor of those perceived to be relatively safe, for example, U.S. Treasury bonds. The cost of insuring against default of bonds issued by the Greek government, as measured by the price of credit default swaps, stood at 4 percent of the concurrent price of the bonds. This was about ten times the cost of buying similar insurance against default in U.S. Treasury bonds. After the euro-currency nations and the IMF put together the rescue package, these indicators of the likelihood of Greek default declined. However, this situation is likely to remain unstable for some time.

3. John Maynard Keynes famously described this process in his brilliant early polemic work, *The Economic Consequences of the Peace* (London: Macmillan, 1918), as follows: "By a continuing process of inflation, governments can confiscate, secretly and unobserved, an important part of the wealth of their citizens ... There is no subtler, no surer means of overturning the existing basis of society than to debauch the currency. The process engages all the hidden forces of economic law on the side of destruction, and does it in a manner than not one man in a million is able to diagnose."

4. The highest U.S. inflation rate for any year since 1800 occurred in 1864, during the Civil War, when prices increased by 24 percent. In the past 60 years, U.S. inflation reached its highest level in 1980, when it peaked at approximately 13 percent. In the 50 years ending in 2010, U.S. inflation averaged 4.1 and 3.6 percent per year, as measured by the consumer price index and the GDP deflator, respectively.

5. Deleveraging is simply the application of leverage on the downside. If a bank traditionally maintains a ratio of loans to capital of 6 to 1 and it gains $100 million of capital, it may expand its loans by $600 million. Its capital is "leveraged" 6 to 1. If bad loans reduce the bank's capital by $100 million, it must reduce loans by $600 million to return to its customary loan/capital ratio. This latter phenomenon is termed "deleveraging." A massive loss of capital in lending institutions led to the enormously damaging phenomenon of deleveraging.

2 The Nature of Banking Crises

1. See two works by Hyman Minsky: *Stabilizing an Unstable Economy* (New Haven, CT: Yale University Press, 1986), and "The Financial Instability Hypothesis," Working Paper No. 74, Jerome Levy Economics Institute of Bard College, May 1992.

2. In the build-up to the Great Crisis, much of the new lending took place in the rapidly expanding "shadow-banking" sector, which by 2007 had grown in magnitude to approximately equal the size of the "regular" banking system.

3. This phenomenon was first witnessed during the manic phase of the enormous late-1990s bubble in technology stocks that drove the NASDAQ 100 index up approximately ten fold in the seven years ending in early 2000.

4. The Federal Reserve advanced the proposition that the surge in credit that fed the U.S. housing bubble was largely the result not of Federal Reserve policy, but of a "global savings glut" that found an outlet in the United States and other nations. In this view, an enormous and persistent capital inflow to the United States and other countries from nations with persistent current account surpluses, like China and India, drove down U.S. interest rates and financed the bubble. See Ben Bernanke's speech, entitled, "Monetary Policy and the Housing Bubble," available at http://www.federalreserve.gov/newsevents/speech/2010speech.htm. This hypothesis is contentious.

5. As the crisis engulfed nations throughout the world, however, fearful investors in more vulnerable nations began liquidating domestic assets and moving funds into the United States, long regarded as the ultimate safe haven. The dollar thus appreciated strongly. This wholesale dumping of assets in many countries perceived to be highly vulnerable disrupted financial markets in those countries, contributing further to the severity of their crises.

6. This is a major theme of an important book of the same name by Carmen Reinhart and Kenneth Rogoff, *This Time is Different: Eight Centuries of Financial Folly* (Princeton, NJ: Princeton University Press, 2009). This book provides a detailed empirical analysis of the history of financial crises, commencing with those of the thirteenth century.

7. Prior to the 2007–2009 financial crisis, both Federal Reserve Chairman Ben Bernanke and his predecessor, Alan Greenspan, were adamant in their opposi-

tion to the view that the Fed should attempt to deflate asset bubbles. However, having experienced the enormous cost of the Great Crisis, Bernanke has revealed a softening of his position on this issue.

8. See Reinhart and Rogoff, *op.cit.*, and "Is the U.S. Subprime Crisis So Different? An International Comparison," *American Economic Review*, 98 No. 2 (2008): 339–344.

9. The increase in the government budget deficit/GDP ratio in the crisis-related recessions experienced by Finland and Sweden were 11.8 and 15.4 percentage points, respectively. In contrast, these budget deficit swings experienced by Mexico, Thailand, Korea, and Indonesia in crisis-related recessions in the 1990s were less than six percentage points, as was the case for the United States during 2007–2010. See Reinhart and Rogoff, op.cit, *This Time is Different*, p. 231.

3   The Panic of 1907 and the Savings and Loan Crisis

1. For a detailed study of nineteenth century U.S. banking panics, see Charles Calomiris and Gary Gorton, "The Origins of Banking Panics: Models, Facts, and Bank Regulation," in R. Glenn Hubbard, *Financial Markets and Financial Crises* (Chicago, IL: University of Chicago Press, 1991).

2. At the peak of the banking crisis a few months later, J. P. Morgan, steel industry magnate and eminent banker, was informed by Mayor George McClellan that New York City was likely to declare bankruptcy the following week. Acutely aware of the blow to public confidence and the fragile banking system such an announcement would cause, Morgan agreed to keep the city afloat by personally buying $30 million of New York City bonds.

3. The Panic of 1907 took a terrible toll on Barney and his family. Although the crisis was over by then and he remained a wealthy man, Barney died in his home of a self-inflicted gunshot on November 14, 1907. For a fascinating account of the personalities and events involved in the Panic of 1907, see Robert Bruner and Sean Carr, *The Panic of 1907:Lessons Learned From the Market's Perfect Storm* (Hoboken, New Jersey: John Wiley and Sons, 2009).

4. In 1981, for example, the 90-day Treasury bill yield averaged 14.2 percent while the 30-year Treasury bond yield averaged 13.4 percent.

5. Had the S&Ls not sharply boosted rates paid to depositors, depositor defection to money market funds and Treasury bills would have forced the S&Ls to liquidate large quantities of mortgages to obtain the funds to pay departing depositors. This would have severely depressed the value of the mortgages on the S&Ls' books. In the absence of a government bailout, this would likely have bankrupted many of them.

6. In December 1981, the low point of S&L valuation, a widely quoted estimate placed the net worth of the S&L industry at negative $100 billion. The 1981 spike in interest rates, by depressing the value of mortgages and bonds on the books of the S&Ls, temporarily put the net worth of the industry at an all-time low. By the end of 1983, long-term rates had come down appreciably from their

peaks and the increase in bond and mortgage values returned the net worth of the industry to positive territory.

7. The infamous "Keating Five" scandal involved five U.S. senators who had collectively received $1.3 million in campaign contributions from Charles H. Keating, Jr., head of the Lincoln Savings and Loan Association in Arizona. Keating had been breaking rules and speculating with depositors' money for years. His S&L bought junk bonds, speculated in currency futures, and looted the company to transfer $30 million to his family. As regulatory authorities prepared to swoop in on Keating the five senators went to bat for him, complaining to top regulators that they were being inconsistent with the regulatory sentiment of the times. Jurisdiction was taken out of control of the Federal Home Loan Bank of San Francisco and Lincoln's books were not examined for more than a year. In 1992, Keating was convicted of numerous counts of fraud and served a sentence in federal prison. The senators were excused with a mild slap on the wrist. Ultimate cost to the Treasury of the Lincoln fiasco was in excess of $3 billion.

4   Development of the Housing and Credit Bubbles

1. Restrictions on institutions that purchased the MBS and related securities often required that only AAA-rated securities were eligible for purchase. Moody's, Standard and Poor's, and Fitch were the principal rating agencies and they were financed by fees collected by the investment banks that issued the bonds. The conflict of interest is palpable.

2. America's homeownership rate jumped sharply in the early post-World War II period from 45 percent in 1945 to about 65 percent in 1957, remained stable until 1994, and then increased to 69 percent in 2005. Hence, this recent increase in the share of American households owning homes can account for only a minor portion of the increase in mortgage debt/disposable income. Typical homebuyers were taking on larger amounts of mortgage debt relative to take-home pay.

3. From 1998 through 2005, the consumer price index increased at an average annual rate of 2.6 percent. In this period, the rate of inflation of houses nationwide averaged 10.4 percent per year. In major urban areas, house prices increased even more rapidly.

4. In the first case, the $10,000 investment led to a gain of $122,102 after five years. The average annual compounded rate of return on the investment is thus $[(\$122,102/\$10,000)^{1/5}-1] \times 100 = 64.9$ percent per year. At 14 percent per year appreciation, it is $[(\$185,083/\$10,000)^{1/5}-1] \times 100 = 79.3$ percent per year.

5. The data plotted in Figure 4-2 are backward-looking 12 month inflation rates. The Case-Shiller 20-City Home Price Index commences only in 2000, which is why the first observation plotted is for the first quarter of 2001.

6. The monthly payments typically increased by more than $300 after the first two years of the loan. Some 15 percent of these "teaser rate" mortgages issued in

2006 featured initial rates of less than 2 percent, while the rate on conventional 30-year fixed-rate mortgages was more than 6 percent.

7. This problem could be fixed by requiring the mortgage originator to retain, say, 20 percent of the mortgages on its books. This would change the pattern of incentives by ensuring that lenders had "skin in the game."

8. An excellent analysis of the subprime mortgage market can be found in Edward Gramlich, *Subprime Mortgages: America's Latest Boom and Bust* (Washington, D.C.: Urban Institute Press, 2007).

9. Tax breaks for homeowners not available to renters include deductibility from taxable income of mortgage interest payments and property taxes, along with favorable capital gains tax treatment, including a one-time exemption of up to $500,000 in capital gains realized on the sale of a principal residence.

10. It is likely that these firms will eventually be totally privatized (thus eliminating any implicit guarantees by the government), de-privatized and returned to their original status as strictly government organizations, left as privately owned GSEs but subjected to increased regulations that reduce the risks they are allowed to take, or maintained as privately owned GSEs but reduced dramatically in size to reduce taxpayer exposure to risk.

11. In 2004 Fannie Mae became engulfed in an accounting scandal, and in December 2006 federal regulators filed numerous civil charges against three top Fannie officials. These officials were charged with fraudulently manipulating Fannie's reported profits for purposes of boosting their annual bonuses. The suit sought to recover more than $115 million in bonus payments paid to these officials during the 1998-2004 period in addition to $100 million in fines for involvement in the accounting scandal. These fraudulent accounting activities appear similar to those engaged in concurrently by such purely private corporations as Enron, Tyco, and World Com, among others.

12. Banks themselves became participants in the shadow banking system during the mortgage boom. They established subsidiaries, so-called structured investment vehicles (SIVs). These SIVs issued commercial paper to finance purchase of a variety of higher yielding assets, including mortgage-backed and related securities. Banks placed these SIVs off balance sheet so they would not be subject to capital requirements on the securities held in the SIVs. By reducing required capital, this tactic enabled banks to increase their leverage.

13. Tim Geithner, remarks at the Economic Club of New York, June 9, 2009, available at http://www.newyorkfed.org/newsevents/speeches/2008.

14. Part of the jump in leverage in 2007 was due to the decline in capital resulting from major losses taken by investment banks that year, especially in mortgage-backed securities. This was particularly true in the case of Merrill and Lehman. The increases in leverage exhibited in 2005 and 2006 can be ascribed primarily to a careless increase in risk-taking as the investment banks got caught up in the manic phase of the cycle.

15. In chapter 11 the Taylor rule is analyzed and used as a benchmark for the purpose of evaluating the level of the federal funds rate set by the Federal Reserve. By the Taylor Rule standard, the federal funds rate was maintained too low on average during 2002–2005 by more than 250 basis points. See the discussion on pp. 210–211.

5   Bursting of the Twin Bubbles

1. Using monthly averages of daily figures, the Treasury securities yield curve has been inverted in only 12 months since 1982. That is, 90-day Treasury bill yields since 1982 have exceeded 30-year Treasury bond yields only in the periods extending from July through December of 2000 and October 2006 through March 2007. In the other 96 percent of the months since 1982 the yield curve has been upward sloping. See the FRED database at http://research.stlouisfed/org/fred2/.
2. Even before banks resorted to SIVs, they were encouraged to sell individual mortgages and purchase MBS by a series of accords known as Basel II. In these agreements, implemented in the early 2000s, bank capital requirements were based on the perceived risk structure of bank assets. Because the regulators who drew up the Basel II agreements believed that these MBS and CDOs were relatively safe instruments, capital requirements applied to them were low relative to requirements on individual mortgages in bank portfolios.
3. Occasionally, short-term Treasury bill yields became negative in 2008. How can this anomaly be explained? Because certain types of loans require that collateral be in the form of the ultra-safe Treasury bills, high demand for these instruments occasionally pushed their prices above face value, thus resulting in a negative yield. The same phenomenon also occurred in the early 1930s, although in that instance the negative yield may have been attributable to absence of federal insurance on bank deposits and the associated relative safety of Treasury bills.
4. For a riveting account of the developments of mid-September 2008, see James B. Stewart, "Eight Days," *The New Yorker*, September 21, 2009. Other readable accounts can be found in David Wessel, *In Fed We Trust* (New York: Crown Publishing Group, 2009) and Andrew Sorkin, *Too Big to Fail* (New York: Viking, 2009).

6   The Great Crisis and Great Recession of 2007–2009

1. The Department of Labor does not attempt to measure the number of frictionally unemployed workers. This number, which fluctuates over time, can only be crudely estimated.
2. The problem of structural unemployment is probably best attacked through massive efforts to improve the educational attainment of children from economically and socially disadvantaged families. In the 1960s President Lyndon Johnson initiated the Jobs Corps program to provide young individuals from disadvantaged families with viable job skills. President Richard Nixon preferred to address the problem through the private sector by offering tax credits as incentives for firms to hire and train workers who would not otherwise have warranted employment.
3. See Douglas Staiger, James Stock, and Mark Watson, "How Precise Are Estimates of the Natural Rate of Unemployment?" in Christina Romer and David Romer, eds., *Reducing Inflation: Motivation and Strategy* (Chicago, IL: University of

Chicago Press, 1997). The authors estimate that in 1990 the NAIRU was 6.2 percent. However, their statistical procedures indicated they could be 95 percent confident only that the true NAIRU was within a range of 5.1 to 7.7 percent.

4. During President Bill Clinton's two terms of office (January 1993-January 2001), the nation's unemployment rate declined in each of the eight calendar years encompassing 1993 through 2000, while the inflation rate also declined in six of these years. To a large extent Clinton was the beneficiary of fortuitous events, several of which are indicated above. However, his administration must be given credit for taking steps to bring down the large budget deficit it inherited, thereby facilitating a low interest-rate environment that was conducive to robust investment spending and economic growth. President Clinton also worked to open up trade and promote globalization, which helped hold down inflation in the United States.

5. Because various business cycle indicators often tell conflicting stories, several months typically elapse before the National Bureau of Economic Research (NBER) feels sufficiently confident to declare the beginning points (troughs) or ending points (peaks) of business cycles. For example, the beginning of the (December) 2007–2009 recession was not designated by the NBER until December 2008. The ending date of the recession (June 2009) was not determined until September 2010.

6. During the Great Depression stock prices ultimately declined by 87 percent. This means that $1,000 invested in the Dow-Jones index in September 1929 had declined to $130 by April 1933!

7. In 2009 and 2010 more than 250 U.S. banks failed, and several of the nation's largest banks (for example, Citigroup and Bank of America) would likely have joined the list had they not been saved by the U.S. government.

8. A more comprehensive index of unemployment takes account of the phenomena of discouraged workers and those involuntarily working part time because they cannot find a full-time job. The discouraged workers are those who give up looking for work and therefore are not counted as being in the labor force or being unemployed even though they prefer to be employed. This more comprehensive measure of unemployment jumped to 17.5 percent in December 2009 while the reported unemployment rate increased to 10 percent.

9. Carroll, Otsuka, and Slacalek, "How Large is the Housing Wealth Effect? A New Approach," National Bureau of Economic Research, Working Paper No. 12746, December 2006.

10. The rising share of GDP constituted by consumption spending since the early 1980s was reflected in a declining household saving rate, defined as the percentage of disposable personal income saved. This rate slowly declined from an average of 10 percent in the 1980s to about 2.5 percent during 2000-2007, before increasing during the Great Recession as households reacted to the financial crisis with rare caution. If the recent increase in the saving rate is sustained, the economic recovery from the Great Recession may be less robust than that of typical economic expansions.

11. The huge Chinese trade surplus vis-à-vis the U.S. facilitates the United States' habit of collectively spending more than its income, enjoying more than 104 percent of the goods and services produced at home in recent years. This has occurred as China has used revenues from its trade surplus to purchase U.S.

government bonds, which has kept the dollar artificially high (and the renminbi considerably undervalued) during the past 15 years. Given the elevated unemployment in the U.S. and other nations in recent years, China is predictably coming under intense pressure from U.S. and other nations' officials to let the Chinese currency appreciate more rapidly as part of a push to restructure the Chinese economy from an export-led economy to a consumption-driven nation.

7   The Framework of Federal Reserve Monetary Control

1. Each member bank is required to invest in shares in the Federal Reserve in an amount equal to a small fraction of the bank's own capital accounts. In return, the Federal Reserve pays an annual dividend to the banks on these shares. While the member banks "own" the Fed, the structure of the Federal Reserve System was deliberately designed so that banks have minimal influence over the conduct of Federal Reserve policy.
2. Relative to the Treasury bonds held in huge quantities by foreign nations, these holdings of the Fed are miniscule and certainly would not in themselves suffice to prevent a severe depreciation of the dollar were there to be a massive run against it.
3. Normally, the Federal Reserve is authorized to make loans only to depository institutions. During the Great Crisis, however, the Fed invoked a provision in its statute that specifies that in rare times of exigency it can lend to other privately owned institutions as well.
4. Each bank is subject to the following reserve requirements: zero on the first approximately $10 million of demand deposits and other checkable deposits, 3 percent on such deposits up to a threshold of roughly $55 million, and 10 percent on all such deposits in excess of this threshold. This graduated reserve requirement system is rationalized as helping very small banks to better compete against larger banks that benefit from economies of scale and other advantages.
5. Note, however, that this action does not increase the monetary base. The increase in Cp you are holding means that the bank now holds less currency and its reserves are therefore now lower by $80. As we will demonstrate, the Fed controls the monetary base. The public has no direct influence over the size of the monetary base.
6. Cp, a major component of M1, is defined as all currency and coins issued by the Fed and Treasury except for those currently held in the Fed, the Treasury, and depository institutions. Some of this Cp is hoarded in rare coin and paper currency collections, and a large part of it (estimated to be more than half the total) is believed to reside outside of the boundaries of the United States.
7. In 2008 Mexico imposed a tax on bank deposits, including checking accounts (DDO). Our analysis suggests that this would induce individuals and firms to hold more cash (Cp) and less DDO. Other things being equal, this increase in k reduces the money multiplier and the money supply. To prevent a decline in M1 and M2 being triggered by the tax, the Central Bank of Mexico would need to take actions to increase the monetary base.
8. In the distant past, the Federal Reserve sometimes changed reserve requirements to initiate significant changes in monetary policy. For example, the Fed boosted

reserve requirements sharply in 1936 and 1937 to remove a large amount of excess reserves from the banking system at a time when the nation's unemployment rate exceeded 12 percent. This controversial action was implemented out of a misguided fear that the excess reserves were likely to lead to rapid money growth and high inflation. This policy error contributed to a severe economic downturn in 1937-1938. On this episode, see Exhibit 9-1 (pp. 162–163).

9. The Federal Reserve lowered its federal funds rate target to a range of 0-0.25 percent in December 2008. In the period extending from that point through this writing (October 2010), the 30-day Treasury bill yield ranged from 0.03 percent to 0.26 percent. This means banks were not sacrificing much income if they simply held large quantities of excess reserves rather than using them to purchase Treasury bills.

10. Note that it does not matter what type of assets the Federal Reserve purchases. If it purchases candy bars from Walmart, the Fed would write a check to Walmart. When Walmart deposits the check in its bank, the bank is paid by the Fed by having its deposit at the Fed credited by the amount of the transaction. Both reserves and excess reserves increase. The Fed conducts its open market operations in Treasury securities because the market for these securities is highly developed. Transactions costs (bid-ask dealer spreads) are quite low in this highly efficient market. The Fed can conduct its large requisite volume of daily transactions in the government securities market with less disruption than would be the case if it conducted a similar magnitude of transactions in other financial markets such as the corporate bond market or the stock market.

11. Many decades ago, New York bankers would actually go in person to the discount window at the Federal Reserve Bank of New York to request a loan of reserves. Now, of course, banks simply contact the Fed and request that their deposit account at the Fed be credited by the amount of the requested loan.

12. One of the important considerations in setting the level of reserve requirements involves the distribution of profits associated with growth in the money supply over time. If reserve requirements are high, the money multiplier is correspondingly low, which means a large monetary base (and large Fed portfolio of securities) is needed in order to produce any given money supply. Because some 85 percent of the Federal Reserve's gross revenues, earned predominantly in the form of interest income from its huge portfolio of securities, are routinely remitted to the U.S. Treasury each year, the taxpayers benefit from high reserve requirements. With a low reserve requirement, the money multiplier is large, necessitating a small monetary base and a small Fed securities portfolio. In this event banks are highly profitable because the reserve requirement tax is low, and they reap most of the profits associated with the growth of the money supply over time.

8   Federal Reserve Policy in the Great Depression

1. A modern view is that important supply shocks also played a significant role. Massive bank failures disrupted normal personal relationships between bank managers and thousands of borrowers. As failed banks reopened under new

ownership and management, previous relationships were severely disrupted. This indicates that a major setback to the financial intermediation process had occurred; this phenomenon may be regarded as an adverse supply shock that reduced potential GDP.

2. Not just homebuilding, but other forms of construction surged in the 1920s as well. For example, many buildings on the nation's older campuses date from the 1920s. Many of our college football stadiums were built in the 1920s and dedicated as memorials to former students who died in World War I.

3. A detailed account of the nonmonetary forces alleged to be the main cause of the depression can be found in Peter Temin, *Did Monetary Forces Cause the Great Depression?* (New York: Norton, 1976).

4. In the period from 1923 through 1929, 2408 of the 4841 banks that failed in the United States were located in seven states that extended northward from Missouri and Kansas to Iowa, Nebraska, Minnesota, and the Dakotas. In this same period only 11 banks in the six New England states failed.

5. This was a classic response of a central bank to crisis during the era of the gold standard. In such a regime each country defines the value of its currency in units of gold. A nation might devalue its currency vis-à-vis currencies of other nations by raising the official price of gold. Anticipation of such an event would lead foreign nations to rush to convert their dollar holdings into gold at the U.S. Treasury, which was legitimate under the "rules" of the gold standard system. To demonstrate its commitment to maintain constant the price of gold and eschew devaluation, the typical central bank response was to announce such a commitment by raising its discount rate. As part of the (later) deliberate policy of the Roosevelt administration and the Federal Reserve of pushing the U.S. price level back up to 1929 levels, however, the U.S. raised the price of gold from $20.67 per ounce to $35 per ounce in January 1934. This measure meant that the dollar had been sharply devalued, an action consistent with the desire to boost the U.S. price level.

6. For a fascinating account of the first 100 days of Roosevelt's presidency, see Jonathan Alter, *The Defining Moment* (New York: Simon and Schuster Paperbacks, 2006). Things were so dire in the early months of 1933 that serious discussion of proposals to grant Roosevelt dictatorial powers to implement measures to lift the nation out of depression surfaced. Roosevelt resisted such proposals, but was highly successful in getting unprecedented legislation aimed at boosting employment through a compliant Congress in his first few months in office.

7. This apparently was essentially a smart psychological ploy by the Roosevelt administration. Clearly, there is no way the government could determine which of the nation's 18,000 banks were "sound" in a one-week period. This successful ploy may have inspired Secretary Timothy Geithner's analogous 2008 announcement of "stress tests" to be administered 19 of the nation's largest banks. In the latter case, as in the former, a psychological lift was given to financial markets when it was later announced implicitly that banks were generally not in as bad shape as had been feared.

8. Fear of deflation is almost certainly the main reason the Greenspan Federal Reserve kept interest rates exceptionally low in the 2002-2006 period in which the housing bubble was inflating rapidly. Inflation had been trending downward to approximately 1 percent by 2003 and adverse demand shocks initiated by the

terrorist attacks of September 11, 2001 and the stock market crash of 2000–2002 meant that risk of deflation was not negligible. Greenspan was essentially taking out an insurance policy against deflation. Unfortunately, these exceptionally low interest rates fed the housing bubble. We will have more to say on this in chapters 9 and 11.

9. The 12-month change in the producer price index was negative for 50 consecutive months, from April 1929 through May 1933.

10. In three steps, implemented in August 1936, March 1937, and May 1937, the Federal Reserve nearly doubled the level of reserve requirements. Economists today view this action as a major policy mistake that contributed to the severe 1937–1938 recession. On this, see Exhibit 9-1 in the following chapter.

11. Annual averages of daily Treasury bill yields were as follows: 1.40 percent in 1931, 0.88 percent in 1932, 0.52 percent in 1933, 0.26 percent in 1934, and 0.14 percent in 1935. These yields of 1934 and 1935 are similar to T-bill yields that prevailed in 2009 and 2010 when, once again, banks were holding a huge amount of excess reserves.

12. Imagine a graph depicting the supply and demand for excess reserves, with the interest rate depicted on the vertical axis and the quantity of excess reserves on the horizontal axis. Assume a vertical supply curve (whose position is determined by the central bank) intersecting a bank demand curve for excess reserves that becomes horizontal at some very low interest rate. The Fed can shift this supply curve rightward by purchasing securities in the open market. Note in this case that the quantity of excess reserves demanded increases to exhaust the increase in supply. In this scenario, banks are willing to hold whatever amount of excess reserves the Fed might supply and do not use any of the excess reserves to extend loans or buy securities.

13. An indicator of the "flight to quality" phenomenon is the spread between yields on risky BAA corporate securities and safe Treasury securities. This spread or risk premium in corporate bond yields increased from 2.3 percentage points in mid-1929 to 7.9 percentage points in mid-1932. (A similar, albeit slightly smaller, increase in this spread occurred in 2008 following the Lehman Brothers' bankruptcy.) In any case, the associated increased demand for government securities artificially depressed yields on Treasury securities, helping create the illusion that the Fed was conducting a policy of "easy money."

14. A minority viewpoint is that top Federal Reserve officials believed that their policy was highly restrictive but thought such a policy stance was appropriate and ultimately beneficial. Proponents of a doctrine known as the "liquidationist theory" believed that in an economic boom bad loan commitments are made which must be liquidated for solid business revival to occur following an ensuing slump. In this view, increasing the money supply during a recession, by preventing this needed liquidation, is counterproductive. Adolph Miller, Governor of the Federal Reserve Bank of New York during the depression, was a proponent of this viewpoint. (Variations of this view appeared again in the recent Great Crisis). On various explanations of the conduct of Federal Reserve policy in the 1930s, see Exhibit 8-1 (pp. 149–150).

15. This is the view presented in a widely cited article by Christina Romer, "What Ended the Great Depression?," *The Journal of Economic History*, December 1992, pp. 757–784.

9 The Federal Reserve's Response to the Great Crisis

1. See, for example, Robert Hetzel, "Monetary Policy in the 2008-2009 recession," Federal Reserve Bank of Richmond *Economic Quarterly*, Spring 2009, pp. 201–233.
2. In the meeting of June 25, there was one dissenting vote against the consensus to maintain rates constant. That vote was cast by Richard Fisher, President of the Federal Reserve Bank of Dallas, who preferred to *raise* interest rates. Fisher was also the lone dissenting member of the FOMC meeting of August 5, for the same reason. The vote at the September 16 meeting was unanimous in favor of maintaining the rate at 2 percent. To view the statements that the FOMC releases at the end of each meeting, as well as the minutes of FOMC meetings (released about three weeks after each meeting), go to http://www.federalreserve.gov/monetarypolicy/fomc.htm.
3. Oil prices are notoriously difficult to forecast. Among the factors that account for this are unexpected changes in weather patterns and the macroeconomic outlook, widespread use of the oil futures market for hedging purposes, and heavy speculative activity in the oil markets.
4. Unlike more than 20 other nations, the Federal Reserve has never adopted an official inflation targeting policy regime. However, economists believe the Fed operates with an implicit inflation target of 2 percent per year.
5. Actually, almost all of the expansion of the Fed's total assets took place in an eight-week period during the height of the panic in fall 2008. Total Federal Reserve assets increased from $905 billion on September 4, 2008 (just prior to the failure of Lehman Brothers) to $2,075 billion on November 6. However, the *composition* of these assets continued to change substantially through the end of 2009 and beyond.
6. On this episode, see the account in Chapter 1 of David Wessel, *In Fed We Trust: Ben Bernanke's War on the Great Panic* (New York: Crown Publishing Group, 2009).
7. As an example, on December 14, 2009 the Fed offered $75 billion in 28-day credit through its TAF program, with a settlement date of December 17. The minimum and maximum allowable bids were set at $5 million and $7.5 billion. In this announcement of December 14, the Fed indicated that the auction results would be published on December 17 on the Federal Reserve Board's website at www.federalreserve.gov/monetarypolicy/taf.htm. On December 17, the website indicated that 102 bidders had offered bids totaling $46.035 billion, for a bid/cover ratio of .61, that is, $46.035 billion/$75 billion. Because the total value of bids fell below the $75 billion offering, all bids were accepted at an interest rate of 0.25 percent, the lowest bid offered.
8. As of the end of 2009, some 240 banks had participated successfully in these auctions.
9. This differs from traditional discount window borrowing, in which banks may obtain immediate credit in their deposit account at the Federal Reserve.
10. Money market mutual funds, an important financial innovation, came on stream in the 1970s. From the 1930s to the 1980s, depository institutions

were limited by statutory ceilings in the interest rate they were allowed to pay depositors. (This regulation, known as Regulation Q, was phased out in the 1980s). Market interest rates increased sharply in the 1970s in response to rising inflation, moving significantly above the ceiling rates payable by depository institutions. Enterprising financial entrepreneurs, noting a good opportunity, invented the money market mutual fund in the mid-1970s. These funds are not subject to the statutory interest rate ceilings, in spite of early banks' lobbying efforts to make them so. Money market funds issue "shares" to the public at the price of one dollar per share and use the proceeds to purchase relatively safe short-term liquid assets such as Treasury bills, commercial paper, and negotiable CDs issued by large banks. Owners of these shares may write checks on their MMMF accounts (albeit not typically in amounts less than $250) and earn interest on the accounts at rates normally higher than those paid by banks on checking accounts. While not insured, money market fund shares had come to be regarded as being safe as bank deposits until the Lehman fiasco.

11. A current list of these 18 firms is available at http://www.newyorkfed.org/markets/pridealers_current.html.

12. Long-term bonds are riskier than short-term bonds because market prices of long-term bonds exhibit greater fluctuations from day to day and month to month than do prices of short-term bonds. In the event an investor is forced to sell prior to maturity, the long-term bond is therefore riskier. Assuming investors are risk averse, this means they must be compensated through a higher expected return in order to induce them to invest in longer-term bonds rather than short-term bonds. This additional yield required on longer-term bonds is known as the term premium. This size of this term premium fluctuates over time as expectations about economic stability change. Greater expected instability increases this term premium. Given the magnitude of the term premium, if financial market participants today reduce their expectations of short-term yields for the next few years, the 20-year bond yield will fall today. Since the financial crisis erupted, the Fed, through its extensive communications, has therefore sought to keep the public's expectations of expected future short-term rates as low as possible.

13. See Joseph Gagnon, Matthew Raskin, Julie Remache, and Brian Sack, *Federal Reserve Bank of New York Staff Reports*, No. 441, March 2010.

10   The Federal Reserve's Exit Strategy and the Threat of Inflation

1. Arthur Okun was an economics professor at Yale University and an economic advisor to Democratic Presidential candidate John F. Kennedy in the campaign of 1960. Kennedy charged that the Republican incumbents had run the economy with too much slack and unemployment in the previous eight years. Okun published a famous article in which he estimated that each one percentage point increase in the nation's unemployment rate resulted in an annual loss of national output of approximately three percent. This relationship became known as "Okun's Law."

2. Productivity growth contains both cyclical and trend elements. To minimize the distorting effect of the cycle and focus on the trend, 1983:1 and 2009:3 were selected as starting and ending dates because each represents the first quarter following the cyclical troughs that were reached in 1982:4 and 2009:2. Choice of these points allows us to examine the relationship over the course of full business cycles.

3. The lone exception was the first of the back-to-back recessions of 1980 and 1981-1982. These recessions were separated by a one-year economic expansion.

4. The U.S. deficit/GDP ratio in 2009 ranked with the most severe of the 16 euro-currency nations. On this, see Table 1-1, page 4.

5. A negative gap means actual real GDP is less than potential real GDP. On the differing estimates of the output gap, See John Weidner and John Williams, "How Big is the Output Gap?," Federal Reserve Bank of San Francisco *Economic Letter*, June 12, 2009.

6. See Athanasios Orphanides, "Monetary Policy Rules and the Great Inflation," *American Economic Review*, May 2002, pp. 115-120. Orphanides argues that the Federal Reserve was fooled into overestimating the size of the output gap by failing to take account of the effect of the adverse supply shocks on potential GDP. This allegedly caused the Fed to err in conducting policy that was too stimulative, thus causing the severe inflation of the 1970s.

7. In many cases, because of regulations mandating that they meet standards governing minimum capital/total assets ratios, banks have no alternative to tightening lending standards. To the extent that a bank's capital has been reduced by write-offs of bad loans in a crisis, the decline in capital may necessitate that the bank reduce its assets, most of which consist of loans.

8. See Edmund Phelps, "U.S. Monetary Policy and the Prospective Structural Slump," speech given at 7th Annual BIS Conference on Monetary Policy, Lucerne, Switzerland, 2008.

9. It should be pointed out that any positive correlation between money growth and inflation in the U.S. environment of relatively low inflation in the past quarter century has been almost nonexistent. For example, broad money (M2) growth increased sharply during 1995-2001 and again during 2005-2010, while inflation trended downward in both periods.

10. In the United States the Federal Reserve is prohibited by law from purchasing newly issued government debt. This does not necessarily prevent the Fed from monetizing government deficits because the Fed is free to purchase previously issued government bonds in secondary markets at the same time the government is issuing new bonds. The effect on the money supply would be the same as if the Fed purchased the new bonds as they are issued.

11. Inflation is less effective in reducing the budget deficit today than in earlier years because our federal income tax is now largely indexed for inflation. Prior to implementation of indexation, rising nominal incomes that kept pace with inflation pushed taxpayers into higher marginal income tax brackets, thus boosting tax revenues more rapidly than nominal income. Indexation prevents this disproportionate response of tax revenues to inflation. Nevertheless, a more stimulated economy with accompanying higher inflation will reduce the deficit to the extent that real incomes are boosted and tax revenues are induced to rise more rapidly than expenditures. And higher inflation more rapidly reduces the

real value of the existing stock of debt, thus benefiting the government's real balance sheet.

12. An additional tool for reducing bank reserves, albeit one that is managed by the Treasury rather than the Fed, is the Treasury Supplemental Financing Program. In this operation, the Treasury issues debt to the public in amounts above the amount used to finance government expenditures. The public writes checks to the Treasury to purchase this debt, and the Treasury deposits these funds in the supplemental account at the Fed. As it credits the Treasury's account, the Fed debits the reserve accounts of the banks on which the checks are written, thus reducing aggregate bank reserves. This procedure is effective in reducing reserves but has limited potential for draining reserves in current circumstances because the Treasury's supplemental account counts toward the statutory federal debt limits set by Congress.

11   The Taylor Rule and Evaluation of U.S. Monetary Policy

1. In the case of the Federal Reserve, it is difficult to find blatant examples of political forces compromising the conduct of its policy in the past 50 years. An often-cited exception involves the rapid growth of the money supply in the year preceding the 1972 presidential election, in which incumbent president Richard Nixon was running against George McGovern. Arthur Burns, who had been appointed Chairman of the Board of Governors by Nixon, presided over double-digit narrow and broad money growth in the 12 months prior to the election. This was followed within 18 months by the onset of double-digit inflation.

2. The reason that two percent, rather than 0 percent, is the inflation objective in the Taylor Rule is that actual inflation will inevitably deviate on both sides of a target level over time. If the target level is zero, we will likely experience occasional episodes of deflation. In such instances, monetary policy might lose traction in stimulating economic activity because of the zero bound on nominal interest rates. If we were to experience deflation of two percent per year along with a depressed economy, even a zero level of short-term interest rates set by the central bank would imply a positive real interest rate of two percent. Such a real rate, although the lowest the Fed can possibly provide, may not be low enough to stimulate aggregate spending in times of depressed economic activity. To avoid encountering such circumstances most economists advocate deliberately operating the economy with a small, positive rate of inflation.

3. Among the three appointees nominated by President Obama in 2010, Janet Yellen was the nominee whose expertise lay in monetary policy. Many analysts pegged her as an "inflation dove," most deeply concerned about the high and persistent contemporary unemployment.

4. Lyndon Johnson, U.S. president during the Vietnam War, was perhaps the most activist and interventionist president of modern times. He was not averse to admonishing Federal Reserve Chairman William McChesney Martin not to be raising interest rates. Johnson pleaded the case that higher rates were disadvantageous to prospective homeowners seeking to take out mortgages. More recent

presidents have exhibited more humility about their lack of expertise in economics and more respect for the political independence of the Federal Reserve.

5. Prior to the 1980s, monetary policy influenced economic activity in different ways than it does today. Regulation Q, which placed restrictions on the interest rates banks were permitted to pay depositors on savings and time deposits, was in place until it was phased out in the mid-1980s. As market interest rates moved above the statutory ceiling rates payable by banks, large amounts of deposits were withdrawn from banks and savings institutions to purchase such instruments as Treasury bills, commercial paper, and money market mutual fund shares. These episodes of disintermediation forced banks to severely reduce loans, including mortgages. In these episodes, housing construction absorbed a disproportionate share of the brunt of declining economic activity. A monetary rule designed for such earlier times may therefore have differed from the Taylor Rule as expressed in equation 11-2.

6. Monetary policy was hardly the sole cause of the inflation of the 1970s. Crude oil prices increased some 12 fold in this decade, rising from $3.35 per barrel in 1970 to a peak of $39.50 billion by April, 1980. The falling U.S. dollar also fed into inflation. To a large extent, the falling dollar resulted from inflationary monetary policy. However, other forces besides monetary policy contributed to the severe weakness of the dollar in the late 1970s.

7. These two viewpoints are expressed in John Taylor, "An Historical Analysis of Monetary Policy Rules," in John Taylor (ed.), *Monetary Policy Rules* (Chicago, IL: University of Chicago Press, 1999) and Athanasios Orphanides, "Historical Monetary Policy Analysis and the Taylor Rule," *Journal of Monetary Economics*, July 2003.

8. Figure 11-2, which uses quarterly data compiled by averaging monthly averages of daily rates, shows a peak of 18.52 percent in April 1981. But the actual FFR reached an intra-quarterly peak of 19.93 percent in July, 1981.

9. This was indeed a remarkable and successful period of economic history. The standard deviation of both real GDP growth and inflation fell sharply during this period. The two recessions in this period (1991 and 2001) were the mildest and the briefest of the 10 post-World War II recessions. As suggested by Minsky's theory, an unfortunate side effect of this exceptional stability may have been the huge bubble in credit and house prices that developed during 2002-2006.

12   Regulatory Reform Proposals

1. For a fascinating account of the frantic deliberations and actions of Fed Chairman Bernanke, Treasury Secretary Paulson, and New York Fed President Geithner in the period immediately surrounding the Lehman decision, see James B. Stewart, "Eight Days," *The New Yorker*, September 21, 2009, pp. 56-81.

2. See Simon Johnson and James Kwak, *13 Bankers* (New York, Pantheon Books, 2010).

3. This is an example of the pervasive phenomenon of "regulatory capture," in which the regulated firm "captures" the regulatory authority. A viable financial reform package must come to grips with this pernicious phenomenon.

4. See Oliver Hart and Luigi Zinglales, "Curbing Risk on Wall Street," *National Affairs*, Spring 2010.

Bibliography

Alter, Jonathan. *The Defining Moment* (New York: Simon and Schuster, 2006).

Bernanke, Ben S. *Essays on the Great Depression* (Princeton, NJ: Princeton University Press, 2000).

Bernanke, Ben S. and Mark Gertler, "Should Central Banks Respond to Movements in Asset Prices?" *American Economic Review*, March 2001, pp. 253–257.

Bordo, Michael D. "An Historical Perspective on the Crisis of 2007–2008," National Bureau of Economic Research, Working Paper 14569, December 2008.

Bruner, Robert F. and Sean D. Carr, *The Panic of 2007: Lessons Learned from the Market's Perfect Storm* (Hoboken, NJ: Wiley, 2007).

Calomiris, Charles and Gary Gorton, "The Origin of Banking Panics: Models, Facts, and Bank Regulation," in R. Glenn Hubbard (ed.), *Financial Markets and Financial Crises* (Chicago, IL: University of Chicago Press, 1991).

Carroll, Christopher, Misuzu Otsuka, and Jirka Slacalek, "How Large is the Housing Wealth Effect? A New Approach," National Bureau of Economic Research Working Paper No. 12746, December 2006.

Diamond, Douglas and Philip Dubvig, "Bank Runs, Deposit Insurance, and Liquidity," *Journal of Political Economy*, 1983, pp. 401–419.

Eichengreen, Barry. *Golden Fetters: The Gold Standard and the Great Depression 1919–1939* (New York: Oxford University Press, 1992).

Fisher, Irving. "Debt-Deflation Theory of Great Depressions," *Econometrica*, 1933, pp. 337–357.

Friedman, Milton and Anna J. Schwartz, *A Monetary History of the United States, 1867–1960* (Princeton: Princeton University Press, 1963).

Gordon, Robert J. (ed.) *The Business Cycle: Continuity and Change* (Chicago, IL: University of Chicago Press, 1986).

Gorton, Gary B. "The Subprime Panic," National Bureau of Economic Research, Working Paper 14398, October 2008.

Gorton, Gary B. "Questions and Answers about the Financial Crisis," National Bureau of Economic Research, Working Paper 15787, February 2010.

Kindleberger, Charles P. and Robert Aliber, *Manias, Panics, and Crashes: A History of Financial Crises*, 5th ed. (Hoboken, NJ: Wiley, 2005).

Gagnon, Joseph, Matthew Raskin, Julie Remache, and Brian Sack, "Large-Scale Asset Purchases by the Federal Reserve: Did They Work?" Federal Reserve Bank of New York, Staff Report no. 441, March 2010.

Gramlich, Edward M. *Subprime Mortgages: America's Latest Boom and Bust* (Washington, DC: Urban Institute Press, 2007).

Hart, Oliver and Luigi Zingales, "Curbing Risk on Wall Street," *National Affairs,* Spring 2010.

Hetzel, Robert. "Monetary Policy in the 2008–2009 Recession," Federal Reserve Bank of Richmond *Economic Quarterly,* Spring 2009, pp. 201–233.

Jarsulic, Marc. *Anatomy of a Financial Crisis: A Real Estate Bubble, Runaway Credit Markets, and Regulatory Failure* (New York: Palgrave Macmillan, 2010).

Johnson, Simon and James Kwak, *13 Bankers: The Wall Street Takeover and the Next Financial Meltdown* (New York: Pantheon Books, 2010).

Keynes, John Maynard. *The Economic Consequences of the Peace* (London: Macmillan, 1918).

Krugman, Paul. *The Return of Depression Economics and the Crisis of 2008* (New York: W.W. Norton, 2009).

Levine, Ross. "An Autopsy of the U.S. Financial System," National Bureau of Economic Research, Working Paper 15956, April 2010.

Minsky, Hyman. *Stabilizing an Unstable Economy* (New Haven, CT: Yale University Press, 1986).

Minsky, Hyman. "The Financial Instability Hypothesis," Working Paper No. 74, Jerome Levy Economics Institute of Bard College, May 1992.

Orphanides, Athanasios. "Monetary Policy Rules and the Great Inflation," *American Economic Review,* May 2002, pp. 115–120.

Orphanides, Athanasios. "Historical Monetary Policy Analysis and the Taylor Rule," *Journal of Monetary Economics,* July 2003, pp. 983–1022.

Reinhart, Carmen M. and Kenneth S. Rogoff. "Is the 2007 U.S. Subprime Crisis So Different? An International Comparison," *American Economic Review,* March 2008, pp. 339–344.

Reinhart, Carmen M. and Kenneth S. Rogoff. *This Time is Different: Eight Centuries of Financial Folly* (Princeton, NJ: Princeton University Press, 2009).

Romer, Christina. "What Ended the Great Depression?" *The Journal of Economic History,* December 1992, pp. 757–784.

Roubini, Nouriel and Stephen Mihm, *Crisis Economics: A Crash Course in the Future of Finance* (New York: Penguin Press, 2010).

Shiller, Robert J. *Irrational Exuberance,* 2nd ed. (Princeton, NJ: Princeton University Press, 2005).

Shiller, Robert J. *The Subprime Solution: How Today's Global Financial Crisis Happened, and What to Do About It* (Princeton, NJ: Princeton University Press, 2008).

Sorkin, Andrew Ross. *Too Big to Fail: The Inside Story of How Wall Street and Washington Fought to Save the Financial System—And Themselves* (New York: Viking, 2009).

Staiger, Douglas, James Stock, and Mark Watson, "How Precise Are Estimates of the Natural Rate of Unemployment?" in Christina Romer and David Romer (eds.), *Reducing Inflation: Motivation and Strategy* (Chicago, IL: University of Chicago Press, 1977).

Stewart, James B. "Eight Days," *The New Yorker,* September 21, 2009, pp. 56–81.

Stiglitz, Joseph E. *Freefall: America, Free Markets, and the Sinking of the World Economy* (New York: W.W. Norton, 2010).

Taylor, John. "An Historical Analysis of Monetary Policy Rules," in John Taylor (ed.), *Monetary Policy Rules* (Chicago, IL: University of Chicago Press, 1999).

Temin, Peter. *Did Monetary Forces Cause the Great Depression?* (New York: Norton, 1976).

Temin, Peter. *The Great Recession and the Great Depression.* National Bureau of Economic Research Working Paper 15645, January 2010.

Weidner, John and John Williams. "How Big is the Output Gap?" Federal Reserve Bank of San Francisco *Economic Letter*, June 12, 2009.

Wessel, David. *In Fed We Trust: Ben Bernanke's War on the Great Panic* (New York: Crown Business, 2009).

Zandi, Mark. *Financial Shock: A 360 degree Look at the Subprime Mortgage Implosion, and How to Avoid the Next Financial Crisis* (Upper Saddle River, NJ: FT Press, 2009).

Index

Page numbers in *italics* refer to notes or illustrations.